TOURISM
AND THE
ECONOMY

... understanding the economics of tourism

JAMES MAK

UNIVERSITY OF HAWAI'I PRESS
Honolulu

© 2004 University of Hawai'i Press
All rights reserved
Printed in
07 06 05 04   6 5 4 3 2 1
Library of Congress Cataloging-in-Publication Data
Mak, James.
Tourism and the economy / James Mak.
p.   cm.
Includes bibliographical references and index.
ISBN 0–8248–2789–9 (paper : alk. paper)
1. Tourism—Economic aspects.   I. Title.

G155.A1M234 2003
338.4'791—dc21
2003048893

University of Hawai'i Press books are printed on acid-free paper
and meet the guidelines for permanence and durability
of the Council on Library Resources

Design by Trina Stahl
Printed by Versa Press, Inc.

I dedicate this book to my parents, Eddie and Patty Mak.

CONTENTS

ACKNOWLEDGMENTS

MANY FRIENDS AND colleagues have read earlier drafts of the book and provided me with valuable comments and insights. Their comments forced me to think hard about what kind of book I wanted to write and which audiences I wanted to reach.

I want to thank the following friends and colleagues for their patience and perseverance in reading the earlier, disorganized drafts and apologize to them if not all their suggestions found their way into the final manuscript: Roger Blair (University of Florida), Doug Frechtling (George Washington University), Chris Grandy (University of Hawaii–Manoa), Sumner La Croix (University of Hawaii-Manoa), Ping Sun Leung (University of Hawaii-Manoa), Juanita Liu (University of Hawaii-Manoa), Sheila Meehan (The International Monetary Fund), Seiji Naya (East-West Center, Honolulu), Alan Tice, M.D. (University of Hawaii-Manoa), Clem Tisdell (University of Queensland), James E. T. Moncur (University of Hawaii–Manoa), Bill Fox (University of Tennessee–Knoxville), Turgut Var (Texas A&M University), James Roumassett (University of Hawaii–Manoa), Chuck Goddner (University of Colorado–Boulder), and Mark Hukill (University of Hawaii–Manoa). Yoav Wachman co-authored Chapters 13 and 14 of this book. Bill Hamilton, Director of the University of Hawai'i Press, gave me strong encouragement and support along the way. I want to thank my librarian wife, Alice, for helping me find information from unusual sources, and for doing all my household chores, which I neglected while working on this book, and Meechai (Robb) Orsuwan for designing the graphs and tables in the book. Bryan Lee, the librarian at the Sunset Reference Room (University of Hawaii–Manoa, School of Travel Industry Management), was always quick to respond to my requests for help and information.

PREFACE

I DECIDED TO write this book after the chairman of the University of Hawaii-Manoa economics department asked me to develop a new undergraduate introductory course on the economics of tourism that can serve our students as well as students from the School of Travel Industry Management. Tourism is the most important economic sector in Hawaii, accounting for over 25 percent of the state's gross domestic product.

Tourism is also an important economic sector around the world. The World Travel and Tourism Council estimates that travel and tourism account for roughly 10 percent of the world's gross domestic product and almost 8 percent of total worldwide employment. Between 1970 and 2000, international tourism grew 1.4 times as fast as the world's economy. Tourism's economic contribution is expected to become even greater in the future. The World Tourism Organization notes that in the world's developing countries, and especially the least developed countries, tourism is "almost universally the leading source of economic growth, foreign exchange, investment, and job creation." Tourism is among the top five foreign currency earners for 79 developing countries. But tourism can do a lot more to improve the material well-being of millions of people around the world. Among the 49 least-developed countries, tourism still accounts for only 1 percent of all international tourist arrivals and only .5 percent of tourism revenues. Many in the tourist industry also believe that tourism can foster global peace by reducing world poverty and promoting cross-cultural understanding.

However, there is growing public concern that uncontrolled tourism growth may overwhelm the Earth's natural, cultural, and social environments. The *Economist* magazine noted (January 10, 1998) that "Travel and tourism is the largest industry in the world. Its potential for making a mess of it is equally large." People have become aware that tourism can be a blight as well as a blessing and are demanding a more careful evaluation of its benefits and costs. Not surprisingly, interest in travel and tourism studies has grown rapidly.

Many benefits can derive from studying tourism economics. The most important contribution of the study of tourism economics is its relevance to the real world. Studying tourism economics can contribute to a better understanding of tourism. Tourism economics can help guide public policy in tourism, and it can help policy-makers evaluate the costs and benefits of alternative policy options.

Economics is a logically rigorous discipline, and studying tourism economics helps students of travel and tourism develop critical thinking skills.

Finally, studying tourism economics also exposes students to many subspecialties in economics including transportation economics, public finance, regulatory and antitrust economics, environmental economics, and international economics.

Tourism and the Economy is written for two audiences. The most important audience, of course, is students in tourism studies, but not only those studying tourism economics. This book can be a valuable supplementary text in introductory survey courses in travel and tourism, tourism marketing, tourism management, tourism planning, and in the sociology and geography of tourism.

Tourism and the Economy is also useful to tourism professionals and policy-makers who want to gain a better understanding of tourism from a "big picture" perspective. It does not, however, provide cookbook remedies to the day-to-day problems faced by travel businesses.

My hope is that *Tourism and the Economy* will also attract interest among a more general audience. Harold L. Vogel states in his recent book (*Travel Industry Economics, 2001*) that "The urge to travel is universal." If this is so, then all of us have an innate interest in tourism. This book is for people who want to be informed about the role of tourism in our economy. Although I use economics terminology when needed, I provide simple definitions, explanations, and examples immediately, and a fascinating compendium of facts about tourism around the world is also included.

I use neither high-level mathematics nor complicated graphs. "Making the complex understandable" is the main goal of this book. I want to share with readers the economic way of thinking about tourism. The emphasis here is placed more on understanding tourism than on teaching the formal tools of economic analysis. In keeping with this objective, I have intentionally left out topics such as tourism forecasting, regression analysis, project evaluation, and other evaluation tools used by tourism professionals and researchers. Those topics belong in a different book for a different audience.

Tourism and the Economy is loosely divided into four parts. Part I provides a definition of tourism and describes the nature of the tourism product. Part II focuses on the tourists. Part III focuses on the tourism suppliers, both businesses and governments. Part IV focuses on the destinations.

Authors of tourism economics textbooks tend to use examples from those countries and destinations that they are most familiar with. Hence, European authors tend to use European examples, and American authors tend to use American examples. I am most familiar with tourism in the United States, Japan, Hawaii, and other tourist destinations in the Asia-Pacific region. Although the venues and the institutional details are different, the economic principles that govern tourism everywhere are the same. The basic messages that come out of *Tourism and the Economy* are readily transferred to other destinations.

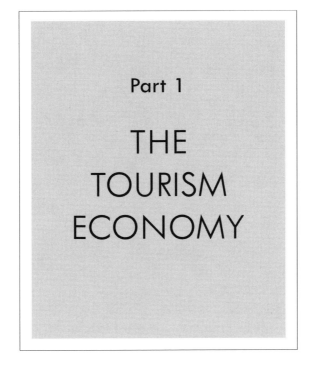

Part 1

THE
TOURISM
ECONOMY

CHAPTER 1

TOURISM and ECONOMICS

To be able to take this very mysterious
world we live in and to illuminate parts of it...
through the use of economics is enormously
intellectually satisfying and challenging.

GARY S. BECKER[1]

TOURISM IS PLEASURE travel. And tourists are people who travel for personal pleasure.

The World Tourism Organization (WTO) uses a broader definition of "tourism." According to the WTO, tourism comprises "the activities of persons traveling to and staying in places outside their usual environment for not more than one consecutive year for leisure, business, and other purposes."[2] Tourism therefore excludes home-to-work commuting trips, but does include travel for pleasure, private and official government business, employment, religious pilgrimage, education, medical treatment, and so on. Leisure and business travel are the main purposes of travel. About 62 percent of international travel is leisure travel, 18 percent business travel, and the remaining 20 percent is for other purposes, including visiting friends and relatives, religious pilgrimage, medical tourism, and so on.[3] In 1999, 69 percent of all domestic and foreign U.S. trips were leisure trips.[4]

Good reasons prevail for why we may want to reserve the term "tourism" to describe pleasure travel only. Tourists travel for a different reason than other travelers. They travel for their own personal pleasure, whereas business travelers, by comparison, travel for the benefit of their employers. Tourists pay their own travel expenses; someone else pays the costs of transportation, lodging, and meals for business travelers. Hence, the factors that influence the travel decisions of pleasure versus business travelers are quite different. The suppliers of tourism services, such as airlines, also regard pleasure and business travel as separate markets and adopt different pricing strategies accordingly. Governments, too, treat pleasure and business travel differently; business travel expenses are "tax deductible," whereas pleasure travel expenses are usually not deductible. Some nations restrict the ability of their citizens to travel to other countries for holiday, but not for business or official government travel. Thus pleasure travel should be studied separately from other types of travel.

On the other hand, good reasons also exist to adopt an inclusive definition of tourism. First, hotels and other tourism businesses serve pleasure as well as other travelers. Second, some trips are dual or multipurpose trips. For example, a business traveler may mix pleasure and business on a single trip. A wealthy foreign visitor comes to the United States for a medical procedure and then stays on for a vacation. Finally, it is difficult to collect data that separate pleasure travelers from other travelers. In countries that restrict their citizens from taking pleasure trips abroad, travelers often lie about their trip purpose to obtain an exit permit, and the official statistics record far fewer than the actual number of leisure travelers. Many countries do not collect information on the travel purposes of outbound visitors at all.

One way to avoid confusion is to use the term *visitor* to correspond to the more inclusive definition of *tourist* employed by the WTO.[5] In this book, this distinction allows us to reserve the term *tourist* to describe a person traveling for personal pleasure. Thus, a tourist is also a visitor, but a visitor need not be a tourist. However, it is important to keep in mind that tourism statistics published by the WTO and destination tourism organizations usually conform to the WTO definition of tourism and include pleasure, business, and other travel purposes.

Difference Between Tourism and Recreation

THE MOST important difference between tourism and most forms of recreation is that consumers must travel to consume tourism.[6] Ian Matley states the distinction between the two as follows:

> Recreation does not necessarily imply travel. A game of tennis or a stroll in a neighborhood park constitute recreation, but the distance traveled to the

location where these acts take place may be minimal. Much outdoor recreation, such as sports of various types, or indoor recreation, such as visits to theaters, cinemas, and clubs may be local in nature. The participant does not travel far and does not leave his home for any lengthy period. Tourism . . . implies the removal of a person away from his habitual place of residence and his stay in another location. This stay or removal is temporary and is motivated by a search for personal pleasure in the shape of rest, relaxation, and self improvement.[7]

Tourism and Economics

ECONOMICS IS about how people make choices. Every day each one of us is confronted with many choices. In the morning, we have to decide what we want to eat for breakfast. What should we wear to go to work or school? Should we go to the gym in the afternoon, hang out with friends, or perhaps take a nap or watch television?

Similarly, choices must be made when we decide to go on vacation. How much money should we budget for the trip? How much time do we plan to be away? Where do we want to go? What do we want to do? Do we take a car, or should we fly to our destination? As we make our individual choices, other people are making their choices as well. Airline officials must decide how many flights and seats to allocate between which cities, and what prices they should charge for these seats. Cruise line companies must decide whether to offer more cruises to Alaska and fewer cruises to Europe this summer. Rental car companies must decide where to locate their cars. Souvenir shops must decide how much inventory they want to order from their suppliers. Government tourist bureaus must decide how much money they should spend in what markets to promote travel to their destinations. Choices must be made because available resources don't permit us to satisfy all our wants. All these examples of people making choices represent economics at work in our daily lives; thus, economics studies how rational people make choices among the available alternatives to meet their goals.

Tourism's many decision makers[8]—tourists, suppliers, and governments—don't share the same goal. Consumers, as the popular cliché goes, want to get "the biggest bang for the buck." Economists use the term *utility* to describe the satisfaction or benefit ("the bang") that consumers derive from the consumption of a good or service. The goal of the tourist is to derive the most satisfaction from the use of her scarce resources—namely, her time and money. A commercial supplier's goal, by contrast, is to maximize profits.[9] In tourism, numerous not-for-profit suppliers also exist, such as the operators of historical attractions, national parks, and museums whose goal may be to maximize the number of tourist visits. Governments have broader objectives: In developing countries, governments may want tourism to generate income and tax revenues, create employment and reduce poverty, and at the same time protect the environment and respect their cultures. In developed countries, an additional goal of tourism development may be to foster better people-to-people understanding and international relations. Tourism may also be exploited to achieve political goals. For example, in the 1970s, the Eastern European countries began to welcome Western tourists on the premise that exposure to communism would convince Westerners of the superiority of their socialist system.[10]

In this book, we examine how tourists, suppliers, and governments make their economic choices regarding tourism and the outcomes of those decisions.[11]

Organization of the Book

THE BOOK is loosely divided into four parts: Part I (Chapters 1–2) explores the attributes of the tourism product; Part II (Chapters 3–6) focuses on the tourists; Part III (Chapters 7–9) focuses on the suppliers of tourism services; and Part IV (Chapters 10–14) focuses on the tourist destinations. Destinations can be local, regional, or global.

Chapter 2 defines and describes the attributes of the "tourism product" and notes that tourists and tourism suppliers have different notions of what this product is. Chapter 3 discusses the most important economic and noneconomic determinants of demand for pleasure travel. Chapter 4 explains why some people prefer to travel on prepaid package tours, and why consumer tastes for package tours are changing. Chapter 5 explains why some people use travel agents to search for travel information and book their travel arrangements. The chapter also examines the impact of the Internet and high-speed computers on consumer demand for travel agent services and on the travel distribution business. Chapter 6 examines the determinants of trip duration and tourist spending at tourist destinations.

Chapter 7 provides a definition of the tourist industries and examines the structure of competition within the U.S. tourist industries. Chapter 8 compares the relative advantages and disadvantages of travel via different transportation modes (such as air versus rail or automobile) and how economic regulation and deregulation in the airline and cruise industries affect the welfare of consumers. Chapter 9 examines how government tariff and nontariff barriers impede international tourism.

Chapter 10 describes the newly developed tourism satellite account and explains how it is used to measure the economic contribution of travel and tourism to the host community. Chapter 11 examines the benefits and costs of tourism to the host community, emphasizing that the benefits and costs of tourism are not etched in stone and can be changed by public policy. Chapter 12 explains the principles of tourist taxation, why destinations may want to levy taxes that fall largely on tourists, and how imposing higher tax rates on tourist purchases is neither economically inefficient nor unfair. Chapter 13 examines the relationship between tourism and the natural environment and evaluates the alternative policy instruments to deal with the negative environmental spillovers from tourism. Chapter 14 examines sustainable tourism: that is, tourism development that balances the need for economic development and the protection of the natural, social, and cultural environments of the host community. Chapter 15 concludes with an examination of the most important factors that will likely shape the future of travel and tourism.

CHAPTER 2

THE TOURISM PRODUCT

When asked what their "product" is... most [suppliers] will
not claim to be supplying a product called tourism.

ADRIAN BULL[1]

The tourism "product" is not the tourist destination, but it is
about experiences of that place and what happens there.

CHRIS RYAN[2]

DEPENDING ON WHOM you ask, the term "tourism product" means different things to different people. If you ask an airline executive what product his
airline is selling, he will most likely reply "air transportation." If you ask
the same question of a hotel executive, his response is likely to be "accommodations." Although both will admit that they are in the tourism or travel
business, neither of them will say that their principal product is "tourism."
However, a pleasure trip is not simply a plane ride, or a night's lodging at a
hotel. Economists M. Sinclair and Mike Stabler define the tourism product
as a "*composite product* involving transport, accommodation, catering, natural
resources, entertainment, and other facilities and services, such as shops and
banks, travel agents, and tour operators."[3] From the suppliers' perspective,
the tourism product is composed of heterogeneous goods and services from
diverse suppliers. Some suppliers, such as carriers, hotels, and visitor attractions, produce (and may directly sell to tourists) the actual goods and services
consumed by tourists whereas other suppliers are middlemen or *intermedi-
aries,* such as travel agents who arrange and sell other suppliers' products.

In contrast to suppliers, consumers have a very different view of the
tourism product. If you ask a tourist what she wants from her holiday trip,
she will probably say, "to relax and have fun" or "to visit famous and histori-

cal places." Most tourists are looking for an experience—that is, something that is "uplifting or out of the ordinary"—while on holiday trips.[4] Orvar Lofgren observes that "to have an experience calls for a situation with a beginning and an end."[5] Economists like to use their own jargon, describing tourists as consumers who want to get the most *utility* or satisfaction from the use of their scarce time and money.

The asymmetry between what producers and sellers sell and what consumers demand is not unique to tourism. It is also seen in the provision of government services.[6] Consider, for example, public education. The output of the schools can be measured by the number of subjects taught, the number of classes offered, the number of students served, and so on. Consumers of public education—the students—by contrast, want knowledge and skills. Two schools offering the same number of subjects and classes and serving the same number of students may not produce the same amount of learning.

To avoid confusion between the two concepts of the tourism product, we label the tourism product demanded by consumers—satisfying trips—as the *consumer product,* and the goods and services produced and sold by the suppliers—transportation, lodging, food and drink—as *seller products.* It should be obvious that tourists must have transportation, lodging, and so on (i.e., seller products) to go on a vacation; but many other factors are also important in determining whether a vacation trip turns out to be a pleasurable experience (i.e., consumer product). These additional factors include the weather, scenery, historical and cultural attractions at the destination, quality of public services, the attitudes of local residents and governments toward tourists, and even the congeniality of the travelers' companions. An airline can ruin a traveler's vacation by delaying or canceling flights or providing poor service, but it can't guarantee that the tourist will have a satisfying trip because the airline doesn't supply and control all the elements that go into making a pleasurable vacation experience.

This suggests that it is possible to measure the tourism product in two ways: measure what consumers value, and measure what suppliers sell. Measures of tourism's "consumer product" could include the number and percent of satisfied visits and the number and percent of returning visits. NFO Plog Research, a large market research firm, conducts an annual survey of American travelers to determine which U.S. states provide the most satisfying vacation experiences. The company explains that its Satisfaction Index "measures the satisfaction with the vacation experience rather than just counting the number of visitors to each destination." For 2002, Plog's "Delightful Dozen" ranks Hawaii at the top of the list, followed by Florida, Maine, Alaska, and California.[7]

Measures of tourism's "seller product" include the total number of units sold (airline passenger revenue miles, hotel room nights, and so on). For a destination, representative measures of the "seller product" include total visitor spending, the number of visitor arrivals, and the total number of visitor days spent at the destination.

Attributes of the Tourism Product

A NUMBER of features can be attributed to the tourism product. These are discussed in the following sections.

Need to Travel to Consume Tourism

The most important characteristic of the tourism product is that consumers must travel some distance and spend some time at their destinations to consume it. This has important implications for tourist destinations and their development. Critics of tourism development as an economic development strategy point to the environmental and negative socio-cultural costs of tourism growth to host communities. For example, airplanes bringing tourists to the destination can create noise pollution over residential neighborhoods. Tourists can create congestion on local roads and beaches and potentially harm the natural habitat. Tourist behavior may clash with local custom and offend residents. In small island countries, even modest numbers of tourists can put enormous environmental and social pressures on the local community.

Crime is another potential byproduct of tourism growth. Tourists are favorite targets of criminals because they often don't report crimes against them or return to the destination to testify against apprehended crime suspects. Thus, increased tourism can mean more crime in the host community. However, it isn't simply a case of more people leading to more crime. Crimes against tourists tend to be disproportionately in favor of property crimes, such as burglary and robbery.[8] Tourists can also commit crime. From society's point of view, crime imposes a cost on society regardless of who is the victim and who is the perpetrator.

As the number of tourists increases, the character of the tourist destination will likely change, often becoming degraded. "See it before they spoil it" is a well known cliché in tourism. Hall of Fame New York Yankee catcher, Yogi Berra once said of the popular Toots Shor's restaurant, "It's so crowded, nobody goes there anymore."[9] He might as well have said that about tourist destinations. Stanley Plog argues that tourist destinations contain the seeds of their own destruction.[10] A destination's popularity initially attracts more visitors, but as time goes on these visitors become less desirable; eventually, the character and appeal of the destination decreases, driving tourists away. H. Peter Gray[11] and Louise Crandall[12] note a positive correlation between tourist density and resident hostility toward tourists; lack of friendliness toward tourists impairs the quality of tourism services and the attractiveness of the destination to tourists. Richard Butler offers the famous theory that travel destinations go through a distinct life cycle that goes from the exploration stage to growth and then to maturity.[13] The gist of his theory is that the growth of tourism at a destination, as measured by the number of tourist visits, eventually slows down; unless the destination takes action to rejuvenate itself, tourism will eventually go into decline. Butler's theory of the tourist area life cycle offers support to those who argue that tourism development needs to be tightly managed. A less transparent implication of Butler's theory is that, as tourism growth must necessarily slow down, in time tourism could become less important as a destination's engine of economic growth.

Nonetheless, as tourism continues to increase worldwide, people in many tourist destinations are asking, "What are the additional benefits and costs of more tourism growth?" And, "How can tourism be developed in a sustainable way?" We explore these two issues in Chapters 11 and 14.

Tourism Product Cannot Be Stored

Tourism is often described as a *service* and not a tangible *good*. Hence, it cannot be stored if it is not sold or consumed. The potential revenue from a hotel room that isn't occupied for the night is lost forever. Because a cost to the hotel operator still remains, even if the room is unoccupied, he has an incentive to try to sell the room by lowering prices. The same is true of airline seats, cruise ship cabins, and other personal services. The inability to store services also means that tourism suppliers cannot build up inventory ahead of peak demand.

Another feature of tourism is its seasonality. Seasonality in tourism can stem from the nature of the tourism product itself. For example, skiing is a winter sport. Not surprisingly, demand for travel to ski resorts such as Aspen

(Colorado) and Whistler (British Columbia, Canada) peaks during the winter months. By contrast, summer is the peak tourist season for Alaska cruises.

Summer is the peak travel season for most people. Summer also coincides with school vacations, and many people prefer to take their longest vacations during those months when school is out. Not surprisingly, prices are generally higher during the peak travel months. Some destinations, such as Hawaii, can have two peak travel seasons, summer and winter.

The presence of seasonality means that supply must be adjusted to changing demand during the year. During the off-season, cruise ships and airplanes are diverted to other routes. However, hotels, souvenir shops, and tourist attractions cannot be moved, although some may be closed to cut operating costs. The seasonality of tourism challenges suppliers to find the most efficient way to use their fixed capital.

Difficult to Compare Tourism Products Before Purchase

Before making a purchase, it is always wise to compare product prices and qualities among competing products. Some goods are fairly standardized or homogeneous (oranges), so they are relatively easy to compare. The consumer can see, touch, and maybe smell or taste a good before deciding to buy it.

On the other hand, services are difficult to compare because consumers cannot examine them first before purchase. The tourism product is composed mostly of services. Those products whose attributes can be determined only after purchase are called *experience goods*. In buying experience goods, the consumer must often rely on the reputation of the seller, a professional advisor, or counselor (a travel agent, in the case of tourism), the experiences of friends and relatives, and her own past experience in making a purchase decision. This attribute of the tourism product presents a difficult challenge to tourism suppliers who must figure out how to inform potential customers about their products. In sum, tourism is largely an information business prior to and through the actual sale of services.[14]

Tourism suppliers have developed innovative ways to promote their products. So that they might influence their clients to visit a destination, *fam trips* bring travel agents (and travel writers) to destinations,[15] either free or at highly discounted prices, to experience the best attractions of these destinations. Travel businesses and destination tourism promoters often co-sponsor travel shows and fairs that go from city to city, much like a traveling auto show, to promote their destination and products to potential tourists. Some travel trade shows are mega-events that attract global participation. For example, at the 2002 World Travel Market in London, 5,000 destinations and companies from over 100 countries displayed exhibits promoting their tourism products.[16]

The International Travel Bourse (ITB), held in Berlin in March 2003, boasted even larger participation, having attracted more than 125,000 trade and consumer visitors and 10,000 exhibitors, including 616 U.S. firms.[17] A unique feature of tourism is that destination promotion has become increasingly a government responsibility rather than the responsibility of the travel industry. Almost all governments worldwide establish government travel offices and use tax revenues to fund destination tourism promotion.[18] However, government funding of destination promotion has come under increasing public criticism. In 1996, the U.S. government discontinued public funding of tourism promotion to attract foreign tourists to the United States.[19]

Tourism Products are Consumed by Local and Tourist Consumers
Goods and services consumed by tourists are also frequently consumed by local residents. Restaurants, retail shops, nightclubs, golf courses, and visitor attractions in tourist destinations cater to local residents as well as to tourists. At times, it is difficult to even characterize some goods strictly as tourist goods or a business as a tourist business. Tourists generally have higher incomes and a greater ability to pay than local residents. They are also generally less price sensitive.

When consumers respond to price changes differently, the seller can increase his profits by charging different prices to different customers, under certain conditions. Specifically, he should *price discriminate* by charging a higher price to the less price-sensitive buyer, if he can. *Price discrimination* is most successful if (1) the seller can identify his customers correctly—by requiring buyers to show their IDs at the time of purchase—and be able to separate them into distinct buyer groups; and (2) products cannot easily be resold, to prevent members of one group from buying at a lower price and then reselling them to members of another group who would otherwise have to pay the much higher price. Not surprisingly, price discrimination occurs most frequently in the sale of services rather than in goods because services, once purchased, cannot easily be resold. Airlines charge higher fares to less price-sensitive business travelers than to leisure travelers. Hotels charge the highest room rates (referred to in the trade as "rack rates") to last-minute walk-in customers and lower room rates to members of select groups (such as the members of the American Association of Retired Persons [AARP]). Movie theaters charge lower admission fees to senior citizens, military personnel, and youths.

In Hawaii, a two-tier price system for tourists and locals is openly advertised at inter-island airlines, hotels, car rental companies, entertainment and visitor attractions, golf courses, and even at publicly owned and operated facilities such as the city zoo, Hanauma Bay Nature Park, and aquariums.[20] Locals pay much lower prices for the same purchases.[21] Locals-only price discounts are usually more readily available during slack periods when suppliers have a lot of excess capacity on hand. In China, it is common (although becoming less so) to encounter a three-tier price system where "foreign" (non-overseas Chinese) tourists pay the highest prices, overseas Chinese visitors pay lower prices, and locals pay the lowest prices.

Openly charging higher prices to tourists, as in Hawaii and China, is not common in other travel destinations, perhaps to avoid angering tourists who may return another day. In many destinations, discriminatory pricing is an "open secret" among local residents who qualify for locals-only price discounts. Travel writer John Flinn vividly relates his own experience in Egypt:

> The first time I encountered this dual-price system, I've got to admit, it made my blood boil. My wife, Jeri, and I were on a bus from Aswan, Egypt, to Abu Simbel, the ancient temple complex near the Sudanese border. We stopped for a break at a dusty, sun-seared desert outpost, and everybody piled into a little shop to buy bottles of Fanta Orange, the only liquid for sale. I noticed all the Egyptians ahead of me in line handing over a certain sum of money— I think it was 5 shillings—but when I got to the front of the line, the clerk looked me right in the eye and quoted a price that was exactly double. "Isn't the price 5 shillings?" I asked.
> "Oh no, my friend, it's 10."
> "But I just saw everyone ahead of me pay five."
> "My friend, you must be mistaken. The price is 10 shillings."
> I handed over the money, then stood to the side and watched as the Egyptian behind me paid the clerk 5 shillings. I glared at the clerk, but he refused to make eye contact with me.[22]

Sometimes, tourists get the better deals. For example, the Japan Rail Pass (and similarly the Eurail Selectpass), which must be purchased prior to departure, gives significant price discounts to tourists for rail travel in Japan (and Europe). The pass must be activated at major JR rail stations, and the tourist must show her passport to prove that she is traveling in Japan on a pleasure trip.[23]

Within travel destinations, it is not uncommon to see higher sticker prices in areas most frequented by tourists; prices are much lower elsewhere where locals shop. A few smart tourists soon learn to get away from these "tourist traps" to find better deals where there are not as many tourists. Most tourists will not, because it doesn't pay to spend their scarce vacation time attempting to find cheaper restaurants, souvenirs, and so on outside the tourist areas. If the time spent in searching and shopping for the best deals is included as part of the prices of the purchases, "prices" are actually lower in the tourist areas for most tourists. In sum, locational price differences are generally not considered price discrimination.

Tourism Relies on Human, Man-Made, and Natural Resources

The production of tourism requires many different kinds of *inputs* or *resources*. The usual inputs include labor, capital, and land. *Capital*, in production, is defined as durable, man-made goods used as inputs to produce other products.[24] Buildings and equipment are examples of capital goods.[25] Except in air and water transportation, capital employed in the production of most tourism services in the United States is composed mostly of structures rather than equipment. "Equipment" represents about 81 percent of the total capital employed in air and water transportation, whereas "structures" represent 54 percent of the capital employed in hotels and other lodging places, nearly 74 percent in retail trade, and 72 percent in amusement and recreation services.[26] Capital goods can be privately supplied (e.g., a privately owned hotel) or publicly supplied (e.g., public airports, harbors, and highways).

Land, broadly defined, includes both the terrain and its natural resources, such as beaches, rivers, forests, mountains, flora and fauna, scenery, wildlife, fish stocks, and the like. Additionally, climate, culture, history, and the residents' way of life are also important resources in the production of tourism.

One important feature of tourism production is that the natural resources used in tourism are often unpriced. These resources are virtually free for use by anyone, usually on a first-come basis: The forests and mountains are open to anyone who wants to hike in them; the oceans are accessible to anyone who wants to swim, surf, or sail in them.

When nature's resources are offered for use at a zero price, they can result in overuse and crowding. Crowding leads to resource deterioration and possible depletion, thus reducing the value of those resources to both tourists and residents. Moreover, in the competition for access to these recreational resources, local residents are often crowded out by tourists.[27] Entrepreneurs, on the other hand, are able to exploit these resources for their own profit. What is the best way to ration the use of these valuable tourist resources to preserve them for future use? Who should reap the profits from the exploitation of these resources? We explore the answers to these questions in Chapter 13.

Is Tourism Labor Intensive?

It is widely believed that tourism is a *labor intensive* product in that it employs more labor relative to other factors of production, such as capital and land.[28] Tourism's labor intensity is attributed to the highly personal service nature of many tourism products. This high ratio of labor to other inputs is an important reason why many less developed countries with abundant labor have chosen to embrace tourism as an economic development strategy. However, divergent views exist, and the evidence varies depending on specific country circumstances.[29] In some, especially island, countries, the start of a tourist industry may require huge up-front infrastructure investments such as an airport, harbor, and roads; the capital cost per tourism job created may be very high. Tourism development can be a very expensive strategy to create jobs.

Concluding Observations

THE TOURISM product is not an easy term to define, because consumers and suppliers have different notions of what it is. Surveys conducted in 1999 of Japanese and North American visitors to Hawaii found that about 90 percent of them indicated that "Much of the real value of a Hawaii vacation comes from things that have no price tag, like the scenery and the people."[30] Suppliers, on the other hand, view the tourism product as the goods and services they sell to tourists.

The tourism product, as viewed by economists, is not a single product like apples or oranges but a composite of highly heterogeneous goods and services. A tourist traveling away from home combines transportation, lodging, food and drink, and entertainment into a holiday trip. In an all-inclusive package tour, all the component parts are obviously complementary. But the apparent complementarity of tourism products can be deceptive because substitutes can also exist: Within narrow product categories, bus transportation can substitute for rental cars, and public transit can substitute for taxi rides. The tourist may even choose to spend more money on food and entertainment and less on museum visits and souvenirs. Hence, suppliers must be aware of substitution possibilities. Likewise, tourist destinations must be aware that, for some people, a Wyoming vacation can substitute for an Alaskan cruise, and a domestic vacation trip can substitute for an overseas trip, and vice versa.

In this chapter, we also saw that "tourism" raises a number of important public policy issues. We re-examine some of these issues in greater detail in later chapters of this book.

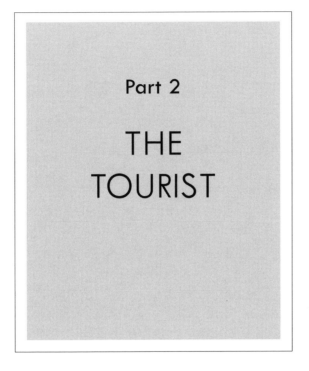

Part 2

THE
TOURIST

CHAPTER 3

DEMAND FOR PLEASURE TRAVEL

The freedom to travel safely and cheaply is one of the
great blessings of our time—something that immeasurably
expands the range of human experience.

MICHAEL ELLIOTT [1]

HAROLD VOGEL STATES that "The urge to travel is universal" because people are born with innate and insatiable curiosity.[2] Historians have traced one
of the first lists of tourist attractions—the seven wonders of the ancient
world—to 146 B.C.[3] During the Roman era, massive road construction facilitated travel from cities to country villas and resorts around the Bay of Naples,
and a stable political environment for two centuries under Roman rule
encouraged travel within the empire.[4] Nonetheless, before modern times,
"travel was pretty much limited to the elite, the nomad, the warrior, and the
pilgrim."[5]

Mass tourism, as we know it, is a relatively recent phenomenon. Indeed,
it took roughly a century (starting in 1850) before vacations became an
opportunity for just about everybody in the Western world.[6] Until the
middle of the twentieth century, pleasure travel was a privilege enjoyed by the
rich, who had lots of discretionary time and income on their hands. Although
lower income people may have harbored a desire to travel, most would not
realize their aspirations until well after World War II, when travel became far
safer and more comfortable and affordable.

During the nineteenth century, the institutions of modern tourism began
to take shape. In the mid-1800s, Thomas Cook founded the modern travel

agency industry in England and quickly turned it into a sizable business.[7] In 1856, he conducted his first Grand Tour of Europe and led his first group of tourists around the world in 1872. The first souvenir postcard may have been issued at the Paris Universal Exhibition of 1889; it depicted the Eiffel Tower.[8] American Express issued the first travelers' checks in 1891. Just before the turn of the century, the Orient Line claimed to be the first ocean liner to provide luxury cruises.[9] The first trans-Atlantic scheduled passenger flight took place in 1919, but it wasn't until 1957 that more passengers crossed the Atlantic by air than by sea. The first nonstop transcontinental flight in the United States occurred in 1923, but American tourists weren't very interested in travel by air until the development of the DC3, with sleeping accommodations, in the late 1930s.[10] By the middle of the 1960s, only about 25 percent of the American population had ever taken an airplane flight either for business or pleasure.[11]

In the United States, steamboats and railroads were the transportation modes of choice for tourists during the nineteenth century. Steamboats—some very large and opulent—were more comfortable than railroads, but they were also slower and more expensive. The automobile freed Americans from their cities in the twentieth century. The automobile provided freedom of movement at relatively low cost; it also made tourism more family oriented. Initially, Americans used their automobiles to escape to the countryside on day and weekend trips. In the mid-1920s, the first motor hotels, or *motels*, were developed. During the 1930s, Americans began to take to the road in increasing numbers in personal automobiles for longer distance vacations. *See America First* became a popular slogan, and America became the camping nation of the world.[12] The building of roads was an important piece of President Franklin Roosevelt's New Deal anti-Depression program. Ironically, after a brief decline at the beginning of the 1930s, vacationing became more, rather than less, widespread in America during the Depression decade, as the practice of paid vacations was extended to about half of the industrial labor force by the latter half of the 1930s.[13] After World War II, a massive road building program knit the country closer together and spurred domestic recreational travel. The *American Traveler Survey*, published by *Travel Weekly*, found that in 1999, 66 percent of U.S. adults took holidays averaging four trips each; 95 percent of leisure trips were in the United States; and 76 percent were made by car or camper.[14]

Occasionally, the diffusion of a technological innovation can change the path of history, as did the introduction of the jet airplane in the case of international tourism. The initiation of scheduled passenger jet plane service in the late 1950s, followed by the introduction of the Boeing 747 "jumbo jet" in 1970, made possible the transportation of large numbers of people quickly, safely, and at affordable prices. Jet air travel has been essential to the development of tourism in the vast region of Asia and the Pacific.

Combined with growing affluence, increasing acceptance, and the support of governments around the world, the golden era of global mass tourism arrived after 1950.[15]

The World Tourism Organization (WTO) notes that nearly 700 million international visitor arrivals were recorded around the world in 2000, and these visitors spent more than $475 billion (U.S.) in the host countries, excluding international transportation payments. By comparison, in 1950, only 25 million international visitor arrivals were recorded, along with $2 billion in visitor spending.

Historically, international tourism meant people from rich countries visiting other rich countries. With the exception of China and Japan, the top ten visitor-generating countries in the world in 2000 were in Europe and the Americas. Germans led the world in the number of international trips, but Americans led the world in visitor spending abroad. Ten countries, among roughly 200 nations and territories, currently account for nearly two-thirds of all visitor expenditures in the entire world.[16] Europe and the Americas account for more than three-quarters of the international visitor arrivals.

By region, Europe continues—as it has since record keeping began—to dominate the world in international outbound travel. Europe leads the world with 59 percent of total international departures, followed by the Americas (19 percent), East Asia and the Pacific (16.6 percent), Africa (2.3 percent), the Middle East (1.7 percent), and South Asia (1 percent).[17] The fastest growing region for international departures since the 1960s has been East Asia and the Pacific.

Most (80 percent) of the international travel worldwide is travel within the same geographic region (Table 3-1). However, big differences are apparent among these regions. Over 85 percent of all the travel in Europe consists of Europeans traveling to other European countries; in South Asia, that percentage is less than 25 percent.[18] Following growing political and economic

TABLE 3-1

INTERNATIONAL TOURIST ARRIVALS: 2000

	Total (millions)	Same Region	Other Region	Same Region	Other Region
		(millions)		%	
INBOUND TOURISM BY ORIGIN					
World	698.8	561.9	136.9	80	20
Africa	27.6	12.8	14.8	46	54
Americas	129.0	94.6	34.4	73	27
East Asia and the Pacific	11.9	87.9	24.0	79	21
Europe	403.3	356.9	46.4	88	12
Middle East	20.6	8.1	12.5	39	61
South Asia	6.4	1.6	4.9	24	76
OUTBOUND TOURISM BY DESTINATION					
World	698.8	561.9	136.9	80	20
Africa	16.1	12.8	3.3	80	20
Americas	133.2	94.6	38.6	71	29
East Asia and the Pacific	115.9	87.9	27.9	76	24
Europe	414.8	356.9	57.9	86	14
Middle East	11.7	8.1	3.6	69	31
South Asia	7.2	1.6	5.6	22	78

Source: World Tourism Organization

integration among the Western European countries, we should consider the intra-European travel by European Union (EU) residents as quasi-domestic rather than international travel.

Although comprehensive statistics on worldwide domestic travel are unavailable, anecdotal evidence suggests that the volumes of domestic travel and related expenditures are much larger than in international travel. The World Tourism Organization estimates that there are ten times as many domestic visitors as there are international visitors.[19] In the United States, residents took nearly 61 million trips abroad in 2000, compared to over 1 billion domestic long distance (person) trips. U.S. residents spent $489 billion on travel within the U.S. in 2000, and only $65 billion on travel abroad.[20] China also has a huge domestic travel market. In 2000, Chinese took 10.5 million overseas trips, compared to 665 million domestic trips of one or more nights in 1999.[21] In France (92 percent) and Italy (85 percent), the overwhelming majority of personal trips in 1998 were domestic trips. However, international travelers tend to spend more money per trip. For example, in 2002, the Japanese took 319 million domestic trips, compared to 16.35 million overseas trips, but Japanese travelers spent 11.8 billion yen on overseas trips compared to 16.9 billion yen on domestic trips.[22]

Why People Take Pleasure Trips

FRANCES BROWN surmises that people travel because they feel a need to "escape from ordinary life."[23] Some travel because they also want to "see the world." Surveys of holiday travelers find that the ten most frequently cited reasons for taking a holiday trip are:

1. To have time for family and friends.
2. To be with others and have fun.
3. For rest and recreation.
4. To discover new places and things or experience a different culture.
5. To experience nature.
6. To broaden one's education (through museum visits, etc.).
7. To get away from bad weather.
8. To eat good food.
9. For excitement and adventure.
10. To visit places one has heard about, or to see famous places.[24]

Whatever the reason for taking a holiday trip, many factors—both economic and noneconomic—determine whether people actually go on a trip. A nationwide survey of American families conducted for *Better Homes and Gardens* asked respondents to identify the main obstacles to their taking family vacations. The top three reasons cited were the costs of transportation, hotels, and meals.[25]

Economic Determinants of Pleasure Travel

A CONSUMER who is considering taking a holiday trip has to weigh the potential benefits of taking a trip against the benefits of spending her money in other ways. The survey by *Better Homes and Gardens* found that Americans who did not travel felt that spending the same amount of money on material things brought them more joy, because things had more "lasting value" whereas the pleasure of travel was perceived to be short-lived.[26]

Time spent on vacation travel also has an *opportunity cost*, measured by its value in the next-best use. The person who takes a trip could be giving up income earning opportunities, or the pleasure from spending the same amount of time doing other things (e.g., gardening or sunning by the pool) at home. If the other activities are valued more highly, the person may choose not to go on a vacation trip.

Economists believe that income and prices are the most important economic determinants of demand for pleasure travel. Economic theory posits that demand for tourism is positively related to consumers' income and negatively related to tourism prices.[27] We examine each in turn in the following sections.

Effect of Income on Tourism Demand

Travel is costly, and it takes people with money to travel on vacations. The median household income of Americans taking pleasure trips overseas in 2000 was $92,400, compared to a median of $42,148 for all U.S. households.[28]

All else being equal, higher income generally means greater demand for pleasure travel.[29] But how much greater? Economists use the *income elasticity of demand* as a measure of the responsiveness of demand to changes in consumer incomes. Specifically,

$$\text{Income elasticity of demand for product X} = \frac{\%\text{ change in demand for product X}}{\%\text{ change in consumer income}}$$

The income elasticity of demand is represented by a number. If the income elasticity of demand for good X has a value of 2, then for every 1 percent increase in consumer income, demand for good X will rise by 2 percent. Demand can be income *elastic* (elasticity greater than 1) or income *inelastic* (elasticity less than 1 but not less than 0). Income elastic products are highly responsive to changes in consumer income, because a small percentage change in income will result in a larger percentage change in demand. The demand for products that are income inelastic are not very responsive to changes in consumer income. The demand for luxuries is income elastic, whereas the demand for necessities is income inelastic. Stephen Witt, Michael Brooke, and Peter Buckley found that, for Americans, most foreign holidays, except travel to Canada and Italy, are luxuries with high income elasticities of demand.[30] By comparison, food, with an income elasticity of demand of only .14, is a necessity.[31] But what defines a luxury or a necessity depends on the consumers' incomes: Gourmet food may be a necessity for people with high incomes, but it is a luxury for people with low incomes. As incomes rise, what was once a luxury may become a necessity.

Effect of Prices on Tourism Demand

The law of demand states that, all else being equal, consumer demand for pleasure travel will be greater (i.e., more trips will be taken) at a lower price than at a higher price. Economists use the *price elasticity of demand* to measure consumer responsiveness to price changes. Specifically,

$$\frac{\text{Income elasticity of demand}}{\text{for product X}} = \frac{\text{\% change in quantity demanded of product X}}{\text{\% change in the price of X}}$$

The price elasticity of demand is represented by a number. If the price elasticity of demand for X has a value of 2, then an increase in the price of X by 1 percent will *reduce* the quantity demanded of X by 2 percent.[32] In this example, buyers are obviously quite sensitive to the price change, because a small price change results in a proportionately larger change in the amount of X demanded. The demand for pleasure travel can be price *elastic* (i.e., price elasticity greater than 1), meaning that consumers are price sensitive, or price *inelastic* (i.e., price elasticity less than 1), meaning that consumers are price insensitive.

But what is that price? In making her final choice, the tourist faces many price comparisons. She no doubt compares the price of going to one destination *relative* to the price of going someplace else—or, staying home. If the airfare to Europe suddenly falls while the airfare to Hawaii remains unchanged, an American tourist who had initially decided to go to Hawaii may now change her mind and go to Europe instead. In sum, consumers make purchase decisions based on *relative* price differences among available alternatives. In addition to the relative price of transportation, the tourist also compares the relative prices of vacation goods, such as hotel accommodations, at each possible destination.

An important price in international tourism is the price of foreign currency or *foreign exchange*. An American tourist visiting Japan must have Japanese yen to spend while in Japan. The currency exchange rate converts the prices of Japanese goods in yen into U.S. dollar equivalents. For example, if a dinner at a Japanese restaurant is priced at 15,000 yen, an American visitor must pay the equivalent of $115.38 for the dinner if the currency exchange rate is 130 yen for $1.[33] If the yen–dollar exchange rate becomes 100 yen for $1, the dollar price of the 15,000 yen dinner rises to $150. Changes in the currency exchange rate alter the prices paid for foreign goods by visitors in their home currencies, even if the sticker prices at the foreign destination remain unchanged. In this example, the yen has *appreciated* against the U.S. dollar; alternatively, the dollar has *depreciated* in value against the yen. A depreciation of the dollar against the yen makes a Japanese vacation more expensive for Americans and may persuade some American tourists to visit another country instead of Japan. At the same time, it may encourage more Japanese to visit the United States.

Real World Demand Elasticities in International Tourism

GEOFFREY CROUCH has reviewed 80 studies of demand elasticities in international tourism and summarized them; his results are presented in Table 3-2.[34]

Although it is difficult to explain the individual differences in demand elasticities among the regions, Crouch's study can be summarized as follows:

- *Demand elasticities vary by country of origin and country of destination.* This should hardly be surprising. For example, residents of large countries, such as the United States, where many domestic tourist attractions exist, might be more price sensitive to the costs of foreign travel than residents of small countries (such as the Netherlands or Singapore), all else being equal. Price elasticities of demand for travel to unique destinations, such as Venice or Paris, are likely to be much lower than travel to beach resort destinations where there are plenty of choices.

- *For most origin and destination regions, international travel is a luxury with income elasticities of demand exceeding 1.*[35] The income elasticity of demand for travel *from* North America (i.e., United States and Canada) to foreign countries has an average value of 1.74, meaning that for every 1 percent increase in income in these two countries, demand for foreign travel increases by 1.74 percent. The income elasticity of demand for travel *to* the United States and Canada averages 2.06 percent.

TABLE 3-2

DEMAND ELASTICITIES IN INTERNATIONAL TOURISM

Region	Income	Price	Exchange Rates	Transport Costs	Marketing
OF ORIGIN					
N. Europe	2.06	-0.37	-1.57	-0.86	0.31
S. Europe/Mediterranean	1.67	-0.54	-1.41	-1.30	0.23
N. America	1.74	-0.58	-1.51	-1.52	0.59
Oceania	2.55	-0.73	—	-1.46	0.20
Latin America	0.28	-0.84	—	-1.26	0.61
Asia (developing)	—	—	—	—	—
Asia (developed)	4.45	-0.74	-0.51	-0.62	0.28
Middle East	—	—	—	—	—
OF DESTINATION					
N. Europe	1.79	-1.73	-0.44	-1.54	—
S. Europe/Mediterranean	2.34	-0.64	-1.34	0.11	0.39
N. America	2.06	-1.42	-1.54	-1.89	—
Oceania	3.35	-0.74	—	-0.98	0.23
Latin America	1.76	-0.58	—	-1.28	0.67
Asia (developing)	4.10	-0.56	0.27	-0.44	—
Asia (developed)	1.17	-1.18	—	-1.61	—
Middle East	2.47	-0.24	—	—	0.16

Source: Crouch (1995), p. 112.

- *Consumers appear to be generally price sensitive to the cost of transportation and currency exchange rates but not very sensitive to destination prices.*[36] Visitors from the developed countries of Asia appear not to be very price sensitive. Because these estimates from developed Asia come mostly from studies of Japanese overseas travel behavior, they suggest that Japanese consumers are not very sensitive to the costs of international travel.

- *Demand for international travel is generally not very responsive to the promotional or marketing expenditures of national tourist offices.*

In a separate study, Crouch found that consumers appear to be significantly more sensitive to the cost of transportation and income in long-haul tourism than in short-haul tourism.[37]

Other Determinants of Demand for International Tourism

THE DEMOGRAPHICS or population profile of a country has an important influence on the demand for travel.[38] Figure 3-1 displays the *travel propensities* for Japanese men and women for travel abroad—defined as the number of yearly overseas trips divided by the total population.[39] The figure shows that Japanese men and women have different travel propensities. Moreover, travel propensities vary at different ages and stages of a person's life. For example, Japanese women have their highest propensity to travel abroad in their twenties; travel propensity falls sharply after they marry in their late twenties and have children, and this propensity rises again after the late forties, when their children are grown or have passed their college entrance examinations. People from different age groups also belong to different birth cohorts, and cohort effects are important in determining Japanese outbound travel. The next generation of the elderly is likely to have a higher propensity to travel abroad than the current generation simply because the young and experienced travelers of today may want to continue to travel when they become older.

Cultural and religious ties between residents of different countries also have an important impact on the demand for international travel. For example,

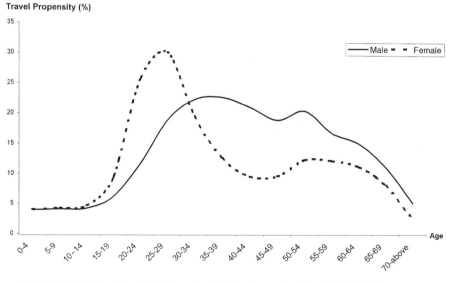

Source: The *Japan Travel Blue Book*, 2001, and the World Development Indicators 2000 CD-ROM.

FIGURE 3-1. Japanese outbound travel propensity.

most visitors to China are Chinese residing abroad. Large numbers of Japanese residents visit South Korea each year, not only because Korea is a cheap country to visit due to its geographic proximity to Japan, but also because many Korean–Japanese want to visit the country of their ancestry.[40] More Australians visit New Zealand than any other country, with the United Kingdom in a lofty fourth place; 24 percent of all Australian trips abroad in 1998 were trips to visit friends and relatives (referred to as VFR trips). American WWII veterans return to Europe in large (but decreasing) numbers each year to visit former battle grounds, just as survivors of the Pearl Harbor attack return to Hawaii each December to remember the event that propelled the United States into World War II.[41] Saudi vacationers, feeling unwelcome in the West especially after the September 11, 2001 terrorist attacks, are flocking to Malaysia, another Muslim country.[42] Catholics travel to Rome to visit the Vatican, and Muslims visit Mecca for "religious tourism."

Geography is another important determinant of the demand for travel. For example, although the Netherlands, the United Kingdom, France, and Italy have similar standards of living, citizens of the Netherlands (107.6 percent) and the United Kingdom (90.7 percent) have extremely high travel propensities, whereas those of France (32.3 percent) and Italy (26.1 percent) have much lower travel propensities.[43] The reason? France and Italy have sun-, sand-, and sea-destinations in their own countries, but the Netherlands and the United Kingdom do not. Citizens of the Netherlands have one of the highest propensities to travel internationally in the world also because of its small area and geographic proximity to other countries; in the Netherlands, no one has to travel more than 100 miles (or 160 kilometers) to get out of the country.

Travel decisions are heavily influenced by personal safety and security concerns.[44] Crime, war, terrorism, and political instability discourage tourist travel.[45] Political instability in Fiji deterred tourist travel to this popular Pacific island destination during the 1980s and 1990s. Likewise, tourism "became virtually nonexistent" in Uganda during the 1970s and the early 1980s due to political turmoil.[46] The first Gulf War in 1991, and the terrorist attacks on September 11, 2001, in New York City and Washington D.C., illustrate dramatically the negative impact of war and terrorist acts on travel. Even when people continue to travel, they tend to take shorter trips and stay closer to home. Abe Pizam and Aliza Fleischer found that the frequency of terrorist acts has a larger impact on tourism demand than the severity of these acts.[47] Moreover, for some destinations, the recovery can be quick—often within a year of the acts. For example, a recent study by the National Capital Area Tourism Research Program (NCATRP) at George Washington University found that seven months after the September 11, 2001, tragedies, lodging demand in New York City and Washington D.C. had recovered to year-earlier levels.[48] Likewise, in Hawaii, arriving passenger counts at Hawaii's airports returned to pre-September 11 levels by spring 2002, although Japanese visitor arrivals—plagued by severe economic problems at home—were still significantly below pre-September 11 levels.[49]

The World Tourism Organization has identified other factors that influence tourism demand; these include technological innovations, infrastructure development, the supply of skilled and experienced workers, and destination product development.[50] In 2003, the contagious and deadly SARS respiratory virus caused havoc with travel in some Asian countries.

Government regulations on pleasure travel have been a significant impediment to international travel. We examine this issue in Chapter 9.

Concluding Observations

STUDIES OF international tourism demand generally confirm that tourism is a luxury good, and that consumer demand for pleasure travel is highly responsive to income growth. Between 1975 and 2000, international tourist arrivals grew at an average annual (compound) rate of 4.9 percent per year, while world real gross domestic product grew at an annual rate of 3.4 percent; thus, international tourism grew 1.4 times as fast as world income.[51] This suggests that as long as the world's economies continue to grow, the continuation of tourism growth around the world is assured. On the other hand, demand for tourism is likely to fall even faster when economies go into recessions. Destinations and suppliers that depend heavily on tourism quickly find tourism is a highly volatile business.

This chapter also suggests that as people's incomes rise, tourism may become less of a luxury and thus less responsive to future income growth. This could mean that tourism will not grow as fast in the future as it has in the past.

Another important finding (Table 3-2) is that in deciding to take a trip, consumers are not as influenced by prices at the destinations as they are by the costs of (transportation) getting there or by changes in currency exchange rates. The insensitivity of consumers to destination prices might be explained by the fact that consumers are generally less aware of local (destination) prices before they leave and hence less influenced by them in making their travel decisions. The result is that the cost of "getting there" and the cost of "being there" don't have the same impact on consumer behavior.

Big gaps remain in our knowledge of domestic travel. For example, we don't know much about the degree of substitutability between domestic and foreign pleasure travel.[52] As well, we know little about the determinants of multidestination travel. Why are some trips multidestination trips, while others are travel to a single destination? More research must be done in these areas.

CHAPTER 4

WHY SOME PEOPLE TRAVEL on PACKAGE TOURS

Tours have never been the most popular way to travel, and never will be.

STANLEY C. PLOG [1]

Pleasure package tours organized by wholesalers: The most common way to go abroad among our people is this method of travel, and it still enjoys great popularity.

JAPAN TRAVEL BLUE BOOK [2]

THE 1969 MOVIE "If It's Tuesday, This Must Be Belgium" (starring Suzanne Pleshette), about a wacky group of American tourists on a 10-day, 18-country escorted European tour, provides one comic episode after another. The movie became synonymous with many viewers' perception—and misperception—of *package tours*. On both sides of the Atlantic, mass-marketed package tours did not present an attractive image. Orvar Lofgren describes tourists who travel on package tours as people who "chose security before adventure and could not tell the inauthentic from the authentic." Yet he acknowledges that it is exactly "its certainty and predictability that made the package tour a mass phenomenon. It opened up international travel for the vast majority of working-class families for whom a trip abroad had previously been a utopia." [3]

In 2001, 17 percent of U.S. residents traveling overseas on pleasure trips and 27 percent of foreign tourists visiting the United States purchased package tours. [4] Package tours are generally more popular among travelers on overseas pleasure trips than on domestic trips. However, the statement that "Tours have never been the most popular way to travel" does not apply to travelers from all countries. For example, most—about two-thirds—Japanese tourists traveling abroad in 1998 were on prepaid package tours.[5]

Millions of tourists around the world travel on package tours. The 17 percent of American tourists traveling abroad and 27 percent of foreign tourists traveling to the United States in 2001 represent 3.4 million Americans and 3.6 million foreign tourists buying package tours.[6] The National Travel Association (NTA) estimates that residents of Canada and the United States took 144 million overnight package trips during 2000, with a total spending of approximately $186 billion worldwide.[7] A Google search of "package tours" pulls up a 75-page listing of package tours and tour vendors around the world.

What Is a Package Tour?

A PACKAGE *tour* combines elements of a pleasure trip, such as air and ground transportation, baggage handling, accommodation, sightseeing, meals, and other items, into a single product that is then sold to the consumer at a single price.[8] These tours are generally put together by *tour operators* and *tour wholesalers*,[9] who purchase the components from their suppliers, such as airlines, bus companies, hotels, restaurants, and other travel-related companies. The tour operators and wholesalers sell the tours either directly to consumers or, more frequently, through retail *travel agents*. Thus, tour wholesalers and tour operators are the middlemen between the suppliers and the retail agents and consumers.

Package tours vary in price, departure dates, trip lengths, and purpose. The tours may be single destination, or multidestination and multicountry tours. These tours also vary in *inclusivity*. Some package tours are very basic (or stripped down), containing perhaps only round-trip airfare, ground transfers, and lodging accommodations; travelers on these tours travel on their own with considerable schedule flexibility. At the other extreme, inclusive tours usually require buyers to travel in a group and stick to a tight schedule: The tours may include a *tour escort* who travels with the group, meals, sightseeing, entertainment, and other travel services. A package tour can be put together to meet just about any consumer demand as long as potential profit induces a tour operator to create it. In recent years, special interest tours such as outdoor adventure tours, eco-tourism tours, gourmet tours, and cruise packages have become very popular among travelers.

The common feature of package tours is that the buyer must pay for the tour in advance. Unless she purchases separate trip insurance, she bears the risk that she may lose most or all the money she paid for the tour if she cannot make the trip. In most cases, she can buy the individual components of the package (e.g., transportation) directly from suppliers, but that would require her to make separate transactions for each item she wants to purchase.

Advantages and Disadvantages of Traveling on Package Tours

WHETHER TO travel on a package tour depends on the perceived benefits (advantages) versus costs (disadvantages) to the consumer. A 1975 survey of over 1,000 U.S. tour purchasers conducted by Touche Ross and Company found that 8 percent of them would not travel if package tours were unavailable, and another 42 percent would change their travel plans. The study found that the principal perceived benefits of traveling on package tours were convenience, cheaper price, unfamiliarity with destination, and the ability to "see more, do more."[10]

Buying a package tour not only reduces the cost to the consumer of finding trip information and booking arrangements, it can be a cheaper way to travel. In putting together tour packages, tour operators typically receive discounts from suppliers ranging from 10 to over 50 percent. Most of that discount may be passed along to the consumer if the tour operator faces vigorous competition from other tour companies. In some cases, the price of a package—including round-trip airfare, lodging, and ground transfers—may be cheaper than the round-trip airfare alone if purchased directly by the consumer.

Stanley Plog cites similar advantages to taking an escorted tour:[11]

1. The most important details of a trip have been taken care of by experts, allowing the traveler to relax and obtain maximum enjoyment from his travels. Even the problem of strange customs and foreign languages are handled by an expert tour guide provided by the tour operator.
2. There are no surprises. Hotels wait for their guests in each city, and they are of a guaranteed level of quality. Restaurants included in the package are safe and representative of what is unique to the local culture.
3. A planned itinerary ensures that all of the "must-see" spots will be visited—places that might be overlooked by travelers unfamiliar with the area.

4. All of this can be purchased at a price well below the cost of making one's own arrangements because of the vast purchasing power of travel providers.

The benefits of traveling on a package tour vary among travelers. A female traveling alone may place a very high value on the companionship and safety of group travel. Frequently, tour operators and travel agents will pair single travelers together to save on the price of a single room. Elderly travelers may value highly the baggage handling service included in many tours.

However, the fact that most (U.S.) tourists do not travel on package tours indicates that their perceived disadvantages outweigh their advantages. The disadvantages of package tour travel also vary among travelers. One of the most important reasons why travelers do not travel on package tours is that there may not be a package tour sold for every imaginable trip demanded by travelers.

Plog believes that package tours (especially escorted tours) are declining in popularity among North American travelers because they suffer from poor consumer image and a changing psychology of travelers. The words "tour" and "escorted" carry negative connotations to many travelers, because they convey notions of "herding" and "too much manipulation and control over the lives of people." At the same time, more senior citizens see themselves as psychologically and physically younger and want to remain independent longer than cohorts from earlier generations.[12]

For many travelers, package tours also may not be a "cheaper" way to travel than independent travel. The savings from buying a package tour may be far less than the difference between the retail price of the tour and what the consumer would have to pay if she were to buy the individual components separately: The buyer may not want all the components of that package tour, because some items in the package may have little or no value to her. For example, if a tour includes the admission fee to a museum or a temple, and the tourist would rather spend the time shopping, she ends up paying for something she doesn't use. A repeat visitor may not want to revisit some of the attractions visited on a previous trip, and thus would not assign much value to those items if they were included in a tour. Many services included in package tours are never used by their buyers.[13] As well, tour packages may include lodging accommodations that are more expensive than what the buyer is otherwise willing to pay if she were booking accommodations for the trip herself. Whether the package tour is the more "economical" way to travel depends on a comparison of the retail price of the package and the price the consumer is willing to pay for that package.

The price that a consumer is willing to pay for any good, whether it be one night's stay at a four-star hotel room in Paris, a meal at a fancy restaurant or street-side cafe, or a visit to the Louvre, reflects the *utility* (or, personal satisfaction) that she expects to gain from that good. The more utility she expects to get from the good, the more she is willing to pay.[14] Thus, the price a consumer is willing to pay for a particular package tour depends on the utility that the consumer expects to derive from the individual components of the package and perhaps some utility from the benefits of traveling in a group (e.g., companionship and safety). The bottom line is that if the retail price of the package exceeds the price the consumer is willing to pay, the consumer will not buy the tour. Obviously, the lower the retail price of the package, the greater the likelihood that more consumers are willing to buy the package. Studies have shown that consumers are quite sensitive to the price of package tours.[15] One implication of this discussion is that people who travel together on an inclusive package tour share similar tour preferences; otherwise, they would buy different tour packages or travel independently. Another implication is that repeat visitors are less likely to return to a destination on an inclusive package tour.

Another potential cost disadvantage of traveling on package tours exists. Package tours are priced on a per person basis, and each person pays the same price. Visitors who travel independently may enjoy *economies of scale* in the purchase of some vacation goods. For example, children accompanying adults can often stay for free in a hotel if they stay in the same room. On a tour, the children may have to pay additional charges. Several people traveling together can economize by driving their own car instead of paying the equivalent of individual coach fares on a sightseeing bus. Thus, one attribute of package tours is that they might be less attractive to large travel parties.

Pauline Sheldon offers three hypotheses on package tours:[16]

1. *More people travel independently than on a basic tour, and more people will buy a basic tour than an inclusive tour.* She found her hypothesis confirmed on package tours from the U.S. mainland to Hawaii. However, had she tested the hypothesis on Japanese overseas travelers, she would have rejected her hypothesis. Among Japanese tourists traveling overseas, those

traveling on escorted, "full package" tours (in which meals and local sight-seeing trips are also included) outnumber those traveling on less inclusive "free-time" package tours (where tourists spend a greater portion of their time doing their own activities); less than 20 percent of Japanese overseas tourists travel independently.[17]

2. *Basic tours offer bigger savings (percentage wise) than inclusive tours.* She reasons that if more people travel on basic tours than inclusive tours, tour operators can negotiate larger discounts from suppliers, and that could mean bigger savings to consumers. Indeed, she found that the retail prices of some package tours in her sample were higher than if the travelers had bought the components separately.[18] Some people who bought inclusive package tours paid a price premium for their packages.

3. *Members of an inclusive tour are more alike in their personal characteristics than those traveling on a basic tour; and those who travel independently are the most diverse.* In other words, people on the same tour must share similar tastes for the tour, and to the extent taste preferences are reflected in their personal characteristics, those who travel on inclusive package tours must share the greatest number of common personal traits. This hypothesis was confirmed when she compared the age, expenditure, and party size of travelers from the United States mainland to Hawaii for the three groups. The buyers of inclusive tours showed the least differences in the three attributes.

Why Are Package Tours So Popular Among the Japanese?

PAUL VARLEY, a renowned scholar of Japanese culture, writes the following about the Japanese people:

> The spread of mass culture tends to standardize tastes and reduce class distinction. The Japanese, with their collective ethos, are probably more susceptible than most people to such standardization... Always one of the world's most ethnically homogeneous people, the Japanese may also have become one of its most homogeneous socially and culturally.[19]

The Japanese are also frequently described as quality-demanding, safety-conscious, and time-constrained travelers. Most Japanese also lack confidence in their ability to speak foreign languages. These attributes may explain why package tours are so popular among Japanese overseas travelers.[20] These constraints are much less important among younger Japanese overseas travelers.

Among Japanese overseas travelers, package tours are more popular among women than men, and more popular among the elderly than the young. Elderly men and women prefer the escorted, inclusive (full package) tours, whereas housewives, single women, and female students prefer the less structured (free time) tours. Free time package tours are preferred by tourists visiting beach resorts.[21]

Concluding Observations

IN RESPONSE to changing consumer demand, tour operators and wholesalers are altering the product mix of package tours they offer. The United States Tour Operators Association (USTOA) notes that package tours today are far more flexible and less regimented. It estimates that 80 percent of all the package tours sold in the United States today are independent tours. Not surprisingly, the average age of the buyer has fallen to around 50 years of age, versus an average of 60 some years ago. Reflecting the interests of younger travelers, more tours today emphasize "doing" rather than "seeing." Multidestination and multicountry tours have become less common, with four out of five tours focusing on a single destination or country. Although the overall demand for escorted, inclusive package tours may have declined, escorted tours are still popular with first-time travelers and with those traveling to remote destinations.[22]

Similar changes are occurring in Japan, where package tours remain the preferred—though declining—mode of overseas travel.[23] Among Japanese tourists visiting Hawai‘i, almost nine in ten still travel on package tours.[24] However, the trend is clearly away from buying all-inclusive, escorted tours and toward more flexible and less inclusive tours. In 2001, fewer than one-third of tour packages included meals and only 12 percent of them included sightseeing.[25] No longer are travelers herded in big buses from one attraction to another by umbrella-wielding tour escorts, as they were in the 1970s. Today's travelers are more likely to be seen sightseeing and shopping on their own, riding city buses and trolleys, and driving rented Mustang convertibles.

CHAPTER 5

WHY SOME PEOPLE
USE TRAVEL AGENTS

We have lost our monopoly on the distribution of travel.

JOSEPH GALLOWAY[1]

TOURISTS PLANNING VACATION trips require information about where to go, what legal requirements must be satisfied (for example, is a passport or a visa required or will immunization shots be needed?), airline and rail fares and schedules, hotel and car rentals, and so forth. They search for information in travel guides and magazines, call or write to government travel bureaus, and even talk to friends and relatives who have traveled to places they are interested in visiting. The information is not free, because it takes time and often money to find the information needed. With the growing use of the Internet, finding travel information has become much easier and thus less costly. If a tourist is making a repeat visit to a vacation destination, she may already have most of the travel information needed.

Once the trip plans are made, the traveler still has to book reservations, apply for passports and visas if traveling abroad, pay deposits, and maybe purchase travel insurance. Making these transactions also requires time and money. Thus, in planning and arranging a trip, travelers can incur both the cost of information search and the cost of making trip arrangements. Travelers may try to find travel information and book travel arrangements themselves. Alternatively, they may use the services of travel agencies.

The Travel Agency and The Travel Agent

THE TRAVEL *agency* (or, its owner/employee, the *travel agent*) is a middleman organization that brings the buyer and seller of travel services together. Like retail stores, traditional "brick-and-mortar" travel agencies are located in shopping and business centers in towns and large cities, serving customers in local geographic markets. In 2001, there were 27,633 travel agency locations in the United States.[2] These businesses provide information and often make recommendations to the traveler, book travel arrangements with suppliers (e.g., airlines, hotels, cruise ship companies, car rental companies, etc.), and sell prepaid package tours and trip insurance. In many cases, the traveler pays no fee to the travel agency for its services; the agency receives a commission from the travel companies (such as airlines and hotels) whose services it sells. For some services, the traveler has to pay the travel agency a fee to make certain travel arrangements, because some travel businesses, such as budget hotels and hostels, and recently major U.S. airlines, refuse to pay base commissions to travel agencies for booking business with them. Increasingly, travel agencies are also charging or raising their service fees to their customers because the commissions offered by the suppliers do not adequately cover the cost of providing some services. In 1999, 68 percent of U.S. travel agencies charged service fees for personal or leisure travel, compared to 42 percent in 1997.[3] In 2002, most U.S. travel agents charged $30 to $40 for issuing an airline ticket.[4]

Legally, the travel agency is the *agent* of the travel company. The travel company is the *principal*.[5] Incentive problems potentially arise when the principal–agent relationship is structured this way. Eric Friedheim observes that "Since the agent only makes money on commissions, the more money spent by the client, the higher the commissions will be. But in many cases, the agent's mandate is to save money, so the harder the agent works to save money, the less money that agent makes."[6]

Let's look at a few examples of how travel agents are motivated by the size of the potential commissions on travel bookings. In 1999, more than half of the travel agencies surveyed by *Travel Weekly* magazine indicated that they sold particular airlines based on the commission rate paid. When asked what factors were most important in encouraging agents to recommend particular destinations to travelers, they listed package prices (78 percent), familiarization ("*fam*") trips (75 percent), and commission incentives (68 percent) as the three leading factors.[7] In 2001, the U.S. federal government set up its own hotel program, the Federal Premier Lodging Program (FPLP), which includes a large number of hotel properties in various cities for use by its staff when they travel,[8] but bookings came in very slowly partly because hotels weren't required to pay travel agent commissions on FPLP bookings.[9] Indeed, if agents have the incentive to sell the more expensive services and products to consumers to maximize commissions, they may not always get the best deals for their clients. Many travelers may opt to arrange their own travel.

On-line travel agencies such as Expedia, Inc., Travelocity.com, Orbitz.com (owned by the five largest airlines in the U.S.—American, United, Delta, Continental, and Northwest),[10] and eBay Travel (the joint venture between Priceline.com and eBay Inc.) are not restricted to specific geographic markets and sell their services globally and around the clock. They can also alert passengers of last-minute delays and cancellations via the Internet. On-line travel agencies began by offering relatively limited services compared to tra-ditional brick-and-mortar travel agencies, primarily booking flights, hotels, and car rentals. But these on-line businesses are expanding the scope of their services and sales rapidly. In 2001, Travelocity.com ($3.1 billion in gross sales) and Expedia, Inc. ($2.9 billion in gross sales) became the sixth and eighth largest U.S. travel agencies. Their shares of total travel agency revenues are rising rapidly.[11]

To Use a Travel Agent or Not

Why do some travelers use the services of a travel agent while others search for and book their own travel arrangements? For the consumer, the decision whether to use a travel agent to find information for trip planning or to book the travel arrangements herself depends on the perceived benefits versus the costs of choosing each option. The consumer wants to find the best deals while expending the least amount of effort in time and money.

To find the "best" prices, the buyer has to search for price offerings from different vendors. How intensively the consumer should search depends on the dispersion of prices and the number of prices canvassed.[12] Obviously, if no price variation exists among vendors, no potential gain is achieved from searching, and the bigger the price spread, the greater the potential gain from additional search. The optimum amount of search effort also depends on the cost of searching. Because not all consumers value their time equally, the cost of searching varies among consumers. For a consumer, the "best" price may not be the lowest price offered by vendors.

Searching for information through a travel agent is one way to reduce the personal cost of the search. Not surprisingly, with the proliferation of airfares following the deregulation of air travel in the United States in 1978, more people sought help from travel agents to plan and book their travel, and the percentage of tickets sold by travel agents rose from 38 percent in 1977 to about 80 percent in 1988.[13]

Generally, the more complicated the trip, the more costly it is for the consumer to find information and make the trip arrangements herself. For example, traveling to foreign destinations may require the visitor to get a passport and a visa; find schedule and fare information on air carriers and local transportation; research the quality, availability, and prices of lodging accommodations; and then make the bookings. In some cases, foreign language proficiency may be required. The cost adds up if the traveler wants to visit more than one country. One travel agent observed that "When people travel internationally, a lot more is involved than simply booking a ticket. There are so many rules and regulations regarding air fares. And even people who plan their own vacations want [an agent's help for] things other than flights."[14] When the consumer can have all her trip arrangements made by a single visit to a travel agency, it might be more costly for her to make them herself.

Some travel services, such as package tours, group tours, and cruises can be purchased more easily through travel agents. (Putting together a single customized package tour is costly.) On the other hand, some travel services are typically not sold through travel agents because the suppliers of those services do not offer travel agent commissions; thus, the agent will not sell those services unless the customer pays a separate service fee. Travelers cashing in their frequent flyer miles for air tickets typically must book their own air travel rather than go through a travel agent.

It is less costly for repeat visitors to find information and make reservations themselves than for first-time visitors. Visitors returning year after year to the same destination and the same hotel may find it more convenient, quicker, and perhaps receive better service to call the hotel directly to book their reservations. Hence, repeat visitors are more likely to make their own travel arrangements, other things being equal.

Travelers who value their time highly (e.g., high income travelers and business travelers) are more likely to use travel agents than those with a lower opportunity cost of time.

The Use of Travel Agents

TABLE 5.1 shows how U.S. travelers going overseas and foreign travelers visiting the United States on leisure trips in 2001 obtained their trip information. Travelers typically used more than one source to find trip information to plan their trips. More travelers rely on travel agents for travel information than any other source.

The State of Hawaii conducts a yearly survey of visitors to Hawaii. The survey of 2001 (January–June) U.S. visitors to Hawaii indicates that they are quite aware of the relative advantage of using travel agents in trip planning (Table 5.2). As expected, repeat visitors are less likely to use travel agents because they have information from prior trips. And not surprisingly, time-constrained business and higher income travelers are more likely to use travel agents. It is harder to explain how education affects consumers' use of travel agents; more educated consumers can find information more easily themselves rather than through a travel agent, but on the other hand, their time is more valuable because they generally have higher incomes and hence might prefer to rely on a travel agent to help them with planning and making travel arrangements.

TABLE 5-1

INFORMATION SOURCES FOR PLANNING FOREIGN TRIPS

	U.S. Travelers (%)	Foreign Travelers to the U.S. (%)
Travel Agent	48	58
Airline	26	16
Internet	28	22
Friends & Relatives	18	20
Company Travel Dept.	4	4
Travel Guides	8	13
Tour Company	6	11
Newspapers/Magazines	3	7
State/City Travel Office	3	6

Source: *Travel Industry World 2002 Yearbook*, pp. 98 and 101.

TABLE 5-2

USE OF TRAVEL AGENTS BY U.S. VISITORS
TO HAWAII IN TRIP PLANNING: 2001

Visitor	Travel Agent Use (%)	
	Yes	No
First Time Visitor	55.6	44.4
Repeat Visitor	45.7	54.3
Pleasure Trip	48.9	51.1
Business Trip	56.3	43.7
Annual Household Income		
Below $50,000	45.8	54.2
$50,000–$99,000	47.8	52.2
$100,000 and over	49.8	50.2
Education		
High School Grad.	55.9	44.1
College Grad. (4 yrs.)	44.1	55.9
Post Graduate Degree	56.2	43.7

Source: State of Hawaii Department of Business, Economic Development and Tourism, Tourism Research Branch. Special tabulation by Mr. Cy Feng.

Figure 5-1 shows how U.S. travelers booked their overseas pleasure trips in 1999 and 2001. Booking through the middlemen—travel agents or tour operators—accounted for more than 50 percent of all bookings on overseas trips, more than the frequency of self-bookings. However, self-booking on the Internet is rising, while the use of travel agents has declined. The dominance of middlemen in booking travel arrangements in overseas travel is perhaps not surprising given the greater complexity of overseas trips.

The Impact of the Internet on Consumers

TRAVEL IS the largest category of retail sales on-line. The Internet has dramatically reduced the cost to consumers of finding travel information and booking trip arrangements personally. For some consumers, shopping on the web is more convenient because they don't have to make a trip to the travel agency, find parking space, and wait for confirmation, and they can shop 24 hours a day and 7 days a week.[15] A March 2001 survey conducted by Plog

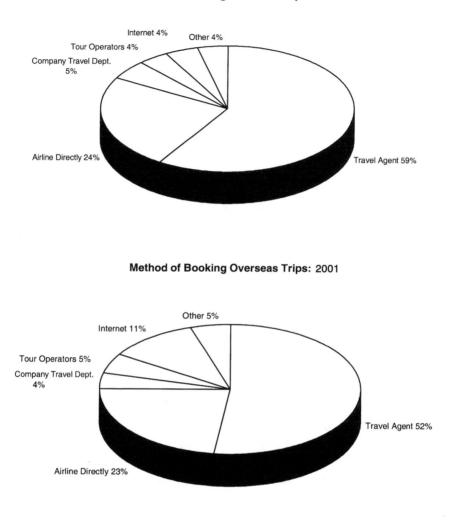

Method of Booking Overseas Trips: 1999

Internet 4%
Other 4%
Tour Operators 4%
Company Travel Dept. 5%
Airline Directly 24%
Travel Agent 59%

Method of Booking Overseas Trips: 2001

Other 5%
Internet 11%
Tour Operators 5%
Company Travel Dept. 4%
Airline Directly 23%
Travel Agent 52%

Source: *Travel Industry World 2002 Yearbook,* p. 75; *2001 Yearbook,* p. 101.

FIGURE 5-1

Research Inc., of on-line air travelers who used the Internet to search and book travel, found that most respondents believed that the Internet "gives [travelers] more control over their itinerary; saves time, and provides unbiased information."[16] The Internet also tends to increase price dispersion, which induces consumers to increase their search effort.[17] The 2002 National Trade

Monitor survey by Yesawich, Pepperdine & Brown/Yankelovich Partners (YSB) noted that nine out of ten travelers responded that the most important reason to use the Internet on travel research was "being able to check the lowest rates for airfares, hotels, and rental car companies."[18]

A similar survey conducted by Forrester Research in 2002 found that 70 percent of American travelers were doing travel research on-line and more than half of them actually made purchases on the web.[19] Credit card security concerns, preference for face-to-face dealings, and customer loyalty continue to induce many travelers to use traditional travel agents to make their travel arrangements. Not surprisingly, younger travelers, who are more comfortable with using technological innovations, are more likely to use the Internet to plan and book their travel. In 2002, three out of ten U.S. travelers still used the services of a travel agent; usage is much higher among older and more affluent travelers.[20]

Reducing transaction costs is not the only reason why some travelers purchase travel products on-line. Airlines often sell tickets at lower prices on-line (called "web fares") on their own web sites (or on Orbitz.com) than through traditional travel agents. Indeed, budget conscious and opportunistic travelers are able to name their own prices for travel services on Priceline.com.

However, a recent study of round trip airfares in the top twenty markets searched thirteen on-line travel sites, including those of traditional travel agents and suppliers, on two specific dates and found that Orbitz.com was able to find the lowest fares more often than either Expedia or Travelocity.com, and that the airlines themselves frequently have the best fares.[21] A similar study of airfares for identical itineraries on the big three on-line travel sites—Expedia, Travelocity, and Orbitz—with airline reservation sites, airlines' toll-free reservation numbers, and a neighborhood travel agency with access to several industry reservation systems found no consistently clear winner in locating the lowest fares.[22] The reason? The pricing of travel services remains highly decentralized, and no single source has access to all the prices from different suppliers.[23]

The Impact of the Internet on Travel Agencies

THE INTERNET has reduced the cost to suppliers of selling services directly to travelers through their own web sites or through on-line travel agencies. Not surprisingly, the Internet has resulted in some *disintermediation* whereby consumers and suppliers bypass the traditional middlemen, the brick-and-mortar travel agencies.[24] As the cost of direct marketing via the Internet falls, suppliers are less willing to pay the same commissions to travel agents as before.

The Internet has dramatically changed the relationship between the major U.S. airlines and travel agencies. Travel agencies and airlines traditionally subscribed to computer reservation systems such as Sabre, Worldspan, Amadeus, and Galileo, which are referred to as global distribution systems (GDS). By subscribing to a GDS, a travel agency can locate information and book and issue tickets. For an airline, subscribing to a GDS enables it to inform travel agencies what products are available. When travel agents make bookings using the GDS, the airlines pay booking fees to the GDS and, in many instances, additional incentive commissions. In 2000, 82 percent of GDS revenues came from booking fees and 87 percent of the booking revenues were derived from airline reservations.[25]

Airlines prefer to sell services directly to travelers through their own web sites, which is their least costly distribution channel[26] or through on-line travel agencies such as Orbitz. Orbitz is developing direct connections to the airlines' internal reservation systems to reduce its dependence on the GDS, hence reducing its distribution costs. Airlines do not pay fees to the GDS or commissions to travel agencies when they book on their own internal reservation systems. Vice President of Orbitz, Carol Jouzaitis, explains that:

> It simply costs the airlines less to sell tickets on-line. Orbitz, for example, enables airlines to reduce the cost of the middleman and pass the savings on to consumers in the form of discounted Web fares. In this case, the middlemen are the computer reservation systems that traditional travel agents use but that add $12 to $15 to the cost of an air ticket, besides the commission charged by the agent.[27]

The major airlines have cut or capped agent commissions several times, beginning in 1995. Finally, in March 2002, Delta Airlines, the third-largest U.S. carrier, eliminated all base commissions to travel agents for tickets sold in the United States and Canada; American, Continental, Northwest, and United Airlines quickly followed Delta's lead. As a result, major airlines' commission expenses have been cut by nearly half between 1995 and 2001.[28]

In response to the earlier rounds of commission cuts, one travel agent remarked that the airlines "want to get rid of us."[29] As a result, travel agencies are currently refocusing their business by de-emphasizing selling airline tickets for leisure travel to selling more "lucrative" travel products like corporate travel, package tours, cruises, and international travel.[30] Agents are also selling more Web fares using "fare scraping" software that automatically searches a large number of Websites for the best fares. These agents charge their clients a service fee.[31]

Unlike the airlines, hotels have yet to make wholesale cuts to travel agent commissions. One reason is that the hotel industry is a lot more fragmented than the airline industry and provides many more choices and keener competition in any given destination. Although many consumers only want the lowest airfares, they also consider amenities and location when choosing hotel accommodations. One hotel executive observed that "Hotels are a much more complex product than airlines. So the travel agent is much more helpful in actually selling the hotel product."[32] But that may soon change. For example, in 2002, five leading hotel companies—Marriott, Hyatt, Hilton, Six Continents, and Starwood—formed their own on-line Website to sell discount hotel rooms directly to consumers.[33]

Concluding Observations

TOURISM IS largely an information business prior to and through the actual sale of the services. The Internet and high-speed computers have dramatically reduced the cost of disseminating information, thus producing an explosion in the number of information brokers in the travel and tourism industry. Not surprisingly, traditional travel agencies have lost ground in the business of travel distribution.

Between 1996 and 2002, the number of travel agency locations in the United States fell from 33,715 to 26,120, a decline of over 22 percent.[34] About 90 percent of the decrease was due to the consolidation of small travel agencies; the rest was due to closings. The decline paralleled the decision by the major U.S. airlines to reduce travel agent commissions beginning in 1995. Major airlines no longer pay base commission fees for travel sold in the United States.[35]

As increasing numbers of Americans go on-line and feel more secure about making purchases on the Internet, the decline in the number of U.S. brick-and-mortar travel agencies is likely to continue as more travelers find it more advantageous to conduct their own information search and book their own travel arrangements. James Koch and Richard Cebula surmise that travel agents "may be an endangered species" because of the 'Net.[36] On-line sites, however, display what they want to sell; by contrast, the traditional travel agent may respond to her client's requests. Thus, an important role for travel agents may still exist. Some services—like tourism—are very difficult to compare, even using the Internet, because they involve distinctive services and atmospheres. In the future, travel agents may find their niche more in the business of providing counsel and planning to travelers requiring these services than in booking basic travel services. One travel agent's recent advice to other travel agents is that "It's not just about selling. If you're not educating and motivating and inspiring, then, yes, you can be replaced by computers."[37] In the future, travel agents will be selling their expertise rather than simply searching for and selling travel services. The age of "commissions" is increasingly being replaced by the age of "service fees." When agents are paid by the consumer rather than the supplier, the future travel agent increasingly will become the agent of the consumer rather than the agent of the supplier.

CHAPTER 6

ONCE THERE

The first condition of understanding a foreign country is to smell it.

RUDYARD KIPLING [1]

WHEN TOURISTS FROM the U.S. West Coast traveled to Hawaii by ship in the 1950s, the journey took more than five days one-way, and they stayed more than three weeks in the islands. Today, the same trip by plane takes about five hours and at a far lower real fare than ship passage, and the typical visitor from the western states stays in Hawaii less than ten days. Visitors from the eastern United States who spend more time traveling to Hawaii and pay higher airfares stay longer than tourists from the western states (about half a day). European visitors to Hawaii stay even longer—an average of twelve days in Hawaii. The law of demand states that, all else being equal, the quantity demanded of a good—in this case, the number of vacation days in Hawaii—should be less at a higher price (i.e., time and money cost). Does the law of demand not apply to vacationing Hawaii tourists? Because this positive relationship between travel cost and length of stay is also observed elsewhere, the law of demand apparently has not been refuted.

To illustrate, Reuben Gronau observed that air trips of 800 miles and less had a duration of four nights or less, whereas trips in excess of 800 miles tended to last more than one week.[2] In 1998, British visitors to France or the Netherlands spent an average of four nights at their destinations. By comparison, British visitors to the United States spent fifteen nights in the United States;

British visitors to Japan spent twenty nights. Canadian visitors to the United States averaged 7.1 nights, Italy 12.4 nights, Australia 29.7 nights, and India 34.1 nights.[3] It is apparent that the further the distance traveled, the longer the trip duration. Gronau explains the disparity in trip durations as follows:

> …the higher the price [i.e., money and time cost] of the trip, the greater the passenger's tendency to prolong his stay and to reduce the number of his trips. On the other hand, the higher the costs of hotels and restaurants and the lower the cost of the trip, the greater is the passenger's tendency to return home quickly and repeat his journey in the future. Since the price of the trip is directly related to distance, one can expect the length of the stay and the trip's distance to be positively correlated.[4]

Determinants of Trip Duration

A SIMPLE explanation exists for the puzzling relationship between trip cost and length of stay at the destination.[5] Consider two individuals: One lives in town and the other lives in a distant suburb and both are planning to attend a theatrical production in town. The price of the theater ticket is the same for both individuals, but it would obviously take more time and money for the suburbanite to travel into town for the show. The suburbanite decides that because it requires so much effort to go into town, it may not be worthwhile only to attend the show. She decides, instead, to extend the trip to an entire day by leaving home early to shop, run errands, have dinner, and then attend the show in town before returning home. Thus, she combines several activities into a single, longer trip. If she only had sufficient time to attend the show, she may decide not to go at all.

By contrast, the individual living in town would think nothing about just going to the show; the shopping and dinner on the town can wait another day, because it requires little effort to make another trip. For her, attending the show can be a brief evening outing. In sum, the person who has the higher cost of travel wants to stay longer.

Now, suppose city officials decide to levy a fee of, say, $5 for each hour the suburbanite remains in town, to be paid at the time she leaves. Because the cost of staying in town now rises with each additional hour she spends in town, it will induce her to use her time efficiently and perhaps even cut out some less valuable activities so that she can leave town quickly.

The same principles apply to pleasure travel. If the cost of travel (i.e., "getting there") is high, a tourist may decide not to go; but if she does go, she would opt for a lengthy stay. And if the cost of getting there were to fall, she might decide that it would even be worthwhile to take a short trip now and return soon for another visit.

On the other hand, if the prices of hotel accommodations, restaurant meals, and entertainment were to rise at the destination (say, due to the government raising its sales tax), she might decide to do less and reduce the duration of her trip.

It follows from this analysis that visitors from the eastern United States would, on average, spend more days in Hawaii than visitors from the western states because of their relatively higher cost of travel to Hawaii. By staying longer in Hawaii, the visitor from the eastern United States is less likely to make another visit soon. Hence, it is not surprising that visitors from the West have taken an average of nearly six trips to Hawaii (lifetime) compared to 3.5 trips for visitors from the East.[6]

In any given year, the cost of travel to a destination is roughly proportional to the trip distance. Over time, however, the time and money cost are a better measure of the cost of travel to a destination than geographic distance. The cost of travel to Hawaii has declined dramatically because of the switch from ships to planes, the higher frequency of scheduled air service, and the lower real fares, even as the distance to Hawaii remains the same. Not surprisingly, the duration of American tourist visits has declined. This decrease in visitor length of stay was greatest during the 1960s and 1970s, immediately after the introduction of jet plane service to Hawaii from the U.S. mainland in 1959. Following the initial sharp decline, the average length of stay (in days) of U.S. visitors to Hawaii has stabilized, as has the cost of travel to Hawaii.

A decline in visitor trip duration is usually greeted by Hawaii tourism officials with disappointment. Officials often do not understand that the long-term decline in the visitor length of stay is offset by more people visiting Hawaii more frequently on shorter vacations. The analysis here suggests that the decision to go on a trip, the choice of the destination, and trip duration are jointly determined and are not separate and independent decisions. Moreover, the price of "getting there" and the price of "being there" have different effects on trip duration. All else being equal, higher destination prices reduce a visitor's length of stay, but a higher cost of getting there increases her length of stay. In multidestination travel, higher prices in Destination A relative to substitute Destination B induces tourists to spend less time in A and more time in B, although first time visitors appear to be much less price sensitive to price differences than repeat visitors.[7]

How do we explain that U.S. visitors to the island of Oahu (Honolulu) stayed an average of 7.72 days in 2001, whereas visitors to Kauai stayed nearly 1 day less, and visitors to the tiny island of Lanai stayed only 5 days? The simple answer is that there's lots more to do on Oahu than on Kauai and on Lanai. Consumer demand for heterogeneous goods is influenced by differences in the physical and qualitative attributes of the goods.[8] For example, car buyers don't want to buy just any car. Their choices depend on the physical and performance attributes of a car: Some consumers prefer four-door sedans to two-door coupes, some prefer an automatic transmission to the standard shift, and so on. Like cars, tourism is a heterogeneous good. Thus, demand for pleasure trips and trip duration are partly determined by the attributes of tourist destinations.[9] This implies that destinations can entice tourists to stay longer by developing more and better tourist attractions.

Finally, differences in social attitudes toward vacations can also account for differences in trip duration among different visitor groups. For example, the typical Japanese visitor to Hawaii stayed only six days in Hawaii in 2001, the shortest trip duration among Hawaii's visitors.[10] Japanese society, unlike European society, still regards with suspicion and disapproval those of its people—and especially white-collar male office workers—who take long vacations. Although the Japanese have about as many yearly vacation days as Americans, the Japanese typically use only half the vacation days to which they are entitled.[11] In 1999, 56.3 percent of all Japanese overseas trips were five days or less.[12] In 2001, the median length of stay of U.S. visitors to overseas destinations was eleven nights.[13] Fortunately for Japanese workers and consumers, social attitudes in Japan toward work and leisure are changing.

Destination Visitor Spending

VIRTUALLY ALL travel destinations gather information on visitor spending to measure the economic impacts of tourism on their economies.[14] For example, the Travel Industry Association of America (TIA) and the U.S. Department of Commerce, Office of Tourism Industries (TI) estimate that in 2000, Americans traveling within their own country spent almost $489 billion on travel-related expenditures (i.e., transportation, lodging, meals, entertainment and recreation, and miscellaneous expenditures). Foreign visitors spent another

$82.0 billion in the United States, plus international passenger fares of $20.7 billion on U.S. flag carriers. In total, these expenditures generated an estimated $173.7 billion in payroll, 7.9 million indirect jobs, and $103 billion in tax revenues in the United States.[15]

In contrast, analysis of individual visitor spending behavior has been neglected. In this section, we pick one destination—Hawaii—and examine tourist expenditure behavior there. Hawaii was chosen because it has a reputation for producing high-quality tourist expenditure statistics. We begin by reviewing the usual (published) visitor expenditure data to understand what these data include and do not include.

Table 6-1 displays spending by visitors in Hawaii in 2001. An individual visitor's total trip spending at the destination is equal to the length of stay (in days) multiplied by the amount spent per day. Although Japanese visitors, on average, spent the most money per day in 2001, they were among the lowest spenders per trip because of their short trip duration. Visitors from the eastern United States, Canada, and Europe individually spent the most money in Hawaii during their vacations.

TABLE 6-1

TRIP DURATION AND PER PERSON DAILY AND TOTAL SPENDING PER VISIT BY HAWAII'S VISITORS IN 2001

Place of Residence	Length of Stay (in days)	x Per Person Daily Spending ($)	= Spending Per Trip ($)
U.S. West	9.89	149.60	1,479.90
U.S. East	10.40	161.20	1,677.40
Japan	6.02	241.20	1,451.80
Canada	12.16	151.90	1,847.10
Europe	12.07	160.30	1,935.20
Australia & New Zealand	8.40	169.10	1,419.90
Other Asia	7.57	174.60	1,322.20
Latin America	10.41	162.50	1,691.20
Other	10.23	154.10	1,575.90
Average for all Hawaii visitors	9.16	175.20	1,605.60

Note: Numbers may not add up due to rounding.
Source: State of Hawaii, DBEDT (2002), p. 5.

Table 6-1 suggests that visitors who stay longer may spend less money per day. But that is deceptive. James Mak, James Moncur, and David Yonamine found that, after controlling for all the factors that influence tourist spending behavior, tourists who incur higher travel costs tend to stay longer at their destinations and also spend more money per person per day.[16] Note in Table 6-1 that among U.S. visitors to Hawaii, visitors from the East stay longer and spend more money per person per day in Hawaii.

Table 6-2 separates daily spending by U.S. mainland and Japanese visitors into finer categories. These expenditures apply to visitors who stayed in hotels or condominiums only.[17] The data do not include pre-trip spending for such goods as luggage and other personal travel items, passport fees, and so on. Thus, the usual visitor expenditure data published by tourist destinations do not include all the money spent on trips, only the amounts spent at the destination.

The expenditure data in Table 6-2 also do not include tourist purchases of big-ticket items such as time-share units or vacation homes. Some researchers argue that these purchases should be included.[18] Because these purchases are "investments" rather than "consumption," they should not be included with food and entertainment expenditures; but when a tourist stays in her own vacation home or time-share unit (or trades her unit elsewhere for one in

TABLE 6-2

PER PERSON DAILY VISITOR SPENDING
OF HAWAII VISITORS: 2001

Spending Category	Spending ($) by Hawaii Visitors from		
	U.S. West	U.S. East	Japan
Lodging*	65.30	67.10	71.90
Food/Beverages	37.80	38.30	32.60
Transportation	14.60	16.60	11.80
Entertainment	10.80	11.80	3.70
Shopping	24.90	26.70	85.70
Miscellaneous	9.00	13.20	39.40
Total	162.40	173.70	245.10
Total excluding shopping	137.50	147.00	159.40

* Applies to visitors who stayed in hotels or condominiums only.
Source: See Table 6-1.

Hawaii), the market rental value of the unit should be estimated and included as her lodging expenditures, even if she didn't spend any money for lodging on the trip. Otherwise, the economic impact of tourist spending—the amount of resources employed in tourism—will be understated.

Unless a tourist is on a shopping tour, spending money is not the chief reason for a tourist to travel. But a tourist away from home must spend money to purchase lodging, food, and other vacation goods and services. Aside from the probable misidentification of some "miscellaneous expenditures" by Japanese tourists, Table 6-2 shows that Japanese visitors vastly outspent American visitors per day, and the biggest difference is in shopping. Visitors from the U.S. East spent more in every category than visitors from the U.S. West. Because all tourists face the same prices, the (total) cost of a standard vacation in Hawaii—*excluding shopping*—should be roughly proportional to its duration. The tourist who spends more money per day is not paying higher prices for the same goods and services, but rather is buying a higher quality (more expensive) vacation. Thus, the Japanese visitor who spent an average of $159 per day (excluding shopping) in Hawaii purchased a slightly higher quality (more expensive) vacation than the California visitor who spent $138 per day. Shopping is excluded in the comparison because the amount of money spent on shopping need not be proportional to how long a tourist stays in Hawaii (more on this later).

This comparison of daily visitor spending in Hawaii cannot be extended to include other tourist destinations because the prices of vacation goods and services vary among destinations. For example, in 2001, overseas tourists visiting the United States spent an average of only $67 per day per person,[19] or less than half the amount for all Hawaii visitors. That does not mean that overseas travelers to the U.S. mainland purchased substantially lower quality vacations than tourists visiting Hawaii. The huge differences in per diem spending between U.S. mainland and Hawaii's overseas visitors are due largely to price, rather than quality, differences. The prices of most goods and services—especially food and lodging—are much higher in Hawaii than in most other places in the United States.[20]

Economic Determinants of Tourist Spending

THE MOST important economic determinants of tourist spending at a destination are the tourist's income or travel budget and the relative prices of goods at the destination vis-à-vis prices for similar goods at home or in other destinations if traveling to several destinations. Virtually all studies show that higher income tourists spend more on their vacations.[21] They spend more partly because they stay longer and partly because they buy higher quality (more expensive) vacations.[22] Studies have also shown that the demand for individual tourism commodities such as transportation, lodging, restaurant meals away from home, auto repairs, parking, tolls, and gasoline is highly sensitive to changes in consumer incomes.[23] In other words, demand for vacation goods is highly *income elastic.*

The impact of prices on visitor spending depends on the *price elasticity of demand* for individual vacation goods. All else being equal, a consumer tends to buy less quantity of a good at a higher price. But if the buyer is not very price sensitive (that is, demand is *price inelastic*), a higher price may not induce her to buy much less, and she ends up spending more money on the good. On the other hand, if the consumer is price sensitive (that is, demand is *price elastic*), a price increase will cause her to cut back her purchases substantially, and she ends up spending less money on the good.

Only few empirical studies have been made of demand elasticities for individual vacation goods. The exception is tourist demand for lodging. Researchers have generally found tourist demand for lodging to be *price inelastic.*[24] In other words, all else being equal, consumer demand for lodging is not very responsive to changes in the price of lodging. Thus, a small increase in the price of lodging results in somewhat fewer nights of lodging demanded on the trip, but increases the total amount of money spent on lodging. The few available studies indicate that tourist demand for non-lodging vacation goods (food and entertainment, etc.) is also generally price inelastic.[25]

Generally, a consumer is more (less) responsive to a change in the price of a commodity when:

- The greater (smaller) the percentage of her total budget spent on the commodity.
- The more (fewer) substitutes there are.
- The longer (shorter) the price change persists, because she will have had more (less) time to learn about the price change and make changes in her purchases.

Changes in currency exchange rates also have significant impacts on international tourist expenditures at tourist destinations.[26] In international tourism, the link between destination and home prices is through the currency exchange rate. For example, if the currency exchange rate between the U.S. dollar and the Japanese yen is 130 yen to 1 dollar, a designer European scarf that's priced at $250 in Hawaii translates into a price of 32,500 yen (=$250 x 130 yen) in Japan. Suppose that the exchange rate between the two currencies becomes 100 yen to 1 dollar; the dollar has *depreciated* in value against the Japanese yen because it now buys fewer yen (1 dollar now buys only 100 yen instead of 130 yen). Alternatively, the yen has *appreciated* against the dollar because it now requires fewer yen (100 yen instead of 130 yen) to buy 1 dollar. The $250 designer scarf is now priced at 25,000 yen to the Japanese tourist, a decline of 23 percent, even though the (dollar) price of the scarf remains unchanged at $250 in Hawaii. In sum, an appreciation (depreciation) of the yen against the U.S. dollar decreases (increases) the yen price of U.S. goods and services. All else being equal, an appreciation (depreciation) of the yen against the dollar increases (decreases) Japanese purchases of goods and services in Hawaii.

Although Japanese tourists may buy more in Hawaii when the yen appreciates in value against the dollar, whether or not they spend more yen on those purchases depends on the relevant price elasticities of demand for Hawaii vacation goods. Assuming (probably correctly) that Japanese demand for most Hawaii vacation goods is price inelastic, then an appreciation of the yen will result in Japanese making more purchases in Hawaii but spending less yen for them.[27] Because the prices of goods and services in dollars haven't changed, Hawaii's tourism receipts (in dollars) rise because sellers are selling more (quantity of) goods to Japanese tourists at the same dollar denominated prices.[28] As the appreciation of the yen makes a Hawaii vacation cheaper for the Japanese, more Japanese are enticed to visit Hawaii, further boosting Hawaii's tourism receipts. Hence, it is not surprising that studies consistently find that an appreciation (depreciation) of a destination's currency is correlated with a decrease (increase) in tourism receipts.

Japanese Shopping Behavior

TOURISTS EVERYWHERE shop! Among overseas tourists visiting the United States in 2001, 90 percent of them shopped while in the United States. More tourists shopped than dined in restaurants (84 percent), went sightseeing in cities (50 percent), visited amusement or theme parks (40 percent) and historical places (37 percent), or visited national parks (24 percent) and art galleries and museums (21 percent each).[29]

Although buying a few souvenirs and gifts and some miscellaneous items for personal use on the trip is expected, Table 6-2 shows that Japanese visitors in Hawaii are particularly big shoppers. In 2001, Japanese visitors spent 3.0 to 3.5 times as much on shopping per day compared to American visitors. An even more appropriate comparison of their shopping behavior is the total— and not the daily—amount spent on shopping during the trip. In 2001, Japanese tourists spent an average of $515 per trip on "shopping" in Hawaii compared to $246 for U.S. visitors from the western states, and $278 for U.S. visitors from the eastern states. Although Japanese visitors may not be the biggest spenders in Hawaii, they are definitely the biggest shoppers.

Why is shopping so popular among the Japanese? One reason is that social custom in Japan demands that returning tourists bring home gifts (*omiyage*) to relatives and friends who gave them send-off money (*senbetsu*) toward their trips.[30] Another reason is that foreign, especially Western name-brand goods, are much more expensive and harder to obtain in Japan and hence are prized by the Japanese.[31] However, not all Japanese overseas tourists are prolific shoppers; shopping is still a discretionary expenditure.

Shopping is particularly popular among the young and usually single Japanese "office ladies" (popularly known as OLs) traveling abroad.[32] Whereas shopping was cited by 30 percent of all Japanese overseas travelers as a purpose of travel in 1999, it was cited by 56 percent of single women travelers, second only to enjoying "nature and scenery" (72 percent). For many single Japanese women, shopping is not incidental to the main purpose of the trip: It is often the main reason for the trip. For them consuming Western luxury goods derives not only *utility* directly but, more important, social status. Because single women make up the largest group of Hawaii's Japanese visitors, it is not surprising that the *average* Japanese visitor spending on shopping is so high in Hawaii. A survey of Japanese travel activities undertaken at overseas tourist destinations revealed that, in 1999, the propensity to shop was highest in Hawaii and lowest in the Middle East, Africa, and China. The Japanese visit China for its historical and cultural attractions and the Middle East and Africa for their natural and scenic attractions.[33]

Japanese shopping in Hawaii declined sharply in the late1990s because of the depreciation of the yen, a prolonged weak economy in Japan, and fundamental changes in the Japanese distribution system that have opened up

Japan's retailing industry to foreign competition. In 1994, the average Japanese visitor spent over $1,000 on shopping in Hawaii, compared to slightly over $500 in 2001.

Concluding Observations

FOR TOURIST businesses, the decisions on how much inventory to stock, where to allocate advertising budgets, and how many workers to hire depend on "a mix of good instincts and hard statistics."[34] Barbara Okamoto, currently vice president of public relations management at the Hawaii Visitors and Convention Bureau, recently underscored the importance of tourist expenditure data by noting that "The data is so fundamental for us. It's sort of like the air we breathe."[35]

Big gaps remain in our understanding of tourist spending behavior. Understanding tourist spending behavior is important because it is essential to formulating better public policies on tourism. For example, knowing how an increase in the hotel accommodation (or, bed) tax affects tourists' trip spending is essential to designing a better destination tax system. Having quality tourism data is required if we wish to analyze tourist spending behavior.

Having quality information on tourist expenditures also helps us to better understand the economic benefits of tourism to host communities (see Chapter 10). From a government fiscal perspective, tourists also impose costs on the governments of tourist destinations. Local governments must provide infrastructure, police and fire protection, and other public services in support of tourism. Is it more or less costly to provide public services for high spending or low spending visitors, and which one yields higher net economic benefits to the host community? Detailed information on tourist spending behavior is needed in tourism cost–benefit analysis.[36]

Travel Journal Inc., a major Japanese travel publisher, recently observed that "Hawaii needs volume of travelers while European countries tend to seek quality."[37] The implication is that Hawaii goes for quantity, whereas the European nations opt for quality. Who are these quality visitors? "Quality" is often associated with upscale or higher spending visitors.[38] Designing a "quality" tourism promotion plan requires information on tourist spending behavior.

Finally, annual aggregate tourist expenditure data are typically presented without adjustment for price changes. The result is that we don't know whether the year-to-year changes in tourist expenditures are caused by changes in prices or changes in demand for tourism goods and services. The main reason why these data are not adjusted for price changes is because we have been slow to develop tourism-specific price indices. This is beginning to change. Nonetheless, the travel price indices developed to date have been used primarily to track changes in the cost of travel and not used to deflate tourist expenditure data. The World Tourism Organization and tourist destinations everywhere continue to publish tourist expenditure data without adjusting for price changes. Thus, it is impossible to tell how fast tourism is really growing worldwide. It is widely recognized that counting visitor arrivals is not a good way to measure the growth of tourism and especially its economic contribution to host communities. It is necessary to complement tourist arrival data with price-adjusted tourism expenditure data. Hence, we need better tourism price information, and better tourism expenditure information.

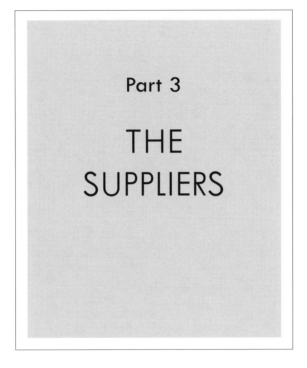

Part 3

THE
SUPPLIERS

CHAPTER 7

COMPETITION IN THE TOURISM INDUSTRIES

Competition is not a desirable end in itself. Rather, it is a very useful means to a desirable end.

ROGER D. BLAIR AND DAVID L. KASERMAN[1]

THE DECLINE IN tourism following the September 11, 2001, terrorist attacks saw rising hotel vacancy rates across America. Hotel operators responded by cutting their room rates to attract customers. However, if demand for hotel accommodations is price inelastic, as most studies have shown,[2] then cutting room rates would generate little additional business. Cutting room rates would decrease hotel revenues, not increase them![3]

Why then would any hotel operator want to cut his room rates in this situation? The answer is because he has no choice if he wants to remain competitive. Although consumer demand for hotel accommodations may be price inelastic, the demand for lodging at a particular hotel is likely to be very price elastic, because other hotels are good substitutes. Facing rising vacancy rates, a hotel operator may decide to cut his room rates to attract customers; if his competitors don't also cut their rates, then he stands to lure customers away from them. Indeed, if competition is alive and well,[4] other hotel operators will have to cut their room rates to keep their customers. The result is that room rates fall at all the hotels. Who are the beneficiaries of hotel competition? The consumers. Economists consider the maximization of consumer welfare to be the most important argument for competition. In this chapter, we examine the structure of competition in the tourist industry. We begin with some basic concepts.

What Is the Tourist Industry?

AN ECONOMY consists of huge numbers of buyers and sellers. These buyers and sellers transact business in *markets*. A *market* consists of a group of buyers *and* sellers buying and selling a particular product. An *industry* consists of "the sellers of a particular product."[5] Thus, an industry comprises only one side of the market, the sellers. This chapter focuses on competition among the sellers of the tourism product.

The definition of an *industry* is relatively unambiguous when it is applied to steel, automobiles, or apparel industries. Its application to tourism, however, is not so simple. We already know from Chapter 2 that the tourism product is not a "particular" product but is, instead, a collection of heterogeneous products from diverse sellers.

Tourism is not one of the 1,170 "industries" in the North American Industry Classification System (NAICS) developed by the United States, Canada, and Mexico to compare production across a uniformly defined set of industries.[6] Scheduled passenger air transportation (48111); rail transportation (4821); deep sea passenger transportation (483112 and 483114); scenic and sightseeing transportation (4871 and 4872); amusement, gambling, and recreation industries (713); accommodation (721); food services and drinking places (722); passenger car rental (532111); travel agencies (561510); and tour operators (561520) are among those that produce travel and tourism services and are recognized as "industries" in the NAICS. "Tourism" is not among them. According to the U.S. Department of Commerce, Office of Tourism Industries (TI), "The travel and tourism sector is a diverse group of industries that supply goods and services purchased by business, and other travelers." Thus, "travel and tourism" is considered a *sector* rather than an industry.[7] Nonetheless, because the terms "tourist industry" or "tourism industries" are so widely used, we continue to use them in this book.

Economic Structure of Tourism Industries

WHEN HAWAIIAN and Aloha Airlines announced in December 2001 that they planned to combine Hawaii's only two interisland scheduled air carriers to form a single, larger airline, it created much public concern that this announced merger might be harmful to the economic welfare of Hawaii's people.[8] The concern was well founded, because the new CEO announced that flight schedules would be cut and fares would eventually be raised on interisland routes to enable the new airline to improve its profitability. Yet, in the same year, when Navigant International (the fifth largest U.S. travel agency in 2000) acquired Sato Travel (the tenth largest travel agency in 2000), vaulting Navigant into third place, no one expressed fears that the merger would harm American consumers.[9] Similarly, no one appears to be concerned that Amtrak is the only provider of long-distance passenger train service in the United States. The proposed Aloha–Hawaiian Airlines merger generated public concerns, while the Navigant International–Sato Travel merger did not, because they occurred in very different market environments.[10]

Businesses operate in diverse market environments. Some markets are very competitive and each seller struggles to make a profit; others have hardly any competition at all, and firms in those markets may make huge profits year after year. The market environment in which businesses operate has an important influence on market prices and outputs and thus on consumer welfare.

Economics organizes sellers into four market types called *market structures*. These structures range from highly competitive to not competitive at all. On one end of the competitive spectrum is *monopoly*, a market dominated by a single seller (the *monopolist*) selling a product for which no close substitutes exist. Hence, no competition occurs in a monopoly. The local water company in most towns and cities is a good example of a monopolist.

On the other end of the competitive spectrum is *perfect competition*, a market of many atomistic sellers selling identical products so that no single seller has any influence over the market price. The entry of new firms and the exit of existing firms are virtually costless in perfect competition. Real world examples of perfect competition are rare. We usually think of a small, family-operated wheat farm as a reasonably good example of a perfect competitor.

Monopolistic competition is similar to perfect competition in that many sellers compete, but each seller is somewhat insulated from its competitors because each sells a somewhat different product. Because the products are imperfect substitutes, each firm can charge a price slightly different from that of its rivals. As in perfect competition, the entry and exit of firms is relatively easy in monopolistic competition. Real world examples of monopolistic competition include golf courses, tennis clubs, and tourist attractions. In the tourism industry, other examples are travel agencies, restaurants and bars, souvenir shops, and independently owned hotels (lodging accommodations).

Oligopoly is a market in which only a small number of sellers (*oligopolists*) compete, and it is not easy for a new competitor to enter the market. The airline, car rental, theme park, and cruise industries are good examples of oligopolies in the United States. Because of the small number of sellers, oligopolies are characterized by a high degree of interdependence among the rivals; thus, one firm's pricing and sales strategies must take into account the pricing and sales strategies of its identifiable rivals. For example, one firm may be reluctant to reduce its price to capture a larger market share because it anticipates that its competitors may follow its price cut, resulting in lower profits for all in the end. With only a few competitors, it might be relatively easy and more profitable for all of them to agree not to compete and, instead, act jointly as a monopolist and charge monopoly prices. Collusive agreements, however, tend to be unstable because individual conspirators have an incentive to cheat on the agreement by secretly offering their products below the agreed-upon monopoly price. Collusion is also illegal in the United States and in most other countries. Nonetheless, the possibility of collusion in fixing prices or allocating market shares, or engaging in other forms of anticompetitive behavior in oligopolistic markets, is always a public concern. It is the reason for antitrust laws.

Instead of explicit collusion, price leadership—in which one firm leads by changing its price and its competitors follow its lead[11]—and other parallel forms of behavior are commonly observed in oligopolies. For example, following months of devastating financial losses after the September 11 terrorist attacks, Continental Airlines announced that it would raise round-trip airfares for leisure travelers by $20 per ticket. All other major airlines followed Continental's lead, except Northwest Airlines. The fare increase was rescinded because of Northwest's decision not to go along with the others.[12] The other airlines feared losing too much business to Northwest.

Rivalry among oligopolists may also produce occasional price wars. For example, following the September 11 terrorist attacks, several major airlines in the United States engaged in a fare war over business travelers. The fare war erupted when American Airlines decided to raise the advance-purchase requirements for its lower priced business fares from three days to seven days. When most of its competitors declined to follow its lead, American Airlines apparently retaliated by cutting its business fares in dozens of its key markets.

Delta and United Airlines eventually matched American Airlines' stricter advance purchase requirements, and in return American Airlines withdrew its cut-rate fares in markets served by Delta and United Airlines.[13]

In addition to the number of firms in a market, the size distribution of firms in a market also matters when assessing the degree of competition in oligopoly markets. For example, it matters whether, in a ten-firm oligopoly, two of them are giants controlling 80 percent of total sales and the other eight firms share the remaining 20 percent, or all ten firms are the same size. The first is said to be highly concentrated; the second is not. The higher the percentage of a market's output that is controlled by a few sellers, the more concentrated it is. A market's concentration measure, along with other information, is used to determine the degree of competition in a particular market.

The most commonly used measure of market concentration is the four-firm concentration ratio. This is the ratio of the sales of the four largest firms in a market to total sales in the market.[14] Concentration ratios are commonly computed for manufacturing industries. (We shall see later that the terms "industry" and "market" do not necessarily mean the same thing.) These concentration ratios are not so common for service industries, but we can illustrate how the concentration ratio is calculated with examples using national data for U.S. travel agencies and car rental companies.

In 1999, the four largest travel agencies in the United States had total sales revenues of $33.2 billion, compared to $143 billion in sales revenues for all U.S. travel agencies.[15] Thus, the four-firm concentration ratio for the travel agency industry is 23.2% (= $33.2 b. /$143 b. x 100%). By contrast, the four-firm concentration ratio in the U.S. rental car industry is 74.4%, based on their revenues of $13.1 billion versus $17.6 billion in total industry car rental revenues.[16]

Are either of these competitive industries? William Shepherd classified each industry into one of four categories: monopoly, dominant firm (a firm with 50 to 90 percent industry share), tight oligopoly (four-firm concentration ratio above 60 percent), and effective competition (the rest).[17] By his classification, the travel agency industry in the United States would be considered a competitive industry, but the car rental industry would be considered an oligopoly.

Similarly, the tour operator industry in the United States has low industry concentration.[18] By contrast, the U.S. scheduled passenger airlines industry is moderately concentrated, with the four largest firms accounting for more than 60 percent of domestic passenger miles.[19] The North American cruise industry is also moderately concentrated, with the top four cruise lines accounting for more than half of total industry capacity.[20] Thus, the tour operator industry is a competitive industry whereas the U.S. scheduled passenger airline and cruise industries are oligopolies.

The degree of concentration in any given industry can also vary among countries. For example, the market for high-end and mid-level hotels in the United States is dominated by chain hotels; by contrast, independent ownership of hotels is the general rule everywhere else.[21]

Why is Competition Preferred?

THE CONVENTIONAL wisdom in economics is that competition is preferable to monopoly. Under competition, sellers supply those goods and services that consumers value most at the lowest possible prices.[22] By contrast, a monopolist will restrict production (below the competitive level) and charge above-competitive prices and earn excess (monopoly) profits. Firms that are able to charge prices above competitive levels are said to have *monopoly power* or *market power*. We can also think of market power as pricing power. Obviously, consumers are better off under competition than under monopoly.

Examples of market power are everywhere. Movie theaters, sports stadiums, and arenas usually don't allow customers to bring in "outside" food. Once inside, customers have no other option but to buy from the in-house food concessions, thus enabling the management to charge exorbitant prices. The managers of the food concessions know that they have market power and price accordingly.

Generally, industries with higher seller concentrations (such as monopolies and oligopolies) possess market power and tend to charge higher prices and reap higher profits than industries with low seller concentrations (that is, competitive industries).

Seller concentration is not the only indicator of the degree of competition in a market. At least two other factors—*product differentiation* and *barriers to entry of new firms*—must be considered.[23]

Product Differentiation

TWO PRODUCTS are differentiated if buyers *perceive* that they are different in some way. Products may be differentiated because of differences in their physical features. Two Chinese restaurants can be differentiated by their menus, by their style of cooking, by their quality, or by their location. Branding and advertising a product—Pizza Hut versus Papa John's Pizza—is a telltale indication that a seller is trying to differentiate its product, at least in the minds of consumers. The Honda Passport and Isuzu Rodeo are the same SUV but carry different brands. Gas stations selling the same brand of gasoline are nonetheless differentiated by the different locations of their stations.

Product differentiation reduces potential competition among sellers. By differentiating his product, a seller hopes to reduce the buyer's price sensitivity toward his product. As long as enough consumers prefer his brand to someone else's brand, the seller can charge a higher price and still sell his product.

What is a respected brand name worth? Apparently, a lot! For example, each year *Business Week* magazine estimates the values of the top 100 brand names in the world. The magazine does not estimate the values of the companies, only the values of their brand names.[24] In 2002, the value of the Disney brand was estimated at $29.26 billion, ranking Disney seventh among the 100 top brands around the world; American Express was in fifteenth place at $16.29 billion; and Hertz was in seventy-seventh place at $3.36 billion.[25]

Differentiation plays an important role in how firms set their prices when product attributes are unique, complicated, or difficult to evaluate and consumer tastes are varied, as in the tourism industries. It would be impossible for someone other than the Walt Disney Company to duplicate a Disney World, thus giving Disney substantial *market power* in the amusement and theme park industry.[26] In North America, the top five theme parks in total attendence are Disney parks. Not surprisingly, Disney is widely regarded as "the most aggressive pricer" in the industry.[27]

Barriers to Entry

WHETHER NEW firms can easily enter a market can also affect the conduct of existing firms and the degree of competition in that market. Imagine a market in which current member businesses are making excess profits. This situation attracts the attention of outsiders who want to enter the market. If they are able to enter the market easily, increased competition would force the existing businesses to lower their prices. But if, for some reason, the new firms are not allowed in, the existing firms can continue to charge their high prices and reap excess profits.

On the other hand, consider a market with only one firm. As an apparent monopolist, one expects the firm to charge high prices. It might not if new competitors can enter the market easily. In essence, this firm has no monopoly power. A small town may have only one small hotel and a few restaurants and retail stores; yet these businesses are easy to get into and potential entrants are always waiting on the sideline to leap in if sufficient demand is there to allow more of them. Markets in which existing firms face competition from potential entrants are *contestable markets*. Pauline Sheldon describes the U.S. tour operator industry as a contestable market.[28] The threat of potential entry could prevent incumbent firms from acting irresponsibly.

Barriers to entry may come from different sources. A sizable up-front capital requirement may be a barrier to entry. For example, it may be difficult for an outsider to secure financing for a 1,900-passenger cruise ship that may cost upwards of $500 million to build in the United States, or to obtain the financing to start a new airline. In some markets, entry is controlled by the government. For example, New York City limits the number of taxicabs that can legally operate in the city. In Hawaii, entrepreneurs who want to provide passenger motor coach (tour bus and ground transfers) service must demonstrate to the Public Utilities Commission that the proposed service meets an unmet demand. United States law allows cruise lines to operate passenger ships between U.S. ports only if the ships are built and registered in the United States and largely crewed by American seamen. A similar law prohibits foreign airlines from providing domestic air service. These restrictive laws, which insulate domestic carriers from foreign competition in the U.S. domestic transportation markets, are known as *cabotage* laws. Roger Blair and David Kaserman note that government control of entry "is the most absolute of all entry barriers because the police power of the state is used to prevent entry."[29]

The Problem of Market Boundaries

WE NOTED earlier that Amtrak is the sole provider of long-distance passenger train service in the United States, but no one is concerned that it is harming consumer welfare by charging exorbitant prices and earning excessive profits. In fact, Amtrak has been losing money year after year since its founding in 1970. In fiscal year 2002, the Amtrak system had an estimated deficit of $1.1 billion. It has been able to remain in business only because of large annual federal government grants or subsidies.[30]

Although Amtrak is the exclusive provider of long-distance passenger train service and is in the passenger rail transportation industry, it faces competition from other passenger transportation industries, such as air and bus transportation, and even private automobiles. In other words, the *product market* in which Amtrak does business does not include only passenger train service; it includes other modes of transportation. Two products are in the same product market if buyers perceive them to be good substitutes. If a sizable number of travelers consider air, bus, or personal automobile travel as good substitutes to train travel, all these forms of transportation are in the same product market. Thus, the boundary of the product market and the boundary of the industry—that is, passenger rail transportation—may not be the same.

In addition to the need to identify the correct product boundary, it is also necessary to identify the correct geographic boundary. Some firms sell their products nationally; some only do business in certain regions of the country or in certain states or cities. The *geographic market* for some firms such as American Express spans nearly the entire world. With the increasing globalization of markets, domestic firms in the tourism industry face increasing competition from foreign firms, and vice versa.

Thus, the first task in assessing the degree of competition in any given market is to ascertain the relevant market in which competition takes place. Amtrak has to consider what other transportation services it competes against and where. The relevant market occurs where the two—the product and geographic markets—overlap. We defined monopoly as a market in which a single seller sells a product for which no close substitutes exist. Amtrak may be the sole provider of long-distance passenger train service in the United States, but excellent substitutes for train travel exist. Hence, Amtrak is not a monopolist in the relevant market in which it competes. Thus, the terms "industry" and "market" are not necessarily the same thing. In assessing the degree of competition, it's the "market" that matters. Industry concentration ratios computed using national sales data that do not adjust for market boundaries may give false information on the actual degree of competition in those markets.

Determining the relevant markets can be a difficult task. To illustrate, in 2001 Carnival Corporation and Royal Caribbean Cruises, the world's largest and second largest cruise companies respectively, began vying to acquire P & O Princess Cruises, the world's third largest cruise company. Because the cruise industry is already moderately concentrated, antitrust officials at the U.S. Federal Trade Commission were prepared to reject both combinations out of concern that either merger would further increase industry concentration, significantly reduce competition, and hurt consumers.[31] But if cruise operators also compete against land tour operators, the relevant market is much larger than just the cruise industry, and a merger between P & O Princess Cruises and either Carnival or Royal Caribbean might not substantially increase market concentration, reduce competition, and harm consumers. Indeed, the president of Carnival Cruise Lines took it one step further earlier when he opined that "Our competition is Las Vegas, Disney World, cars, jewelry. . . ."[32]

How do we know if cruises and land tours, cars, and jewelry are in the same market? One way to determine if cruises and, say, jewelry are in the same product market is to examine the response of consumers to a small cut in the price of cruises on the demand for jewelry. Although there may be a few people who will switch from buying jewelry to buying a cruise when the price of a cruise vacation is reduced, for the two goods to be in the same product market there must be a *significant* number of people who decide to switch. Thus, if a small percentage price cut on cruise vacations induces a larger percentage increase in the number of people to switch from buying jewelry to buying cruise vacations, then the two goods are in the same product market.[33] Defining the boundaries of a relevant market usually requires the help of economic experts to perform careful analyses of consumer behavior and product attributes.

Horizontal Integration

HORIZONTAL INTEGRATION occurs when two or more companies selling the same product consolidate or coordinate their business operations. A merger of two companies in the same industry, such as the merger between American Airlines and TWA in 2001, and a merger between Carnival and Princess Cruises, is a *horizontal merger* and is one type of horizontal integration. To be considered a horizontal merger, it is necessary that the two companies be rivals in the same market prior to their consolidation; that is, both must sell the same product in the same geographic market.[34] In a merger, one of the competitors disappears. Whether a merger between two former rivals harms consumer welfare depends a great deal on the market environment in which the firms do business.

Why do companies in the same line of business want to merge? One motive is to lessen competition. This could raise public concerns and invite government antitrust scrutiny. Another motive is to increase profits by cutting costs through economies of scale. For example, in the United States, three-quarters of all hotels are part of a chain. J. T. Kuhlman, the head of Inter-Continental Hotels and Resorts, notes that, "Take two hotels standing side by side, offering the same level of service. One is flagged, the other stands alone. The one that's part of a chain will win, every time."[35] This is because the more rooms a hotel has, the lower the cost of operating each room.

Similarly, following the Chapter 11 bankruptcy of Budget car rental company in 2002, the Cendant Corporation received court approval to acquire Budget. Because Cendant already owned Avis, the deal would make Cendant the second largest car rental company in the United States, although Cendant announced that it would maintain separate brands for the car rental companies.[36] Nonetheless, combining Avis and Budget would enable Cendant to realize substantial economies of scale via consolidation of their back-office and administrative functions.[37] If cost reductions are passed along to consumers under pressure of competition, consumers actually benefit. Mergers that result in increased efficiency enhance the economic welfare of consumers and society.

Horizontal integration does not necessarily imply mergers only. Airline *alliances*, in which a group of airlines agrees to collaborate and coordinate their marketing, scheduling, and other business activities but remain as separate companies have sprung up quickly since 1996. In the trans-Atlantic routes, United Airlines formed the Star Alliance with the German airline, Lufthansa, and several other European airlines; Delta formed an alliance with Air France and Alitalia (Wings); and Northwest Airlines formed the SkyTeam alliance with KLM. Airline alliances typically agree to coordinate their marketing, routes and *code sharing*, in which one airline is allowed to use its flight designation code on a flight operated by its partner. Another marketing coordination involves *frequent flyer reciprocity*, whereby airline partners combine their frequent flyer programs. On the surface, these *alliances* do not appear to lessen competition because they are agreements between firms in substantially different markets. They may actually increase economic efficiency to the benefit of consumers. An alliance between United Airlines and its foreign partners increases convenience to passengers by creating a seamless travel itinerary. Nonetheless, allowing potential competitors to engage in marketing and scheduling coordination clearly raises anticompetitive concerns, especially if the partners have overlapping routes. Such cooperation could also discourage potential entry of new firms. Because of the costly penalty of antitrust violation, U.S. airlines proposing alliances with foreign carriers typically seek government antitrust immunity first before implementing their agreements.[38]

Vertical Integration

A COMPANY becomes vertically integrated if it acquires another "company" that either supplies inputs to it (*backward integration*) or purchases from it (*forward integration*). For example, a *backward* integration occurs when a hotel operator decides to start its own in-house laundry department instead of contracting the hotel laundry to an outside firm. The same applies to in-house accounting, pool cleaning, landscaping, and even secretarial services; all of those services, and many more, can be purchased from outside firms. To some extent, all businesses are vertically integrated.

Note that the hotel doesn't have to start its own internal laundry department from scratch; it can merge with another company that is already in the laundry business. When this occurs, it is a *vertical merger*. A vertical merger enables a firm to extend its business beyond the boundaries of its previous market.

A *forward integration* occurs, for example, when an airline starts its own tour operator company to sell its own package tours, which obviously would include the airline's transportation services as a key component of the tours. For example, American Airlines has its AmericanAirlines Vacations, Northwest Airlines has its Northwest Airlines World Vacations, and other airlines have "Their" Airlines Vacations.

How can vertical integration affect competition? In the tourism industries, integration can result in lower marketing and distribution (selling) costs. Vertical integration can reduce a firm's tax liability in jurisdictions (e.g., Hawaii) that tax business transactions at each stage of production and sale. By vertically integrating backwards, firms can also eliminate the cost of having to frequently negotiate the terms of supply with outside firms. If these economies are large enough, they can give the integrated firm a competitive advantage over a nonintegrated firm. However, because large, vertically integrated firms in the tourism industry co-exist with small, nonintegrated firms, the cost advantages of integration are obviously not large enough to drive the small, nonintegrated firms out of business. Because the tourism product is highly heterogeneous, small firms can survive simply by finding the right niche markets through product differentiation.

Often, the object of backward vertical integration is to enable the firm to have control over the supply of its key inputs to minimize supply risks. A large tour operator like Pleasant Hawaiian Holidays wants to have its own hotel in Hawaii to ensure that it will have enough rooms to accommodate its U.S. mainland package tour customers. By owning its own hotel, it has a certainty about its source of room supply. An advantage of forward vertical integration is to provide better quality control of the final product. Larry Dwyer et al. note that vertical integration (forward and backward) is particularly important to Japanese tourism investors in Australia because the Japanese are extremely quality conscious.[39] Vertical integration has an important disadvantage in that a vertically integrated firm loses some flexibility in conducting its business. If sales turn out to be less than expected, a hotel that contracts with an outside laundry service can cut its order; if it owns its own laundry department, it still has to pay the fixed costs. It shouldn't be surprising that vertically integrated firms have a greater fear of market instability.

Conglomerate Integration

A THIRD category of integration, *conglomerate integration,* is also quite common in the tourism industries. Conglomerate integration or conglomerate mergers can be of several types. Consider an airline that merges with a major hotel and a motor coach company to provide airport transfers and tours at its destinations. The airline has become a multiproduct firm. It has extended its product line by acquiring companies that produce products that are natural complements to its airline business. Because the hotel and motor coach services are not direct inputs to the production of air transportation services, these mergers cannot be considered vertical mergers. They are *product extension* mergers.[40] Another term is *complementary integration.*[41]

A good example of complementary integration is the Cendant Corporation, the largest hotel franchiser, having hotels such as Howard Johnson and Days Inn. It also owns the Avis rental car company; the discount ticket vendor, Cheap Tickets; and the travel reservation company, Galileo International Inc., as well as thousands of affiliated time-share properties. By acquiring these disparate companies, Cendant hoped to have them sell services to each other's customers. In other words, Cendant aims to take advantage of "synergism" among its diverse companies. One financial analyst observed that "Cendant is all about marketing. They have many distribution channels." [42]

Mergers can also extend geographic markets. A motor coach company in Honolulu on the island of Oahu decides to acquire a similar company on the island of Maui. The acquiring company is still selling the same product—tours and transfers—but it is now in another geographic market. This is a *market extension* merger. Because product extension and market extension mergers combine firms not previously rivals in the same market, these mergers are generally not a threat to competition.

Sometimes, one company acquires another company that is in a totally different line of business. For example, in 2001, the Japanese financial institution Nomura International acquired Le Meridien Hotels. [43] Such a merger is a *pure conglomerate merger* and generally is not a threat to competition.

Multinational Corporations in Tourism

MULTINATIONAL OR transnational corporations do business in more than one country. Because international tourism involves travel in many countries, it is not surprising that multinational companies play an important role in the tourism industry. International corporate hotel chains are an excellent example of multinational companies in the tourism industry. In 2001, the well-known Hilton Hotels Corporation—headquartered in the United States—operated 1,986 hotels with 327,487 hotel rooms around the world. [44] Note that to expand one's business abroad also amounts to making a *direct foreign investment.* [45] Hence, to understand why businesses expand abroad, one must also understand why they want to invest abroad.

The main reason for a domestic hotel (or any firm) to expand (invest) abroad is to grow its business beyond its home market, especially if the foreign market is large and expanding. A hotel may expand overseas by following its domestic customers abroad. For example, in the 1970s, the Japanese traveled overseas in rapidly growing numbers. Because of their proximity to Japan, Saipan, Guam, and Hawaii soon were among the most popular overseas destinations for the Japanese. Japan's Prince Hotels (among others) acquired luxury hotels in Hawaii and became a multinational hotel corporation, in essence, by following its customers to Hawaii.[46] In Guam and Saipan, where Japanese comprise more than 90 percent of all tourists, almost all the luxury hotels are Japanese owned.

Another reason for a domestic hotel to expand abroad is to capitalize on the value of its *proprietary assets*, such as its brand name, its reputation for quality and standardized service, and its reservation system.[47] Hilton Hotels is a name that is recognized worldwide. By operating hotels in many countries, it is able to extend its market power or low costs at home to foreign markets.

How do multinational corporations affect competition in tourism? Studies of multinational manufacturing corporations find that they tend to be large firms operating in concentrated industries, thus enabling them to earn excess profits.[48] Nonetheless, anecdotal evidence indicates that they are also competitors. If they operate in oligopolistic markets abroad, multinational corporations are less likely to conspire with their host country rivals to fix prices and outputs. Richard Caves notes that "There is no decisive evidence that multinational status either does or does not feed back to make industries still more concentrated or less competitive."[49] In the generally less concentrated tourism industries, the entry of foreign firms can only give consumers more choices, and in the process stimulate rather than dampen competition.

Concluding Observations

WITH A few important exceptions, the tourism industries in the United States—and, indeed, just about everywhere else—are dominated by small businesses with modest capital requirements and ease of entry and exit. These characteristics ensure that most markets are quite competitive. Dwyer et al. surmise that "the world market for tourism services approximates a monopolistic competitive market."[50] Even in those markets and industries where concentration ratios are high—such as the airline and car rental industries in the United States—visibly keen rivalry exists among the firms.

In the U.S. scheduled passenger airline industry, individual city-pair markets (with some exceptions) are highly contestable, because airline companies can reallocate their planes from route to route. A number of formerly big or well-known players such as Braniff, Eastern Airlines, Western Airlines, People's Express, and most recently TWA (America's longest flying airline), have either gone bankrupt or have merged with financially stronger airlines.

Between 1985 and 2001, the number of major airlines in the United States has fluctuated annually between eleven and fifteen, and all "other" carriers fluctuated between fifty-six and eighty-nine.[51] Moreover, U.S. airlines clearly have not been making excess profits. The overall profitability of American airlines has been well below the average of American industries generally.[52] Warren Buffett, the billionaire American investor, remarked that "the money that had been made since the dawn of aviation by all of this country's airline companies was zero. Absolutely zero."[53] This record of financial performance is generally not expected of a highly concentrated and uncompetitive market.

Keen rivalry also characterizes the moderately concentrated car rental industry. It wasn't too long ago that Avis aired a television commercial that boasted, "When you're No. 2 [after Hertz], you try harder." Today, Avis is only the fourth largest car rental company in the United States, and Hertz has fallen to second, after Enterprise Rent-A-Car.

However, competition may not be equally vigorous in all areas of the country. Firms in tourism industries do business mostly in local or regional markets rather than national markets. Hence, it is likely that the degree of competition could vary greatly in different parts of the country. In the airline industry, the limited number of take-off and landing slots and gates at some major U.S. airports, especially in the Northeast and Midwest, block potential entry, and the few incumbent firms with control over those slots and gates exercise considerable monopoly power in those markets.[54] Small communities tend to have the least amount of airline service and competition. Some may only have one airline, or none at all. Not surprisingly, fares on many short-haul and low-density routes can be much higher than fares on the more competitive transcontinental routes. Despite the unevenness of competition across the country, the overall picture of U.S. tourism industries is one of a generally high degree of competition and a consuming public pretty well served by diversity of choices.

CHAPTER 8

GETTING YOU THERE

America is a nation on wheels.

WENDELL COX AND JEAN LOVE[1]

The airlines are the C drive of the travel industry. We're all
a directory below those guys.

ARTHUR TAUCK[2]

How to get there—by air, rail, car, bus, or ship? According to the World
Tourism Organization (WTO), air and road transportation are the most
widely used modes of transportation in international tourism. In 1998, air
transportation accounted for 43 percent of international tourist travel, road
transportation 41.4 percent, sea 7.8 percent, and rail 7 percent. However, the
mode of travel varies greatly from country to country, depending on the available options and their relative costs. For residents of island countries like
Japan, Australia, and New Zealand, air travel is the only viable mode of travel
abroad. By contrast, railroads play a significant role in Europe, where an
extensive rail network covers almost the whole of the continent, and the
introduction of high speed trains has helped to stave off competition from auto
and air travel. Even so, automobile travel is gaining rapidly at the expense of
rail travel in Europe.[3]

If air transportation is the leading transportation mode in international
travel, road transportation is more important in domestic travel. Table 8-1
displays the transportation modes chosen by long-distance travelers in the
United States in 1995.[4]

In 1995, American households made over 650 million long-distance trips
in the United States, representing over 1 billion person trips, of which about

60 percent were pleasure trips.[5] Table 8-1 shows strikingly the dominance of automobiles (personal use vehicles) in long-distance domestic travel, accounting for eight out of ten such trips. Without too much exaggeration, America is, indeed, a nation on wheels! Nearly 90 percent of all auto trips were less than 1,000 miles round trip. As the trip distance increases, the dominance of auto travel declines (Figure 8-1). Beyond 1,000 miles round trip, less than half of the household trips were in automobiles. Air travel accounted for nearly 20 percent of all trips. The other modes of transportation—railroads, buses, and ships—were of negligible importance. Thus, long-distance travel in America generally means either automobile travel or air travel.

Determinants of Consumer Choice of Travel Modes

A NUMBER of factors determine a consumer's choice of travel mode, among them comfort, safety, freedom, convenience and flexibility of travel, price, and time cost of the journey. In sum, different modes of travel yield different consumer *utilities* and impose different money and time costs of travel. Time spent on the journey can be decomposed into waiting (buffer) time, travel time to and from transport stations and terminals, and the journey time, which is a function of speed. Consider the tradeoffs among three modes of transportation: (1) car, (2) rail/bus, and (3) airplane.

TABLE 8-1

CHOICE OF TRANSPORTATION MODE IN LONG-DISTANCE TRAVEL IN THE U.S.*

Mode of Travel	Household Trips (%)	Person Trips (%)
Personal-use vehicle	77.0	81.3
Airplane**	19.7	16.1
Bus***	2.6	2.0
Train	0.6	0.5
Ship, boat, or ferry	0.1	0.1
Total	100.0	100.0

*   Round trips of 200 miles or more (*100 miles or more, one way*), U.S. destinations only.
**   Under airplane travel, the percentages for commercial plane travel are 19.0% and 15.6%, respectively.
***   Under bus travel, the percentages for charter or tour bus travel are 1.8% and 1.4%, respectively.
Source: U.S. Department of Transportation, 1997, Chapter 1, Table 1-33.

The chief advantages of car travel stem from the freedom, flexibility, and convenience that the traveler enjoys. The traveler can depart and return when she wants, change the travel itinerary at the last minute with relative ease, enjoy almost door-to-door service, and the privacy of her own or chosen company. Additionally, she incurs no buffer time before she leaves on the auto trip; nor does she have to spend time traveling to and from air, bus, or train terminals.

By contrast, if she decides to travel by air, she loses the advantages of car travel, but she gains speed. As the length of the trip increases, more time is spent traveling between her home town and the final destination relative to the buffer time and travel time to and from terminals. The advantage of speed becomes very apparent. At some distance, the time saved by the faster speed of air travel eventually overcomes the flexibility of car travel. In the United States, that distance threshold is approximately 1,000 miles, round trip (Figure 8-1). Not surprisingly, air transportation has captured a larger market share than road transportation in international tourism because the distances traveled are, on average, longer than in domestic tourism and speed becomes more important in determining the mode of travel.[6]

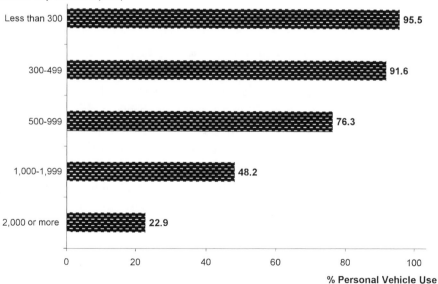

Round-Trip Distance (miles)

Less than 300 — 95.5
300-499 — 91.6
500-999 — 76.3
1,000-1,999 — 48.2
2,000 or more — 22.9

% Personal Vehicle Use

Source: Calculated from U.S. Department of Transportation, 1997, Chapter 1, Table 1-33.

FIGURE 8-1. Personal vehicle use by trip distance.

Trains and buses[7] do not possess the advantages of either car travel or air travel. Traveling by train or bus still requires passengers to incur buffer time and to travel to and from terminals as in air travel; hence, in short-distance trips, trains and buses cannot outperform car travel. On long-distance trips, they do not have the speed of airplanes.[8] The main advantages of trains and buses are that they are cheap and, as one well-known bus commercial touted, "And you can leave the driving to us." Thus, these forms of transportation occupy a small market niche between the car and the airplane and provide important transportation services to those who do not have access to cars or cannot afford to fly. Moreover, any improvements in car or air travel further squeezes the demand for train and bus travel. For trains and buses to compete successfully against cars and airplanes, they must reduce the buffer time by scheduling more frequent service, reduce the travel time to and from the terminals, and/or increase their speeds. Not surprisingly, the introduction of high speed trains in France has given a boost to train travel there.[9] But passenger train service in Europe, as in the United States, loses money and requires government subsidy. In the absence of similar political commitment in the United States, one can understand why cars and airplanes are the dominant modes of domestic passenger transportation in the United States today.

Indeed, the attraction of automobile travel even for extremely long-distance trips (Figure 8-1) is a testament to the efficiency of America's 42,500-mile interstate highway system, built under the Interstate Highway Act of 1956.[10] This super-highway system represents slightly over 1 percent of total U.S. road mileage, but accounts for nearly one quarter of all road traffic. The system has cut travel times by 20 percent or more between cities.[11] The only threat to the popularity of car travel in the United States is an occasional spike in the price of gasoline, and, even more importantly, the availability of gasoline. During the Arab oil embargo of 1973, when gasoline was in short supply, many Americans left their cars at home and utilized public transportation (plane, bus, and rail) for their long-distance vacations; others took vacations closer to home or canceled their vacation plans altogether.[12] The security measures at U.S. airports since the September 11, 2001, terrorist attacks, combined with the public's increased fear of flying, have shifted some competitive advantage away from air travel to cars, buses, and trains. A nationwide survey of 2,400 frequent travelers since October 2001 by D. K. Shifflet & Associates found that people were willing to drive twice as long (or about 8 hours) compared to before the September 11 attacks to avoid airport hassles.[13]

The number of people taking commercial flights for trips between 200 and 400 miles fell by 22 percent in the year after the terrorist attacks.[14]

Cruise Tourism

SPEED IS not an important factor in consumers' decision to take a cruise. The objective of taking a cruise is not to get from Port A to Port B and back to Port A as quickly as possible. On a cruise, the journey itself may be the largest part of the vacation experience. Cruise passengers get transportation combined with an all-inclusive resort experience. The cruise ship is the destination. On some luxury cruise ships, so much entertainment and activity is available on-board, plus food around the clock, that some passengers never leave their ships during the trip. Gerd Hertel of the Norwegian Cruise Line observed that "Food is the most important, most popular thing on a cruise."[15] Cruise travel is also physically less strenuous, has fewer hassles (cruise lines boast that you only have to unpack and pack once on the trip), and is generally more relaxing than air and land travel. Not surprisingly, it has wide appeal among older travelers. But that too is changing. Today the average age of cruise passengers is 42, and the fastest growing segment is family travel, as rich baby boomers bring their children along in increasing numbers.[16] A survey conducted by Plog Research in 2002 found that the most important reason why Americans do not take a cruise vacation is that it is perceived to be too expensive.[17]

The growing popularity of cruise tourism has made the industry one of the fastest growing tourism industries. Between 1980 and 2000, the North American cruise market saw an average annual passenger growth of 8.4 percent, reaching a total of 6.9 million passengers in 2000;[18] by comparison, international tourism growth has averaged about 4.5 percent per year during the same period. In the early 1990s, North America accounted for over 80 percent of the world cruise market of three days or more,[19] but that is also changing as the popularity of cruise travel is spreading to the rest of the world. In 1991, only 9 percent of the industry's ship capacity was cruising in Europe; today that percentage has risen to nearly 21 percent.[20] A Google search of "cruises" turns up nearly 100 pages of advertisements for cruises in virtually every part of the world. The International Council of Cruise Lines (ICCL) reported that in 2001, the cruise industry carried 8.4 million passengers worldwide with 6.9 million cruise passengers coming from North America.[21]

An important advantage of the cruise industry over the lodging industry is that cruise ships are mobile and can be moved from one route to another. Thus, on any given route, the supply response to changing market conditions is very high. Although that makes individual markets (routes) potentially very competitive, it also means that cruise line owners can quickly reallocate their ships in response to changing consumer demand to generate the highest returns from their expensive capital assets. Indeed, within one month of the September 11 terrorist attacks, most major cruise lines rescheduled their ships away from the Mediterranean and closer to the United States by scheduling more Alaska, Mexico, and Caribbean sailings, thereby enabling their mostly American passengers to drive, instead of fly, to board their ships.[22]

Cruise lines, however, cannot simply decide to operate wherever they want to operate. In the United States, the Passenger Services Act (PSA), passed in 1886, prohibits foreign cruise lines from carrying passengers between American ports without making a stop in a foreign port. The law requires passengers traveling only between U.S. ports to be carried in ships built and registered in the United States and manned largely by American crews. Specifically, the PSA allows foreign cruise ships to be based in U.S. ports, but they are required to stop at a foreign port if traveling round trip between two U.S. ports, and they are prohibited from providing one-way passenger cruises between U.S. ports. The original intent of this *cabotage* law was to protect domestic shipping and to safeguard the American merchant marine fleet in the event of war. But the new, big, and luxurious ocean-going cruise ships today are built more cheaply in foreign shipyards and manned by lower-wage foreign labor. The law clearly affects how cruise lines operate their businesses.

For example, the popular seven-day Alaska inside passage cruise leaves not from Seattle, Washington but from Vancouver, Canada, and the mostly American passengers must drive or take a bus to or fly into Vancouver. It has never been illegal to base a foreign cruise ship in Seattle to ply between Seattle and Alaska, but the ship must stop at a Canadian port in between, thus making it impractical to fit the travel schedule into a typical seven-day cruise. The impractical finally became practical when the Norwegian Cruise Line announced, in 1998, that it would build a fast ship that could make the seven-day round trip between Seattle and Glacier Bay (Alaska) with a stop in Vancouver, prompting the mayor of Seattle to remark that, "Technology saved us; Congress didn't."[23] Not entirely, because the Norwegian Cruise Line still cannot carry passengers who want to cruise only one way to explore the Alaska interior and then fly back to the United States. The competing Holland America Line, which operates most of its Alaska cruises out of Vancouver, reports that about one-third of its Alaska cruise passengers only go one way. Alaska cruise passengers from the United States who want to cruise only one way must still drive, bus, or fly into Vancouver.[24]

The PSA clearly forces the cruise industry and its passengers to expend valuable economic resources on less productive activities. The Norwegian Cruise Line's *Norwegian Star*, based in Honolulu, makes a 1,200-mile round-trip dash to Fanning Island in the Republic of Kiribati on each seven-day Hawaiian islands cruise. The atoll of 13 square miles, with a population of 1,600, was one of the most isolated places in the world before the arrival of the cruise ship. During the seven-day cruise, four days are spent cruising in open sea to and from Fanning Island, with a six-hour layover there. When American Classic Voyages Inc. operated its U.S. built and American staffed cruise ships in the Hawaii cruise market, Fanning Island was never a scheduled visit. American Classic Voyages operated three- and four-day, as well as seven-day, cruises in the Hawaii cruise market. The PSA prevents foreign cruise lines offering Hawaii interisland cruises only, or cruises between San Diego and Seattle, or between Boston and Miami.

Following the bankruptcy of American Classic Voyages Inc. in 2001, which sidelined the *Independence*, no large American-built ocean-going cruise ships remained in service.[25] This prompted Congress to re-examine the merits of the PSA. Thus far, however, efforts to repeal the law in Congress have been unsuccessful. One lawmaker noted that the PSA also protects the thousands of small passenger vessels providing inland cruises, dinner cruises, and ferry service, thus ensuring their financial stability.[26] No evidence exists that these American "small passenger vessels" require economic protection from potential foreign entrants, nor is it evident that such protection enhances consumer welfare or the national security of the United States. As an alternative to scrapping the PSA, Congress passed legislation in February 2003 granting the Norwegian Cruise Line the exclusive right to offer Hawaii interisland-only cruises using three foreign-built ships operating under the U.S. flag; the ships would be required to employ an American staff, comply with all U.S. laws, and cannot be repositioned to operate in Alaska, the Gulf of Mexico, or the Caribbean Sea.[27]

Economic Regulation of U.S. Air Travel

REGULATION OF industries in the United States began in the late nineteenth century because Americans believed that large firms had abused their market power, stifled competition, and harmed consumers. The Great Depression of the 1930s further undermined American confidence in the market economy and led to a surge in new regulations imposed on many industries including domestic transportation, securities and banking, and agriculture.

In 1938, the U.S. Congress passed the Civil Aeronautics Act of 1938, which created the Civil Aeronautics Board (CAB) to regulate airline fares and entry and exit in the U.S. airline industry. CAB regulation was imposed only on carriers providing interstate service and not on carriers providing only intrastate service.[28] Under this act, a potential carrier must demonstrate that entry on a route was *required* by public convenience and necessity. Between 1938 and the passage of the Airline Deregulation Act in 1978, the CAB did not permit the entry of a single trunk carrier. It denied 79 applications for entry between 1950 and 1974. From 1965 to 1978, fewer than 10 percent of the applications by existing carriers to provide new service were approved. In high density markets, the CAB preferred additional entry rather than reductions in airfares. As a general rule, the CAB preferred not to have more than two or three carriers on the same route.

Although the CAB imposed strict regulations on airfares and entry, flight frequency was not explicitly regulated. As a result, U.S. domestic carriers competed vigorously via nonprice avenues, such as providing extra in-flight amenities and buying more and bigger planes to increase flight frequency.[29] Although passengers found flying more comfortable because of emptier planes, fares were necessarily higher under CAB regulation. Contrary to expectations, airlines did not profit from regulation because potential excess profits from restricted entry evaporated due to costly nonprice competition.

Movement toward Deregulation in the United States

Deregulation of industries in the U.S. was triggered by the oil crises of the 1970s. Sharp increases in oil prices in the 1970s, coupled with expansionary monetary policy, resulted in the acceleration of domestic inflation in the United States. Politicians believed that deregulation of key American industries would be a politically attractive remedy. Through deregulation, formerly regulated firms would face competition; this would result in lower prices.

Competition would also encourage productivity improvements that would promote economic growth. In the case of the airline industry, one major airline—United Airlines—favored deregulation of the industry, thinking that it could improve its stock in a deregulated environment. Thus, beginning in the mid-1970s, growing popular support for market deregulation led to an easing of restrictions on pricing, entry, and exit in the transportation, finance, communications, and energy industries. After forty years of tight control, Congress passed the Airline Deregulation Act of 1978, which provided for the eventual total deregulation of the U.S. airline industry. The CAB was abolished on January 1, 1985.

Effects of Airline Deregulation in the United States

An important effect of airline deregulation was the acceleration in the development of the hub-and-spoke system in the industry.[30] Under this system, travelers frequently must first take flights (spokes) from smaller outlying airports to major airports (hubs) from which they take connecting flights to their final destinations. Because most city-pair markets were not large enough to offer frequent direct service, under the freer deregulated regime, carriers adopting the hub-and-spoke system were able to offer enhanced single-carrier service to their connecting passengers. All things being equal, passengers prefer direct service to connecting service, because direct service saves travel time. On the other hand, rerouting and consolidating traffic enabled airlines to use larger aircraft from their hubs; larger aircraft had lower operating costs. A more competitive, deregulated environment would ensure that at least some of the cost savings were passed along to consumers in lower airfares.

Deregulation brought a flood of new entrants into the airline industry in the late 1970s and early 1980s. In the late 1980s, however, the industry underwent significant consolidation. Nonetheless, Steven Morrison and Clifford Winston found that, at the individual route level, generally more competition existed than before deregulation.[31] They also found that between 1978 and 1993, the number of "effective competitors" increased on routes longer than 2,000 miles, but fewer effective competitors existed on routes of less than 500 miles.[32]

Deregulation also has led to a proliferation of air fares. Fares range from discount fares with numerous restrictions to much higher fares with no travel restrictions. The Internet and high speed computers have made it possible for airlines to practice price discrimination—referred to in the industry as "yield management"—at the level of high intensity they could not before. James

Koch and Richard Cebula note that "using quantitative techniques, airlines routinely post hundreds, even thousands, of different prices for airline tickets. The price one is quoted depends on who one is, when one asks for the price, how many other requests the airline has received, and its previous selling and pricing experience with this or similar flights."[33]

Alfred Kahn, the acknowledged "father" of U.S. airline deregulation, explains that a lot of the airline price discrimination is beneficial to all travelers:

> In part it reflects wide differences in real costs as between long and short, dense and thin routes and by hour of the day and day of the week, as well as of holding seats open for last-minute availability. Moreover, to the extent that the fare differentials are discriminatory, they make it possible to use larger, more efficient planes and offer more convenient scheduling on a greater number of routes than would have been possible if all fares had to be uniform. . . . the offer of heavily discounted tickets to discretionary and/or leisure travelers, in order to fill the seats that would otherwise go empty, while charging higher fares to demand-inelastic travelers, is beneficial to both of them.[34]

Consumers in the United States enjoyed falling airfares even before deregulation, in part stemming from rising efficiency in the airline industry. Since fare deregulation began in 1976, average real[35] airfares have declined by 40 percent while full fares, paid on only 6 percent of total miles flown, have increased over 70 percent. In the same period, the number of passenger miles flown has tripled.[36] Steven Morrison and Clifford Winston estimated that increased competition from existing carriers accounted for 18 percent of the savings to consumers from lower real fares since deregulation, competition provided by Southwest Airlines (a low-fare airline) accounted for 31 percent of the savings, competition from new entrants accounted for 10 percent of the savings, and improvements in airline operating efficiency accounted for the remaining 41 percent of the savings.[37] In sum, deregulation has accounted for nearly 60 percent of the observed decrease in real airfares. The entry of low-fare Southwest Airlines accounted for over half of the savings from deregulation. Southwest Airlines built its success by providing service on short-haul routes; even today, about 80 percent of its flights are less than 750 miles.[38]

Deregulation also contributed to an increase in the load factor—that is, airlines now fill more seats on a given flight. This was expected. Thus, one trade-off under deregulation was that consumers gave up some comfort for lower prices. Higher load factors have also meant that some passengers have difficulty getting seats on preferred flights.

Although deregulation was expected to reduce flight frequency, in fact, overall service frequency has increased in most markets. The General Accounting Office (GAO) found that the number of scheduled departures increased by 50 percent at airports serving small communities, 57 percent at airports serving medium-sized communities, and 68 percent at airports serving large communities.[39] As a result, consumers now trade longer travel times due to the necessity of rerouting under an expanded hub-and-spoke system for lower airfares and greater choice of departure times.

Concern that deregulation would induce airlines to economize on maintenance and hence threaten passenger safety turned out to be unfounded.[40] Eco-nomic deregulation did not mean safety deregulation; the Federal Aviation Administration (FAA) continues to monitor and enforce safety regulations in flying.

Not all passengers have shared equally in the benefits of airline deregulation. Long-distance air travelers on high density routes have generally benefited more than short distance travelers on low density routes. Some travelers have fared worse under deregulation. Under CAB regulation, airfares were set above cost in long-haul markets to subsidize fares that were set below cost in short-haul markets; not surprisingly, for some travelers airfares actually increased and service quality decreased following deregulation. Morrison and Winston found that, whereas average real fares have decreased, they have increased on distances of less than 800 miles and decreased for greater distances.[41] The GAO's 1994 survey of 112 airports found that real airfares had decreased at 73 airports and increased at 33 airports since deregulation.[42]

Overall, Morrison and Winston estimated that aggregate annual welfare gains to consumers from airline deregulation totaled around $18.4 billion in 1993 prices (Table 8-2).[43]

Frequent flyer programs are another byproduct of airline deregulation. American Airlines introduced its AAdvantage program in 1981; by 1986, all major U.S. airlines had their own programs. The typical frequent flyer program awards a paying passenger points for each mile flown. The passenger can redeem accumulated points toward future free travel, an upgrade to a higher level of service (e.g., from coach to first-class travel), or even merchandise, hotel accommodations, car rentals, and cruises. Today, nonairlines such as credit card companies, hotels, car rental companies, long-distance telephone companies, and others are partnering with airlines' frequent flyer programs.

Are frequent flyer programs a marketing strategy by airlines to reward their good customers by giving them quantity (volume) discounts? Or, are they employed to reduce potential competition? The answer is "yes" to both questions. For pleasure travelers who pay their own fares, frequent flyer programs are essentially a quantity discount.[44] At the same time, they give the large airlines a competitive advantage over small airlines because large airlines provide passengers a greater opportunity to earn award miles on their extensive route systems and redeem them for travel to diverse destinations. Morrison aptly describes the small carrier disadvantage as follows:

> Consider, at one extreme, the disadvantage faced by an airline that serves only one destination. Having accumulated enough miles for a free trip, the traveler is rewarded with another trip to the same place![45]

Also, frequent flyer programs are designed so that passengers with more miles qualify for better awards, an incentive to fly with one airline. Alaska Airlines has a unique program that adds "bonus miles" to a passenger's account at various threshold miles flown during the year. Some airlines impose expiration dates on their award miles, providing even more incentive for travelers to accumulate and redeem their miles quickly on a single carrier.

In summarizing the impact of airline deregulation in the United States, Alfred Kahn recently concluded that "It has meant—you may put it in a favorable way—the democratization of travel."[46] Nonetheless, many travelers complain that the current pricing system is both confusing and unfair, espe-

TABLE 8-2

ANNUAL GAINS TO CONSUMERS FROM AIRLINE DEREGULATION IN THE U.S. (in billions of 1993 dollars)

Source of Gain	Amount
Lower fares	12.4
Greater travel restrictions	-1.1
More flight frequency	10.3
Higher load factor	-0.6
More connections	-0.7
Mix of connections (single carrier of interline)	0.9
Greater travel time	-2.8
Total	18.4+

Source: Morrison and Winston (1995), p. 82.

cially to business travelers. The chief executive of one major airline finally admitted that the current airfare structure is "broken." Faced with growing competition from cut-rate airlines such as Southwest Airlines and Jet Blue, some U.S. carriers are experimenting with "simplified" fare structures by slashing their highest fares and reducing the number of coach fares.[47] But as long as travelers are willing to pay different fares to fly, it is unlikely that the major airlines will scrap the discriminatory pricing model that has been a key feature of a deregulated U.S. airline industry.

Deregulation Spreads to International Aviation
Deregulation of the airline industry in the United States, featuring total removal of price, entry, and exit regulations, has provided a positive model for regulatory reform in other regions such as in Europe, Australia, and Japan. At the same time, deregulation has had the ancillary effect of increasing the productivity of U.S. airlines in international markets and weakening the competitive position of foreign carriers. Thus, deregulation provides strong incentives to foreign governments to deregulate their aviation industries.[48] Regulated firms cannot compete successfully against firms that are subject to the discipline of market competition. Efficiency gains from aviation deregulation have also helped to weaken the monopoly power of the international aviation *cartel*, the International Air Transport Association (IATA), and diminished its ability to enforce its fare-fixing agreements in international aviation.[49] For many governments, the first step even before deregulation is the privatization of their inefficient national carriers. Governments in the rest of the world are generally wary of the free-for-all U.S. approach to airline deregulation that has produced winners and losers among carriers and the wide dispersion and volatility of airfares. In the rest of the world, domestic aviation deregulation will likely mean a highly managed form of competition. Nonetheless, in Europe and Japan, regulatory reform has opened the door to start-up low-fare airlines.[50]

International Aviation: Open Skies and Airline Alliances

SINCE WORLD War II, international aviation has been governed by a network of bilateral agreements that has essentially limited competition among foreign carriers. Under this regime the governments of two countries—say, the United States and Japan—negotiate with each other to determine which U.S.

airlines can fly into Japan (and vice versa) and how frequently, and whether these U.S. airlines are authorized to pick up passengers in Japan to fly them to a third country (say, China).

It is obvious that these restrictions on the global movement of air passengers are antiquated. With commerce becoming increasingly global, and international tourism growing rapidly, consumers and businesses demand global services in air travel. While the world has adopted a multilateral (multicountry) approach to remove barriers to free trade, international aviation continues to operate under a patchwork of approximately 4,000 separate country-to-country aviation agreements.[51] International aviation agreements remain largely bilateral; international air passenger traffic is not.

In 1992, the Netherlands became the first European Union (EU) country to reach an open skies agreement with the United States. This was followed by a similar agreement between the United States and Switzerland in 1995.[52] The United States now has open skies agreements with ten EU countries. Between 1992 and 1999, the United States signed thirty-seven such agreements with foreign nations. These (still bilateral) open skies agreements permit airlines of each country to fly to, from, and beyond the other's territory.[53]

A related development is the emergence of airline alliances between U.S. and European airlines on trans-Atlantic routes. Airline alliances are agreements between airlines to form networks that link the activities of individual airlines.[54] In the 1990s, United Airlines partnered with the German Lufthansa airlines (and others) to form the Star Alliance; Delta quickly followed with its own alliance with Air France and Alitalia (Wings), and Northwest Airlines formed the SkyTeam alliance with KLM. These alliances enable the partners to code share,[55] coordinate their marketing and flight schedules, and to integrate their frequent flyer programs.

Strategic airline alliances have received the official blessing of the U.S. government. The *United States International Air Transportation Policy Statement*, issued in 1995, recognizes that "the trend toward expanding international airline networks is an inevitable response to the underlying network economics of the airline industry." All three trans-Atlantic alliances received antitrust immunity from the U.S. government.

Until the airlines began to form these strategic alliances, most flights involving connecting service abroad required passengers to change airlines. This was inconvenient to passengers because interline service did not provide convenient schedules, flight frequency, through check-ins, and more complete pricing structures. Alliances allow airlines to provide near seamless travel service to consumers. They also reduce the cost of doing business to airlines. In sum, alliances enable airlines to bypass the patchwork of restrictive bilateral aviation agreements to achieve higher efficiency through networking; this potentially benefits both the airlines and consumers.[56] Alliances also circumvent restrictions on foreign direct investment in domestic airlines. Although open skies agreements are not a necessary requirement for the development of strategic airline alliances, they facilitate their development because they allow airlines to significantly expand their capacity across the Atlantic.

To confirm the existence of their beneficial economic effects, in 1999 the U.S. Department of Transportation conducted a study to ascertain the economic effects of the U.S. open skies agreements and trans-Atlantic airline alliances.[57] Its findings can be summarized as follows:

1. Passenger traffic has grown dramatically since the formation of these trans-Atlantic airline alliances. A large part of the growth in traffic is new traffic and not a diversion of traffic from other carriers. Hence, airline alliances over the Atlantic have stimulated passenger demand.
2. As alliances grow, they begin to overlap each other, thus resulting in a more competitive industry structure.
3. Airline fares have fallen significantly under open skies liberalization and the resulting alliance expansion. City-pair markets under open skies agreements experienced the largest fare declines (13.7 percent between 1996 and 1998). To the extent that airline alliances provided more competition than before, non–open skies markets also experienced (less dramatic) fare reductions.

Bilateral negotiation to reach open skies agreements is a slow and arduous process. Some believe that the next logical step is to take a multilateral approach. It won't be easy. As Sumner La Croix and David Wolff point out, "while free trade is usually superior to protected trade, it also generates losers. Until a method is devised for compensating the losers, Open Skies proposals are unlikely to fly." [58]

Concluding Observations

PHINEAS FOGG and Passepartout went "around the world in 80 days"—an extraordinary achievement in 1872—traveling by train, hot-air balloon, sailing ship, Chinese junk, and steamship. Today, they could circumnavigate the globe in speedy jet planes in far less time and, no doubt, for less money. Or, they could cruise around the world in exquisite luxury on the *Queen Elizabeth 2 (QE2)* in about the same number of days. Technology has made it possible for faster, more comfortable, and safer travel, and economic growth has made it affordable for huge numbers of people to travel for pleasure. This chapter has shown that "getting you there" depends not only on developments in transportation technologies and economic growth, but also on government investments in transportation infrastructure and subsidies and national and international transportation regulation. Most people in the United States would agree that domestic airline deregulation is a success story. Recreational travel, or tourism, has enjoyed the largest reductions in the cost of travel as a result of deregulation. Residents of other countries are beginning to enjoy the same benefits as their governments design and implement their own transportation liberalization programs. Governments can facilitate or impede travel. In the next chapter, we further examine the various legal barriers to international pleasure travel.

CHAPTER 9

BARRIERS to INTERNATIONAL TOURIST TRAVEL

Tourism depends on economic development and open, free
societies.

GRAHAM TODD[1]

AMERICANS HAVE THE right to travel for pleasure to virtually any place in
the world where no imminent threat to personal safety or public health
exists—except to Cuba. American journalists, professional researchers, and
educators can apply to the U.S. Department of Treasury for a license to visit
Cuba, but not tourists. The ban on tourist visits to Cuba falls under the U.S.
trade embargo against the country, authorized by the Trading with the Enemy
Act of 1917, which grants the President the power to prohibit financial transactions in time of war.[2]

American tourists can travel to South Korea without a visa for visits up
to three months; but Koreans must incur the time and expense of applying
for a U.S. entry visa.[3] Until 1986, the United States had among the most
restrictive entry visa requirements in the world. After persistent complaints
from foreign countries, the United States implemented a "visa waiver program," eventually allowing visitors from twenty-eight qualifying countries to
enter the United States for up to ninety days without a visa; South Korea is
not among the qualifying countries.[4] In 2002, the State Department used an
"emergency termination" provision to unilaterally remove Argentina—the
eleventh largest source of foreign visitors to the U.S.—from the program
because too many Argentine visitors to the United States had stayed beyond

their time limit in the aftermath of Argentina's latest financial crisis. In April 2003, Uruguay was also removed from the program for the same reason.[5]

Although the United States preaches open markets, it, like other countries of the Organization for Economic Cooperation and Development (OECD), requires majority local ownership of its domestic airlines.[6] Foreign investors may buy land in the United States to build tourist facilities, such as resorts and golf courses, but they may not do so in Fiji or the Commonwealth of the Northern Marianas (CNMI), two of the most popular tourist destinations in the Pacific. In the small island countries of Oceania, foreign investors may lease but not buy land from the native owners.

Restrictions on foreign tourist travel and foreign tourism businesses and investments are not uncommon among nations. In 1979, the OECD established a tourism committee to examine barriers to international tourism in the OECD countries.[7] The OECD Tourism Committee examined forty different types of possible obstacles and solicited comments from its member countries. The list is long and contains both direct obstacles that hinder tourist travel and indirect obstacles that affect the ability of foreign firms to provide tourist services to facilitate travel. Among the responses, nineteen indicated that at least one country had created obstacles that at least one respondent considered to be a substantial impediment to competition.

These responses indicate that the area of the greatest concern is the entry and exit restrictions placed on tourist travel. Among such restrictions, the most important were entry visa requirements for nationals from certain countries to control growth of asylum seekers and illegal immigrant workers, and limits on the amount of money (foreign currency and sometimes domestic currency) residents could take abroad.[8] On the supply side, the greatest concerns related to market access and the right to establish a business in the foreign country. This chapter focuses on obstacles to individual pleasure travel with specific examples from selected Asian countries.

Restrictions on International Tourist Travel

BARRIERS TO the international movement of tourists can either be tariff-like barriers or nontariff barriers.[9] A tariff is a tax on *imports* (foreign purchases) that increases the price of imports to domestic consumers. A tax on *foreign exchange* (foreign currency) purchased by tourists to spend abroad would be considered a tariff-like barrier, as are hefty airport departure taxes or exit taxes levied on residents of a country traveling abroad.

Nontariff barriers place direct restrictions on the number of people who can travel abroad or how much they can spend abroad. Some countries, like China and the Sultanate of Oman,[10] restrict the number of foreign tourists who can visit their countries. Bhutan's Tourism Plan restricted the number of tourist visits by requiring all non-Indian tourists to come on prepaid package tours; no individual tourists were allowed. The government also established minimum daily spending requirements for tourists.[11] Clearly, nontariff barriers are more restrictive of foreign travel than tariff-like barriers. A "tax" on foreign travel may discourage some people from foreign travel, but will not prevent them from traveling abroad if they want and can afford to. By contrast, a prohibition against foreign travel or a limit placed on how much foreign exchange residents can purchase to spend abroad can put a stop to foreign travel.

Many nations limit the amount of foreign exchange residents can purchase to spend abroad.[12] In some countries, the government also sets the price of foreign exchange. Countries impose currency restrictions on foreign travel mainly to conserve foreign exchange. Most countries obtain foreign exchange by *exporting* (selling) goods and services to other countries. Countries covet foreign exchange because it enables them to pay for the high-priority imports needed for modernization and economic development. Exchange controls are placed on tourism because foreign pleasure travel (in contrast to business or official government travel) is a luxury and not a necessity. Even high-income, developed countries like France and New Zealand have at times in the past imposed unpopular foreign exchange controls on tourist travel abroad for balance-of-payments reasons.[13]

Limits on foreign exchange purchases do not necessarily prohibit travel abroad, unless the ceilings are set extremely low; they only limit how far tourists can travel and how much they can spend abroad. A direct ban on pleasure travel abroad can stop foreign travel altogether, except for those who find clever ways to circumvent the ban. For example, for ideological and political reasons and until the fall of Communism, few residents of the Eastern bloc countries were allowed to leave the bloc for holidays.[14] For them, holidays meant travel either to domestic or intra-bloc destinations.

To ascertain how travel restrictions affect foreign pleasure travel, we examine how the lifting of travel bans and foreign exchange restrictions have affected tourist travel in selected Asian countries.

South Korea and Taiwan

SOUTH KOREA, a nation frequently plagued by balance-of-payments deficits, is one of the Asian countries that restricted its citizens from traveling abroad for pleasure. Until 1983, Koreans could travel abroad on private and government business and even to work abroad (for example, in Saudi Arabia), but could not legally travel abroad for tourism. In 1983, the South Korean government finally granted exit tourist visas, but only to citizens aged 50 years or older (ostensibly for national security reasons). Applicants must deposit 2 million won (over U.S.$2,000) in a local bank for at least one year, and travel was restricted to one trip per year. In 1984, only 2,576 Korean outbound trips, or .5 percent of total overseas trips, were pleasure trips; 36 percent were for employment.[15] Following the 1988 Olympic games held in Korea, the government eliminated all overseas travel restrictions as of January 1989. In the first year of unrestricted outbound travel, overseas trips grew by 67.3 percent: from 720,000 in 1988 to 1.213 million in 1989. Two years later, nearly 60 percent of the 1.856 million overseas trips were pleasure trips. In 1999, South Korea's 47 million residents took 4.3 million trips abroad.[16]

Similarly, Taiwan allowed its citizens to travel abroad for tourism beginning in 1979, except for men between the ages of 16 and 30 who had not completed their compulsory military service. Each traveler could take two trips per year and purchase up to the equivalent of U.S.$2,200 per trip. Travel to China was still banned until November 1987. On July 1, 1988, the age ceiling on males was reduced to 26 years from 30 years, the number of trips permitted was raised to three from two, and the tourist exit and entry tax was reduced by half from NT$4,000 to NT$2,000.[17] Helped by easier travel rules, Taiwanese outbound travel more than tripled from 485,000 to 1.6 million between 1980 and 1988. By 1991, nearly half of all outbound trips were holiday trips. Taiwan is currently encouraging its citizens to travel abroad because it sees foreign travel as a way to improve its image abroad and to foster better relations with the rest of the world. Due to Taiwan's political isolation, it is not always easy for Taiwan's 20 million citizens to travel abroad. Nonetheless, in 1999, Taiwan citizens took nearly 6.6 million overseas trips.[18]

Although Taiwan allowed its citizens to visit China, it did not permit

Chinese citizens to visit Taiwan. Finally, in 2001, the government announced new rules that would allow Chinese citizens to visit Taiwan on pleasure trips. The new rules only allow Chinese citizens studying overseas or having permanent residency in a foreign country to visit Taiwan, and only in tour groups of five or more for visits of up to ten days.[19]

Japan

THE BIG story on the liberalization of tourist travel in Asia is Japan, a nation of nearly 127 million people. Japan is currently the leading tourist-generating country in Asia (or, East Asia and the Pacific, using the World Tourism Organization's classification of regions) with 16.35 million visitors going abroad in 2002, according to Japan's Ministry of Justice.[20] The World Tourism Organization reports that the Japanese were the fourth largest spenders on international tourism in 2000 ($31.5 billion, excluding international transportation payments), after the Americans ($65 billion), the Germans ($47.6 billion), and the British ($36.6 billion).[21]

After World War II, Japanese citizens were not allowed to go abroad for tourism until 1964. In addition to the lifting of the foreign pleasure travel ban in that year, the Japanese government also began to liberalize foreign exchange limits on overseas travel. By 1978, all foreign exchange controls were abolished. The liberalization of foreign tourist travel—combined with Japan's growing post-War affluence, a strong *yen*, and the introduction of the jumbo jet in 1970 that enabled the mass marketing of prepaid package tours so popular among the Japanese—produced a spectacular explosion in Japanese overseas tourist travel. Until the first global energy crisis in 1973, Japanese outbound travel increased at an average annual rate of 40 percent, rising from 160,000 in 1965 to 2.3 million in 1973. In 1965, only 28 percent of Japanese overseas trips were pleasure trips; by 1973, most overseas trips were holiday trips.[22] Today, nearly two-thirds of all Japanese trips abroad are for "sightseeing."[23] Unlike governments in other Asian nations, the Japanese government took special steps to encourage its residents to go on foreign trips to help solve an embarrassingly large and growing trade imbalance between Japan and the rest of the world. For example, in 1987, the government announced the Ten Million Program to increase the number of Japanese visitors traveling abroad from 5.5 million in 1986 to 10 million in 1991. The target was actually achieved one year ahead of the plan. Whether the attainment was due to the Program or due to other factors, such as economic growth, has not been determined.

China

SINCE THE days of Marco Polo (1254–1324), Westerners have held a curious fascination for China. But unlike governments in other Asian countries, which competed to attract Western tourists and their foreign exchange, China's Communist government kept foreign tourists out of the country. Tourism wasn't even regarded as an economic activity between the 1950s and early 1970s; it was considered "a part of foreign affairs."[24] Following the end of the Cultural Revolution in 1976, the Chinese government shifted its policy focus from politics to economics, which eventually led to opening the country to outsiders. China was finally "opened" to foreign tourist visits in 1978.[25]

Despite a huge pent-up demand for visits to China, the Chinese government kept tight control over inbound tourism. The tourist industry was operated as a state monopoly, and it wasn't until 1985 that collectives and private citizens were allowed to operate travel agencies. Foreign tourists could only visit certain cities and regions of the country. As the monopolist of tour services, the government set all tour prices. The relative price of Chinese tourist services tended to be higher and the range and variety of attractions were less than in neighboring competing countries.[26] Higher prices were charged to "foreign" (i.e., non-Chinese) tourists, in part because they received the best accommodations and services, whereas overseas Chinese tourists received lower quality services and paid between 20 to 30 percent less for their tours.[27]

The restrictions on where foreign tourists could visit stemmed in part from the lack of adequate tourist facilities and services; as the necessary improvements and investments were made, more cities and regions of the country were opened to foreign visits.[28] The number of foreign tourist visits to China increased from 1.8 million (including 229,646 non-Chinese) in 1978 to 31.7 million (including 1.8 million non-Chinese) in 1989, when the Tiananmen Square incident temporarily reversed the decade of dramatic tourism growth.[29] In 1999, nearly 73 million tourists arrived in China.[30] China has also opened its tourism sector to foreign investors, even allowing overseas operators to hold majority stakes in joint ventures or own tourism businesses outright. For example, in 2002, Hertz opened eight car rental offices in Shanghai, Beijing, and Guangzhou; but unlike the typical "U-drives" elsewhere, each Hertz rental car in China—for about U.S.$121 per day—came with its own chauffeur. Hotel chains such as Days Inn and Four Seasons, as well as the Starbucks coffee chain, have also gained footholds in China's major cities.[31]

Chinese citizens wishing to travel abroad as tourists faced both legal obstacles at home and abroad. At home, the Chinese government maintained a tight control over overseas travel to minimize the outflow of foreign exchange. Until the mid-1990s, Chinese wishing to travel abroad were required to produce invitations from foreign sponsors to attend official or business meetings abroad. Not surprisingly, many would-be pleasure travelers had to lie about the purpose of their trips and creatively manufacture overseas invitations. At the same time, barriers began to come down, although the government still maintained a policy of encouraging domestic tourism.

Outbound tourist travel from China really began in 1991, when its citizens were allowed to travel on tours to Hong Kong, Malaysia, Singapore, and Thailand. Before that, Chinese were only allowed to visit Hong Kong (since 1983) and Macau (since 1984) for family visits. In 1998, Chinese were allowed to join tours to visit Australia, New Zealand, and South Korea. In some cases, only residents of certain cities and regions were permitted to travel abroad.[32]

China is still reluctant to relinquish entirely the control of outbound tourism and prefers to negotiate bilateral tourism agreements with foreign nations to designate them as approved destinations. In 2002, China approved designation status (ADS) for twenty-two destinations, most of them with other Asian nations. The United States and the European Union (EU) have not yet received the approved designation status. Only sixty-six Chinese travel agencies are permitted to promote outbound tourism to the countries having ADS; without this designation, travel companies in China are not permitted to advertise travel to those destinations. Despite the lack of ADS designation, Chinese citizens spent 1.5 billion euros (equivalent to U.S.$1.3 billion) in the European Union in 2000. An ADS agreement between the European Union and China has been held up by the Union's demand that it be allowed to repatriate Chinese who travel to Europe for tourism and then stay on to work.[33]

For Chinese desiring to travel abroad, legal obstacles at home are compounded by obstacles abroad, because some foreign governments make it difficult for Chinese to qualify for tourist entry visas. One Chinese woman recounted her own extraordinary attempt at the Italian embassy in Beijing several years ago to obtain a visa for her family to visit Italy:

> I said we were taking our boys to see the Pope. Of course it was a lie. I'm a Communist Party member and don't believe in religion. But there was no other way to get a visa to Italy.[34]

Despite remaining obstacles, the Chinese took about 10.5 million trips abroad in 2000, and over half of them were pleasure trips, making China one of the largest tourist-generating countries in Asia. But relative to the size of its population of nearly 1.3 billion, the Chinese propensity to travel abroad is well below that of other Asian nations (less than 1 percent).

Impact of Travel Bans and Currency Restrictions on Travel

JAMES MAK and Kenneth White estimated the impact of limited travel bans and currency restrictions on foreign travel and tourist spending for twelve countries in East and Southeast Asia, Australia, and New Zealand.[35] They found that travel bans reduce the residents' propensity to travel abroad, but do not reduce per capita tourist spending abroad. Conversely, foreign exchange restrictions tend to reduce travel spending, but not the propensity to travel abroad. Thus, imposing foreign exchange restrictions on foreign travel is an effective tool to conserve foreign exchange reserves. Not surprisingly, it has been a widely used travel restriction in international tourism.

Exit and Departure Taxes

EXIT AND departure taxes can also act as barriers to international tourist travel. Little empirical evidence shows how effective they are in deterring foreign travel, because they are usually set at modest levels. However, anecdotal evidence indicates that high exit taxes can discourage foreign travel. For example, in November 1982, Indonesia imposed a stiff exit tax of Rp150,000 (about U.S.$140) for residents traveling abroad. This is a huge tax in a country where the annual income per person averages only a few hundred dollars (U.S.). Not surprisingly, the number of Indonesians visiting nearby Singapore fell sharply to 296,000 from 455,000 in the following year.[36]

Departure taxes levied at some international airports are not necessarily intended to discourage foreign travel, but are instead an airport *user charge* (passenger services facility charge) to pay for airport-related costs. It is rather curious that the new Kansai International Airport in Osaka (Japan) levies a passenger services facility charge of 2,650 yen (about U.S.$20) on adult passengers[37] leaving on international flights but not on domestic flights. The discriminatory fee at the airport—given that there is no charge on domestic flights—suggests that it is partly a user charge and partly a tax on international air travel to subsidize domestic air travel.

Duty-Free Allowance

VIRTUALLY ALL countries place limits on how much foreign goods residents can bring back with them from their foreign trips. Duty-free allowances vary substantially among countries. Separate limits are usually placed on tobacco and alcohol products. For example, returning Japanese are permitted to bring home duty-free three bottles of alcoholic beverages; by contrast, Koreans are permitted to bring back only two bottles and Taiwanese one bottle. Curiously, returning Japanese tourists are permitted to bring home only 200 cigarettes duty-free, compared to the 300 cigarettes that American and other foreign tourists can bring into Japan.[38] Passengers are assessed hefty import duties beyond the amounts of goods allowed.

In addition, countries also set allowances on the value of foreign goods returning visitors can bring home duty-free. Japan has a very high duty-free allowance of 200,000 yen (about U.S.$1,550) per returning resident, whereas the United States has an allowance of $800 for persons who have been out of the country for at least 48 hours and have not claimed an exemption within the past 30 days. In-flight surveys of returning passengers suggest that low duty-free allowances do discourage tourist shopping abroad.[39]

Some countries also place restrictions on the importation of specific goods. For example, returning Koreans may bring home up to five medicines, two items of sporting goods (cheaper than 100,000 won), one watch, one cassette radio, one stereo, one camera, twenty items of cosmetics, five blank videotapes, and three prerecorded videotapes, but all these items are subject to duty. They may not bring home color TVs, VCR/camcorders, communications equipment (e.g., cellular phones), textile material in excess of 5 square meters, and luxury goods.[40]

Duty-free allowances may be deliberately set low by a country that borders another country that offers more attractive shopping opportunities. For example, in 1992, the Mexican government lowered the duty-free allowance of Mexicans returning from the United States *via land ports of entry* from $300 to $50. Too many Mexicans were crossing the border into the United States to make purchases, either because prices were lower, qualities were higher, or because the choices were more abundant in the United States.[41] Cross border trips may also combine shopping and pleasure. Because the reduced allowance applies only at land ports of entry, the new policy is apparently designed to address not a national problem but a regional or local problem, namely to protect Mexican businesses located along the U.S. border. The problem is similar to that of two bordering states with different sales tax rates. Studies have consistently shown that the state with the higher sales tax suffers a small reduction in sales.[42] Although the negative statewide economic impact of the higher sales tax may be small, its impact on border towns may be substantial. Lowering the duty-free allowance is equivalent to imposing a sales tax on imports (above the allowance). Consistent with research findings elsewhere, this should discourage Mexicans living along the U.S. border from making purchases in U.S. border towns.

Victor Davila and his co-researchers, however, suggest that the new lower Mexico duty-free allowance may produce exactly the opposite consequences intended by lawmakers.[43] First, Mexicans will continue to cross the border to shop because their demand for U.S. goods are price inelastic. Second, they will circumvent the lower allowance by making more trips or taking more people along; that means higher trip-related expenditures (such as on food and gasoline) across the border. Thus, the total spending by Mexicans in the United States might actually be higher under the new lower allowance than before. More careful research needs to be done on this issue.

Concluding Observations

ECONOMISTS GENERALLY agree that nations can reap significant economic benefits by removing barriers to trade in goods and services. Benefits come from a more efficient use of resources within and between countries, reduction of consumer prices, and expansion of available choices. This notion is the basis for the movement toward a freer global trading system in goods since World War II. The idea is finally catching on in international trade in services, including tourism. In virtually all countries, tourism development remains a lower priority goal than preserving national security, limiting immigration, and protecting domestic jobs. This is not about to change soon. Nonetheless, we have seen in this chapter that barriers to international tourist travel are being dismantled. More people than ever before can travel where they want to, and can afford to, with far fewer restrictions. A freer travel regime has helped Asia to become the fastest tourism growth region in the world since the 1960s.

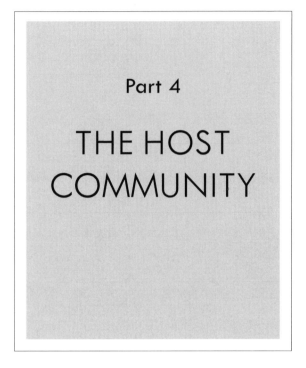

Part 4

THE HOST
COMMUNITY

CHAPTER 10

TOURISM'S PLACE in the HOST ECONOMY

Tourism satellite accounting is the only way to have an overall view of tourism's impact on the economy on an equal footing with other areas of household consumption.

ENZO PACI[1]

BECAUSE OF THE growing importance of tourism as an economic activity, a number of countries, including the United States, currently develop their own travel and tourism (or simply, tourism) satellite accounts (TTSAs or TSAs) to measure the impact of tourism on their economies. Currently, tourism is not separately identified in the nations' aggregate income and output accounts (see Q&A sidebar). Stephen Smith and David Wilton identify three objectives of tourism satellite accounting:

1. To describe the structure of a nation's tourism activity.
2. To measure its economic size and contributions.
3. To collect and interrelate statistics describing potentially all quantifiable data related to a nation's tourism activity.[2]

Understanding these accounts requires a basic understanding of how we measure a nation's total output: that is, its gross domestic product (GDP). We begin with a brief description of gross domestic product accounting.

A Primer on Gross Domestic Product (GDP) Accounting

THE MOST widely recognized measure of a nation's overall economic activity is its *gross domestic product* or GDP. The GDP is the value of all final goods

Q & A: The U.S. Travel and Tourism Satellite Accounts (TTSAs)

Q. *Where is travel and tourism measured in the economy?*
A. It isn't.

Q. *Why isn't it measured in the economy?*
A. There are many industries that provide goods and services to travelers and tourists. Expenditures on travel and tourism cut across many types of industries that do not fit neatly into a single product North American Industrial Classification System (NAICS) code from which most economic sectors are measured.

Q. *Then how do you measure the significant contribution of travel and tourism to the U.S. economy?*
A. Through the development of a new economic tool, Satellite Accounts for Travel and Tourism (TTSAs).

Q. *What are satellite accounts for travel and tourism?*
A. Travel and Tourism Satellite Accounts (TTSAs) are a relatively new economic statistical method to measure more accurately the impact of the travel and tourism industries on the U.S. economy.

   The uniqueness of this method is that it is able to link the tourism purchases of goods and services (demand) to the outputs of the industries that produce those goods and services (supply).

   TTSAs also allow us to segregate the shares of travel and tourism goods and services sold to travelers versus those sold to local residents.

Q. *What's measured in these accounts?*
A. TTSAs measure the purchases by travelers of air fares, lodging, meals and beverages, shopping, and other travel activities. TTSAs then link these expenditures to the industries that produce them.

   They also measure the contributions (i.e., *value-added*) of the producing industries to the gross domestic product (GDP) of the country. In addition, TTSAs also provide the ability to compare travel and tourism to other industries.

Source: The U.S. Office of Travel and Tourism Industries (TI), August 20, 1998.

and services produced in the economy during a specific period—usually one year. To avoid counting the same goods more than once, only *final* goods and services are counted. Goods that go into the making of other goods—called *intermediate goods*—are excluded from the tally.

For example, in computing the GDP for the United States, we don't count both the value of the wheat produced on the farms and the value of the flour that's manufactured from the wheat. The value of the flour already includes the value of the wheat.[3] The wheat contained in the flour is an intermediate and not a final good and, hence, not counted separately. Otherwise, it would be counted twice.

Another way of computing GDP is to add up the value added at each stage of production. A *value-added* amount is obtained by subtracting the value of the intermediate purchases used in production from the market value of the final good. Consider the following example:

Final Output Method		Value-Added Method	
Farm level: Value of wheat produced	$10,000	Value-added at Farm level	$10,000
Mfg level: Value of flour produced	$15,000	Value-added at Mfg. level	$ 5,000
Value of final good (flour) produced	$15,000	Total value-added	$15,000

If wheat produced by a farmer is valued at $10,000 and the manufactured flour is valued at $15,000, the value added at the farm level is $10,000[4] and the value added at the manufacturing level is $5,000 (= $15,000 for the flour - $10,000 for the wheat). The total value added at both levels of production is $15,000—which is equal to the $15,000 value of the flour (the final good). Hence, the GDP equals the value of all the final goods and services produced by all industries, or the GDP equals the *value-added* by all industries. Both these methods of computing GDP focus on the *output* of goods and services by suppliers/industries; namely, the supply side.

GDP can also be measured from the buyers'—or, the demand—side. Because everything that's produced in the economy must be "bought" by someone, the total value of final goods and services produced (GDP) *in the economy* must be equal to the total purchases (or, expenditures) by domestic households, businesses, governments, and nonresident buyers of final goods and services *minus* what they spend on imports. Specifically,

	Domestic			Government				
GDP =	Household	+	Investment	+	Spending on	+	Exports	−	Imports
	Spending		Spending		Goods & Services			
	(C)		(I)		(G)		(X)		(M)

Exports (X) are purchases of U.S. goods and services by foreigners, whereas imports (M) are purchases of foreign goods and services by U.S. residents. Tourism debunks the common perception that exports must be goods sold (and sent) abroad, and imports are goods brought into the United States. In tourism, foreign tourist expenditures in the United States represent U.S. exports, whereas U.S. resident tourist expenditures abroad are imports.

U.S. Travel and Tourism Satellite Accounts (TTSAs)

THE ACCOUNTING framework used to compute the GDP for the United States can be used to calculate the satellite account for travel and tourism. Basically, travel and tourism satellite accounts separate out from a nation's GDP those parts that can be attributed to travel and tourism. The first travel and tourism satellite accounts for the United States were estimated for 1992 and published by the U.S. Department of Commerce, Bureau of Economic Analysis (BEA) in July 1998.[5] Follow-up estimates for 1996 and 1997 were published in July 2000.[6] The results for 1997, presented in a large number of tables, can be distilled down to a few essential findings.

The Demand Side

It all starts on the demand side. Tourism demand in the United States is composed of travel-related expenditures within the United States by foreign and domestic visitors before, during, and immediately after each trip taken. Visitors include U.S. residents, businessmen, government employees, and international visitors to the United States. In 1997, travel- and tourism-related spending by these four groups of visitors totaled $461.2 billion (Table 10-1).[7] Subtracting the amount spent on travel and tourism by U.S. residents abroad ($53.5 billion) yields the total amount of travel- and tourism-related spending in the United States at $407.7 billion.

The $116.2 billion spent by businesses on travel and tourism are considered purchases of intermediate goods and services and cannot be counted (again) in the GDP. All other purchases represent purchases of final goods and

TABLE 10-1

TRAVEL AND TOURISM SPENDING IN THE U.S.: 1997
(in billions of dollars)

Total spending by all visitors	461.2
Minus U.S. visitor spending abroad (i.e., tourism imports)	53.5
Total visitor spending in the U.S. for four visitor groups	407.7
U.S. household spending on travel & tourism	174.9
U.S. business spending on travel & tourism	116.2
Government spending on travel & tourism	20.4
Foreign visitor spending in the U.S. (i.e., tourism exports)	96.2
Minus business spending on travel & tourism (i.e., intermediate purchases)	116.2
Total visitor spending on final goods and services in the U.S. (i.e., tourism final demand)	291.5

Source: Kass and Okubo (2000).

services. Thus, domestic travel and tourism's *final demand* for goods and services in the United States, in 1997, totaled $291.5 billion (= $407.7 billion - $116.2 billion) or about 3.5 percent of U.S. gross domestic product. U.S. households account for the largest percentage—60 percent—of domestic tourism's final demand;[8] foreign visitors, 33 percent; and government employee travel accounts for the remaining 7 percent. Domestic travel is a much bigger slice of the American economy than foreign travel in the United States. Note, however, that capital investment spending in travel and tourism is conspicuously absent in the spending figures.[9]

The Supply Side

The unique feature of the travel and tourism satellite accounts (TTSAs) is the linkage of visitor spending to the industries that produce tourism goods and services. Money spent by visitors in the United States is also revenues (or, receipts) of U.S. businesses (Table 10-2). Hotels and lodging places captured the largest percentage of total visitor spending in 1997 ($74 billion, or 18.2 percent), followed by domestic passenger airfares ($64.9 billion, or 15.9 percent),

TABLE 10-2

RECEIPTS BY TOURISM INDUSTRIES IN THE U.S.: 1997
(in billions of dollars)

	Receipts ($)	% of Total
Lodging	74.2	18.2
Domestic airfares	64.8	15.9
International airfares	45.3	11.1
Eating and drinking	61.2	15.0
Recreation and entertainment	32.2	7.9
Auto and truck rental	21.2	5.2
Other	108.8	26.7
Total	407.7	100.0

Source: Kass and Okubo (2000).

eating and drinking places ($61.0 billion, or 15 percent), international passenger air fares ($45.1 billion, or 11.1 percent), recreation and entertainment businesses ($32.2 billion, or 7.9 percent), auto and truck rental companies ($21.1 billion, or 5.2 percent), and "other." Most of the money spent by visitors went to "tourism industries"; that is, industries that sell a significant portion of their output to visitors (such as hotels and airlines);[10] some also went to "nontourism industries" (such as gas stations and tourist purchases of souvenirs at university book stores).[11]

Industries' contributions to the nation's gross domestic product is measured by their value-added amounts. In 1997, the value added by the U.S. "tourism industries" totaled $178.7 billion, or 2.2 percent of U.S. GDP. By comparison, the contribution of U.S. agriculture, forestry, and fishing industries was 1.6 percent, and of manufacturing, 16.6 percent in the same year.[12]

Those tourism industries that made the largest contributions to GDP were hotels and lodging places ($54.6 billion), air transportation ($46.1 billion), eating and drinking places ($26.7 billion), retailing ($14.1 billion, excluding eating and drinking places and gasoline stations), and auto and truck leasing ($11.2 billion). Note that each industry's value-added amount to GDP is much smaller than the amount spent by visitors in that industry. For example, visitors spent $74.1 billion on lodging, but the value added by the hotels and lodging industry was $54.6 billion.

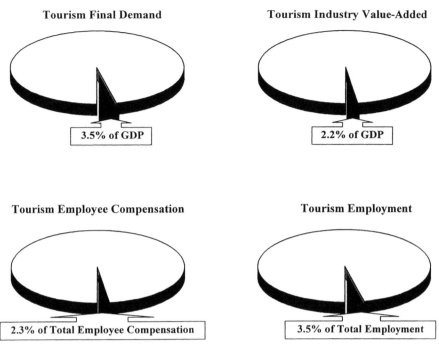

Source: Kass and Okubo (2000).

FIGURE 10-1. Tourism's place in the U.S. economy: 1997.

Figure 10-1 summarizes the contribution of travel and tourism spending to the U.S. economy in 1997.

Tourism Employment and Compensation

SPENDING ON travel and tourism created nearly 4.5 million jobs, or about 3.5 percent of total employment in the United States in 1997.[13] Those tourism industries with the largest number of employees were hotels and lodging places (1.474 million), eating and drinking places (1.327 million), air transportation (.565 million), retailing (.384 million, excluding eating and drinking places and gasoline stations), and automotive rental and leasing (.126 million).

Tourism industries are widely perceived to be low-wage industries.[14] This is confirmed in the travel and tourism satellite accounts. In 1997, the average annual compensation of employees in the U.S. tourism industries was

$23,475 compared to $35,944 for all industries. Although employment in the tourism industries comprised 3.5 percent of total employment in all U.S. industries, the compensation of tourism industry employees represented only 2.3 percent of total employee compensation in all U.S. industries. Lower pay in the tourism industries is generally attributed to a number of factors, among them the high percentage of unskilled jobs and the prevalence of seasonal, casual, part-time, transitory, and female employment.[15]

Growth of Travel and Tourism in the United States

THE U.S. travel and tourism satellite accounts also reveal the following:

1. Visitor spending on final goods and services (final demand) in *nominal* dollars (i.e., not adjusted for inflation) grew at an average annual rate of 6.9 percent between 1992 and 1997, and its share of GDP grew from 3.3 percent to 3.5 percent. Spending on travel and tourism grew faster than the overall growth of the U.S. economy (nominal GDP), which grew at 5.6 percent per year.
2. Value-added amounts from travel and tourism industries grew at an average annual rate of 7.5 percent (again, not adjusted for inflation). Value-added amounts from travel and tourism industries also grew faster than nominal GDP.
3. Employment in the travel and tourism industries grew at an average annual rate of 2.7 percent compared to the 2.0 percent average annual growth of employment in all U.S. industries.
4. Compensation of employees (e.g., wages, salaries, and fringe benefits) in travel and tourism grew at an average annual rate of 4.7 percent between 1992 and 1997, compared to 5.1 percent growth for all U.S. industries.

In sum, output and employment in the U.S. travel and tourism industries grew faster than in other industries between 1992 and 1997. Only compensation in the travel and tourism industries grew slower.

The "Ripple" or "Multiplier" Effects of Visitor Spending

THE U.S. travel and tourism satellite accounts do not explicitly include the "ripple" or "multiplier" effects of visitor spending on the economy.[16] The Bureau of Economic Analysis (BEA) estimates that each dollar of (direct) visitor spending on travel and tourism in 1996 generated an additional (indirect) $.68 of sales in all U.S. industries for a total of $1.68 in direct and indirect business sales in the economy. One dollar of the $1.68 is the revenue from the (direct) sale to the visitor; the remaining $.68 represent (indirect) purchases by businesses from other businesses generated by the initial visitor spending.

Tourism's multiplier effects also vary by industry. For example, each dollar spent in restaurants and food services in 1996 generated an additional $1.05 of sales in agriculture, food-processing, distribution, and other industries. By contrast, each dollar spent on hotel lodging generated an additional $.76 in sales by all industries. Thus, the multiplier effect of money spent in restaurants and food services is larger than if the same amount of money were spent in hotels for lodging services.

Economic Importance of Travel and Tourism for the Entire World

THE WORLD Travel & Tourism Council (WTTC) publishes annual satellite accounts for travel and tourism for the entire world, covering over 160 countries and over one dozen regions.[17] Its methodology is more inclusive than that used by the BEA in developing the U.S. accounts in that the WTTC includes a broader coverage of expenditures in its estimates. In the BEA accounts, tourism demand consists of travel-related spending by travelers only. The WTTC travel and tourism satellite accounts also include capital investment spending by tourism businesses and governments and expenditures by government agencies for such items as tourism promotion, aviation security, sanitation services, and monies given to museums and parks to make up the shortfalls between entrance fees and operating costs. More distantly, the WTTC satellite accounts include "nonvisitor" exports of consumer goods that are subsequently resold to travelers abroad, as well as exports of investment goods such as aircraft, cruise ships, and automobiles, where these are used for travel and tourism by travel companies abroad. Because of the inclusiveness of its satellite accounts, the WTTC provides separate estimates of the economic contributions by (1) the "travel and tourism industries" (T&T Industry) that sell directly to visitors, and (2) the contributions of the broader "travel and tourism economy" (T&T Economy), which include capital investment, government expenditures, and trade exports. The WTTC satellite accounts also include the "indirect effects" (i.e., multiplier effects) of tourism-related spending on the economy.[18] Without going into further methodological detail,[19] the main findings of the WTTC travel and tourism satellite accounts for the world in 2002 can be briefly summarized as follows:

1. Worldwide, travel and tourism spending by visitors and nonvisitors is estimated at U.S.$4,211.1 billion in 2002. Travel-related spending by individual consumers exceeds $2,500 billion, or about 50 percent of the total.
2. The travel and tourism industries (T&T Industry) are estimated to contribute $1,195.1 billion, or 3.6 percent of the world gross domestic product, and generate 2.8 percent of total worldwide employment.
3. The broader travel and tourism economy (T&T Economy) is estimated to contribute $3,282.5 billion, or 10.0 percent of the world gross domestic product, and generate 7.8 percent of total worldwide employment.[20]

Concluding Observations

VISITOR DESTINATIONS are mostly interested in the economic contributions of nonresident visitors to their economies. Travel and tourism satellite accounts have much broader objectives in that they try to ascertain the relative importance of tourism in nations' economies, not only the impact of nonresident visitor spending on host economies. The development of travel and tourism satellite accounts is a significant advancement in our understanding of the place of travel and tourism in our economies. That TTSAs became available only recently is attributable to the extreme difficulty in obtaining the detailed data needed to produce the estimates. For example, producing the U.S. TTSAs requires data on the amount of money spent by all types of travelers (domestic and foreign, business, official, and personal) on travel and tourism, what they spent their money on, and at what types of businesses. Obtaining such data usually requires expensive surveys. For most countries, even the most basic data (e.g., the volume of domestic travel and spending) are not available.

Not surprisingly, the U.S. travel and tourism accounts offer a range of estimates—"high," "medium," and "low"—reflecting the BEA's uncertainty about the correct values of important variables. Hence, BEA limited its study to answering much narrower questions: What are the direct economic contributions of spending by domestic household, business, government, and international travelers in the United States? And, what is the size of the U.S. travel and tourism "industry"?

By contrast, the WTTC takes a bolder step by attempting to answer a different and much broader question: What is the total economic contribution of travel and tourism—in its broadest definition—to the economy? The data requirements to calculate the WTTC's estimates of world travel and tourism satellite accounts "for over 160 countries and over one dozen regions" are enormously challenging and no doubt required numerous heroic assumptions and judgments about the values of many critical variables. Its estimates have been severely criticized as well as defended by reputable scholars.[21]

Finally, it is important to be aware that travel and tourism satellite accounts can only tell us the relative importance of travel and tourism in the host economy at a given point in time. They can't tell us what would happen to the economy if there were no tourism. In other words, they can't tell us the "economic benefit" or "net value" of travel and tourism to the host community. Douglas Frechtling defines "an economic benefit as a gross increase in the wealth or income measured in monetary terms, of people located in an area over and above the levels that would prevail in the absence of the activity under study."[22] In his excellent article, Frank Mitchell explained that the resources employed in tourism may have other uses.[23] If tourism did not exist, the resources currently employed in tourism could be employed in other economic activities. In sum, "If all resources are priced at their opportunity cost, the net value of tourism will consist of (1) indirect taxes paid on goods purchased by tourists, *plus* (2) receipts to government for services provided, *less* (3) the cost to government of providing the services used by tourists and promoting tourism."[24] That would provide a minimum estimate of the net value of tourism.[25] The actual net value could be higher, if, for example, persistent unemployment plagues the economy and tourism development increases employment among local residents; in that case, the additional labor earnings from tourism should be counted in the net contribution of tourism. With reasonable adjustments, Mitchell surmised that the net value to East Africa of foreign visitor spending, in 1967, amounted to between 5 and 10 percent of tourist receipts. In sum, tourism's net value to a community is a mere fraction of tourism spending.

Appendix

Understanding Tourism Multipliers

Economic impact analyses of tourism extend beyond the contribution of travel and tourism to the aggregate economies of travel destinations. Numerous economic impact studies using "multiplier"[26] analyses have been performed on convention centers, museums, and resort developments; specific tourism activities such as sporting and cultural events, casino gambling, festivals, and expositions; different types of tourists, and so on. Yet, much confusion remains on what tourism multipliers mean and how to use them correctly. Misuses and misinterpretations of tourism multipliers are common occurrences and have led, in many cases, to gross exaggerations of the economic contributions of tourism activities.

The problem largely stems from the public confusion over the economic concepts of "output" and "income."[27] "Output" is production or sales. "Income" includes wages and salaries, interest earned, rents, and profits (including corporate profits and incomes of proprietors, such as self-owned businesses). Ask any businessman, and he will acknowledge that his "sales" (or, output) are not the same as his "income."

To illustrate, imagine a tourist spends $10 at the Oceanfront Shoppe for a beach towel. The store records sales (or output) of $10. But that $10 is not the store's "income" from the sale. From that $10, the Oceanfront Shoppe has to pay the Paradise Wholesale Co., its supplier, for the beach towel ($5). The Oceanfront Shoppe also has to pay for supplies, utility expenses, and the purchases of other intermediate goods and services ($1) and wages, interest expenses, and rent ($3). What's left ($1) is profit. The total amount of income generated in the economy is $4: $3 of wages, interest, and rent, and $1 profit. Hence, $10 of business sales (output) generates $4 of income in the economy.

The Paradise Wholesale Co., too, has to pay for the towel, which it imported from China ($2), and pay for other business supplies and expenses ($.50). It pays $2.00 in wages, interest, and rents, and retains $.50 in profit. The money sent to China can no longer circulate and create additional spending in the local economy. Let's summarize the impacts of the $10 spent by the tourist on output and income in the host economy:

The initial $10 spent by the tourist generates $10 worth of *direct* sales (i.e., business to tourist) by the Oceanfront Shoppe and an additional $5 of *indirect* sales (i.e., business to business) by the Paradise Wholesale Co. to Oceanfront for a total of $15 in direct + indirect sales. The direct + indirect tourism "output" multiplier has a value of 1.5 (= $15 in direct and indirect sales ÷ $10 of tourist spending). Hence, for every dollar spent by a tourist, direct + indirect business sales (output) increases by the direct + indirect "output multiplier" (1.5) x $1, or $1.50. Economists refer to the direct + indirect multipliers as "Type I" multipliers. In this example, the Type I "output" multiplier has a value of 1.5.

By contrast, direct + indirect income generated by the $10 spent by the tourist is equal to income from the Oceanfront Shoppe ($4) plus the income from the Paradise Wholesale Co. ($2.50), or a total of $6.50. The direct + indirect (or, "Type I") tourism "income" multiplier is .65 (= $6.50 of direct and indirect income generated ÷ $10 of tourist spending). Hence, for every dollar spent by a tourist, direct + indirect income in the economy increases by the "income multiplier" (.65) x $1, or 65 cents.

In our example, the Type I tourism "output" multiplier is larger than 1 (1.5), whereas the Type I "income" multiplier is less than 1 (.65). Dollar for dollar, tourist spending generates more business sales/output than income. Too many people, unfortunately, confuse "output" with "income" and assume that the "output" multiplier is the same as the "income" multiplier. The result is wildly exaggerated claims about the economic impacts of tourist spending—for example, "A dollar spent by a tourist generates $1.50 of income in the economy."

Finally, the $10 of tourist spending also generates additional household incomes. Part of the additional income is spent on goods and services, thus generating even more business sales and incomes in the economy. Economists call these additional sales and incomes the *induced effects* of visitor spending. Thus, the total economic impacts of visitor spending include the direct + the indirect + the induced effects. Input-output (I-O) modeling systems of local economies are able to generate *total tourism multipliers*—called "Type II" or "total" multipliers—which capture the total economic effects of tourist spending on business sales (output), household income, and employment in an economy.[28]

To show the relationships between the multipliers, Table 10-A1 presents the Type I (direct + indirect) and total or Type II (direct + indirect + induced) input-output (I-O) multipliers for selected visitor-related industries in

TABLE 10-A1

TOURISM MULTIPLIERS FOR SELECTED VISITOR INDUSTRIES IN HAWAII

Industry	Output	Earnings	Employment
Accommodations			
Direct + indirect	1.42	.44	16.8
Total (=direct + indirect + induced)	1.92	.57	22.4
Eating and drinking establishments			
Direct + indirect	1.46	.42	27.0
Total	1.95	.56	32.6
Air transportation			
Direct + indirect	1.41	.30	8.2
Total	1.76	.40	12.2
Sightseeing transportation			
Direct + indirect	1.34	.45	19.4
Total	1.85	.59	25.2
Automobile rental			
Direct + indirect	1.60	.28	12.0
Total	1.92	.37	15.6
Travel arrangements & reservations			
Direct + indirect	1.34	.52	19.9
Total	1.93	.68	26.7
Amusement services			
Direct + indirect	1.39	.36	21.2
Total	1.80	.47	25.9
Golf courses			
Direct + indirect	1.45	.45	20.2
Total	1.97	.59	26.0
Museums & historical sites			
Direct + indirect	1.38	.51	30.2
Total	1.97	.67	36.8

Source: State of Hawaii, March 2002, Table 5.1, pp. 39–43.

Hawaii. Table 10-A1 shows that total multipliers, which include the induced effects of household spending on the economy, are larger than multipliers that include only the direct (business to tourist sales) and indirect (business to business sales) effects. The total multipliers for the accommodations industry indicate that $1 million spent on visitor accommodations generate $1.92 million in total business output (sales) in Hawaii's economy, $.57 million in household earnings, and 22.4 jobs.[29] By comparison, $1 million spent in eating and drinking establishments generate $1.95 million in business sales, $.56 million in household earnings, and 32.6 jobs. Among Hawaii's industries, museums and historical places have the highest, and air transportation the lowest, output and employment multipliers. By contrast, travel agencies have the highest, and car rental agencies the lowest, household earnings multipliers.

The size of the tourism multipliers depends on how much of the visitor expenditure dollars remains in the economy. Multipliers are larger if more of the money circulates at home instead of being sent away to purchase imports. It should hardly be surprising to find that tourism multipliers for the highly diversified U.S. economy are larger than multipliers for a single (less diversified) state that depends heavily on imported goods and services. For example, the 1995 RIMS II multipliers for the United States, produced by the U.S. Department of Commerce, Bureau of Economic Analysis (BEA), shows the following total multipliers for the U.S. hotels and lodging establishments (i.e., accommodations): 3.13 for output, .98 for earnings, and 45.7 for employment.

Multipliers can also vary by type of visitors. For example, young tourists backpacking their way around the world may spend less money per day than their parents, but more of their travel money spent tends to stay in the local economies. For example, it has been estimated that 70 percent of backpackers' vacation spending in Indonesia goes to locally-owned businesses—such as small hotels and unpretentious eating and drinking places—compared to 30 percent of the money spent by "mass tourists" staying in foreign-owned luxury hotels.[30] Thus, dollar for dollar, tourism multipliers for backpackers may be higher than those for upscale tourists.

CHAPTER 11

BENEFITS AND COSTS OF TOURISM TO THE HOST COMMUNITY

Tourism can be both a blight and a blessing.

FRANCES BROWN [1]

WHEN PEOPLE TAKE vacation trips, they expect to have a good time, and by and large, most do. Of course, travel isn't free because it costs time and money. Thus, tourists receive benefits and incur costs when they travel. Likewise, businesses that supply goods and services to tourists expect to receive benefits (i.e., earn profits) and incur costs. Economists refer to these benefits and costs as *private benefits* and *private costs* because they accrue to the two private parties.

Another important group of people are affected by tourism—the residents of tourist destinations. A tourist destination can be a city, a state, or a nation. Travel decisions made by tourists can affect the residents of tourist destinations for good or bad in many ways. The tourist who takes an Alaska cruise probably did not take into account in her decision that she may contribute to the pollution of Alaska's ocean waters and thus impose a cost on its residents; or that her demand for native arts and crafts may help to perpetuate Alaska's native culture, a benefit to Alaskans. Economists refer to these spillover effects that affect the other members of the community (namely, the public) as *externalities.*[2] *External benefits* are benefits that accrue to people other than the buyers of a good. *External costs* are costs that are not borne by producers or sellers of a good but by other people. Externalities arise when the activities of one person create costs or benefits for other people which are not reflected in the activities' prices.[3] Generally, activities that produce harmful (or, negative) externalities are underpriced and oversupplied. For example, if driving your car pollutes the environment, and you are not charged for it, you would drive too much. By contrast, activities that produce beneficial (or, positive) externalities are undersupplied.

In assessing the benefits and costs of tourism, it is generally acknowledged that the welfare of destination residents is of primary concern.[4] In this chapter, we examine the benefits and costs of tourism as they affect the residents of tourist destinations. It is assumed that residents of host communities want to maximize their net total benefit from tourism.

Economic Benefits from Tourism

SUPPORT FOR tourism development is usually based on the perceived economic benefits that tourism can bring to a community. Many people equate the direct benefits of tourism with tourist spending. When tourists spend money, they create demand for local goods and services and generate income, employment, and tax revenues in the community. The construction of tourist facilities also creates income, employment, and tax revenues in the community. Tourism might not generate the most lucrative or the most satisfying employment, but in many cases, it is the only kind available. Foreign tourists also bring valuable foreign exchange to the host country, which is needed to pay for imports.[5] Foreign (nonresident) direct investment in the local tourist industry can increase the host economy's productive capacity and business know-how.[6]

Tourism also can provide indirect economic benefits. Because total demand for goods and services in the host community is greater with tourism than without, bigger demand means bigger markets, which can mean lower prices for many goods and services because of economies of scale. Larger markets also can support more firms, thus resulting in keener competition and greater variety of choices. Tourism development can help to balance economic opportunities and incomes in different regions of a destination or country. The development of tourism in declining rural areas can halt population drift to the cities and narrow the income disparity between urban and rural residents.[7] It can be a catalyst in the development of other complementary industries.

For example, tourism development may provide stimulus to local agriculture by generating additional demand for local food production.[8] It can help to rejuvenate parts of inner cities or run-down harbor-front areas as it did in Baltimore (Maryland), Savannah (Georgia), Darling Harbour (Sydney, Australia), and Yokohama (Japan).[9]

Economic Costs of Tourism

TOURISM ALSO imposes direct and indirect economic costs on the host communities. A destination's resources—land, labor, and capital—are used to provide goods and services to tourists and tourism businesses. Because resources employed in tourism may have other uses, usually a cost is accrued to the community when these resources are diverted from their previous uses and employed in tourism.[10] In some developing countries, tourism development can have an adverse impact on traditional agriculture by diverting agricultural labor to tourism. While tourism receipts rise, agriculture's output declines. Once the loss of agricultural output is subtracted from the gross tourism receipts, the net economic contribution of tourism may only be a small fraction of its gross receipts.

Governments also incur direct costs when they provide public services—roads, airports, police and fire protection, lifeguards and park rangers, garbage pick-up, and sewage disposal—to support tourism. Governments incur indirect costs when they provide public services (police and fire protection and public education) to accommodate the net increase in the population caused by labor in-migration induced by the growth of tourism.[11]

Factors Affecting Tourism's Economic Benefits and Costs

THE MAIN factors that affect the economic benefits and costs of tourism to host communities can be summarized as follows:

Taxes and Subsidies

If an excise or sales tax is levied on a good or service that is sold to a tourist at a price above its cost of production, a net benefit accrues to the local economy. Similarly, if the government levies a *tariff*[12] on a good that is subsequently resold to a tourist, another net gain to the economy occurs. An entry tax or fees levied on tourists increases the cost of a visit to tourists; but the higher tax receipts represent a net benefit to residents. By contrast, if a good purchased by tourists is subsidized by the government (for example, local public transportation), there is generally a net cost to the economy.

Government Revenue Effects

Increased tourism usually produces higher net government revenues. Indeed, governments often design their fiscal systems to generate disproportionate amounts of revenues from their export industries.[13] By shifting taxes to non-residents, *tax exporting* enables the governments of tourist destinations to reduce taxes (tax rates) and/or provide more public services elsewhere in the economy, thus resulting in a net benefit to residents of the host communities. For example, the gaming industry (directly and indirectly) generates most of the tax revenues collected in Nevada; residents of Nevada pay no state income taxes.[14] Nevada residents enjoy public services largely funded by tourists and tourist businesses.

Sometimes tourism growth actually produces lower net government revenues. This may occur if tourism is heavily subsidized. The subsidy of private investment in tourism is practiced in many countries, especially among developing nations.[15] The Republic of Belau, a small island nation located in the middle of the Pacific Ocean, is an extreme example of public subsidy of tourism. The fiscal system in Belau was not designed to generate revenues to finance government functions such as education, road maintenance and construction, police and fire protection, and the like; it was designed mainly to finance the operation of its legislature. Most of the Belau government's revenues comes from U.S. economic aid and transfers. Thus, aid money and transfers from the U.S. are used to subsidize tourism.[16]

Increased tourism can also produce lower net government revenues if the cost of providing public services to accommodate more tourists increases at a faster pace than government revenues. This may occur for at least two reasons: (1) if the cost of providing public services increases at a faster rate than the general price level in the economy, a not uncommon situation; and (2) if the labor requirements of a growing tourist industry must be met increasingly by in-migrants who require substantial public provision of health, education, and other services.[17] Hence, it is important for destination governments to regularly monitor whether tourists and their suppliers pay their own way.

Market Power of Local Tourist Businesses

If local tourist businesses possess market or monopoly power and can charge prices to tourists that are substantially above the cost of production, a gain to the economy occurs.[18] For example, in Chapter 9 we noted that when China was opened to foreign tourist visits beginning in 1978, more people wanted to visit China than could be accommodated by available tourist facilities. The Chinese government operated tourism as a state monopoly. By exercising its monopoly power, China's government-owned and -operated tourism enterprises, some catering exclusively to foreign visitors,[19] were able to charge prices substantially above their costs. High prices levied on tourist purchases were a benefit to China's economy.

Likewise, exclusive concessions granted by destination governments to restaurants, hotels, duty-free shops, recreation equipment rental shops, and other tourist businesses at airports and public parks confer substantial market power to these businesses and enable them to charge exorbitant prices and potentially earn huge profits. If the governments set concession fees and rents at levels that extract most of these monopoly profits from the concessions for the benefit of the general public, there is a net gain to the community.

Price Effects

Tourism growth means an increased demand for destination resources, such as land to build more hotels and tourist attractions and workers to staff them. Local landowners benefit as the value of their property rises. If unemployment exists in the economy, there will be added benefit from higher employment in the economy. Workers in the tourist industry may also be able to demand higher wages, thus inducing workers from other industries to seek employment in tourism,[20] and thus pulling up wages in all industries. Hence, local workers also benefit from tourism growth. The reallocation of land, labor, and capital from lower-valued uses to higher-valued uses in tourism is a benefit to the economy.

An increased demand caused by tourism growth can also contribute to general inflationary pressures in the host economy. Price increases over a wide range of goods and services benefit some people (i.e., sellers), but they also can adversely affect many residents. Thus, tourism can be a blessing to some people in the community and a blight to others. Likewise, inflation increases the cost to the government of providing public services to tourists and tourist businesses. Although higher prices in the private sector may yield higher tax revenues, to the extent that costs of providing public services to tourists may rise even faster than inflation, the net effect of inflation will be to reduce tourism's public sector benefit–cost ratios. Thus, increasing tourism demand can be a mixed economic blessing. Although the economic stimulus provided by rising tourism demand creates additional employment and higher incomes in the host community, the negative inflationary impact of tourism growth offsets some of the aggregate economic benefits.

Environment and Society

Tourism can also yield many nonpecuniary benefits to the residents of travel destinations. Among them are a greater variety of entertainment for local residents, contributions to cultural exchange, more historical and cultural attractions, a positive feeling about their own community, more parks and other recreational opportunities, better maintained roads and public facilities, and a revival of traditional art forms.[21]

Critics of tourism development usually focus on the potential negative environmental, social, and cultural costs of tourism on the local population.[22] Tourism growth may exacerbate urban congestion, decrease accessibility to recreational areas for local residents, and contribute to environmental degradation.[23] It can also lead to the loss of cultural and community identity, create conflict in traditional societies over the use of community-owned land and natural resources, and increase antisocial activities, such as crime and prostitution. Sex tourism is a popular form of tourism in some Southeast Asian countries such as Thailand and the Philippines, and worldwide concern is growing over the effects of tourism on child prostitution. If tourism development is concentrated in urban population centers, as is the case in Asia, it can contribute to urban migration and widen the distribution of wealth and income between urban and rural dwellers.

Tourism's impacts on the environment and the society of host communities are difficult to measure. Hence, studies have generally focused on residents' *perceptions* of tourism's impacts rather than on its *actual* impacts.[24]

How Much Tourism?

WE ARE so accustomed to seeing tourist destinations spend millions of dollars on tourism promotion each year that we tend to overlook the fact that the residents of some destinations don't want more tourists. In Majorca (Spain), the local government requires that, before any developer builds a new hotel, another hotel with more beds must be demolished first.[25]

Nonetheless, whereas some people may harbor strong antitourism feelings, probably few residents of tourist destinations would do away with tourism altogether. When a sample of Hawaii residents were asked if they thought tourism has been "good or bad" for their island, nearly three out of four (74 percent) thought that tourism has "brought more benefits than problems."[26] However, most respondents also did not want more tourism growth. On balance, they liked what they had, but they also perceived that further tourism growth would likely cause more harm than good. In sum, the *marginal cost* (to the community) of more tourism development is expected to exceed its *marginal benefit*.[27]

Hawaii residents' responses illustrate a very important point about the cost–benefit analysis of tourism—namely, how much tourism is best for the community is determined by evaluating the *incremental* or additional benefits and costs of increasing tourism by a small amount, or a little at a time. The net total benefit from tourism is maximized when the additional (marginal) gain from a few more tourists equals the additional (marginal) cost. Tourism development has gone too far if additional tourist visits contribute lower incremental benefits than costs to the host community.

This is illustrated in Figure 11-1(a), where the optimum level of tourism development is shown at the level of V1 tourist visits and the net total benefit of tourism is the shaded area. In Figure 11-1(a), the marginal cost of tourism (MC1) is assumed to rise, while the marginal benefit (MB1) of tourism is assumed to decline with more tourist visits. Beyond V1, marginal cost is greater than marginal benefit to the community, thus reducing the *net total benefit* of tourism. Similarly, decreasing the number of tourists below V1 reduces marginal benefit more than marginal cost, again reducing the net total benefit of tourism. Thus, the net total benefit of tourism is greatest at the level of tourism development, V1, where the marginal benefit to the host community equals marginal cost, i.e., MB1=MC1 at V1 in Figure 11-1(a).

The notion that, to attain the maximum net total benefit, you should carry on an activity until its marginal benefit equals its marginal cost is not an obvious one to many people. It can, however, be illustrated using a simple example. Imagine that you are invited to a party at which tuna *sushi* is served by the host. Because the *sushi* is free, you want to eat enough of it to achieve the maximum net total benefit (utility). Do you know how many

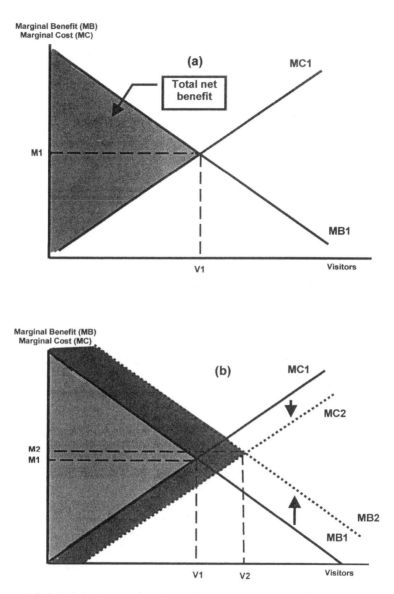

FIGURE 11-1. Marginal benefits and costs of tourism to the host community.

sushi you expect to eat when you first enter the room? Probably not. Instead, you eat one *sushi* at a time, and after eating each one decide whether or not you want to eat another one. Suppose that you can assign a personal satisfaction value to each *sushi* you eat, measured in "utils." The following illustrates the relationship between your satisfaction from eating your last *sushi* (marginal benefit) and the total satisfaction (total benefit) from all the *sushi* you have eaten, including the last one:

Sushi Eaten	Marginal Benefit	Total Benefit
1	10 utils	10 utils
2	8	18
3	6	24
4	4	28
5	2	30
6	1	31
7	0	31
8	-2	29

The numbers under Marginal Benefit indicate the amount of satisfaction you get from eating each *sushi*. Hence, the first *sushi* gives you 10 utils of satisfaction; the second *sushi* gives you 8 utils of satisfaction, and so on. The column of numbers under Total Benefit indicates that by eating two *sushi*, you obtain 18 utils of total satisfaction, 10 from the first one and 8 from the second one.

Because the *sushi* is free (i.e., its marginal cost = 0), how many should you eat to maximize your net total benefit? The answer is seven.[28] When you have eaten the seventh *sushi*, you realize that it gave you no pleasure, and so you eat no more. Your total benefit from eating the seven *sushi* is 31 utils, the maximum attainable.[29] You would have eaten too many if you had eaten the eighth *sushi* because it would have made you feel sick (marginal benefit = minus 2 utils), and your net total benefit actually falls. Like Hawaii residents' attitudes toward more tourism growth, what you have consumed (seven *sushi*) is fine, but you don't want any more. In tourism, the net benefit from tourism development is at the maximum when you cannot obtain any more (net) benefit from having a few more tourists.

Figure 11-1(b) shows that the total net benefit of tourism to the host community would increase by the amount depicted in the dark shaded area if the marginal benefit of tourism rises (from MB1 to MB2) and the marginal cost of tourism falls (from MC1 to MC2). When this occurs, the community would be better off with more tourism development (at V2 instead of V1). This leads to another important point about tourism's benefits and costs to the host community: To the extent that tourism's benefits and costs can be changed by public policy, the optimum number of tourist visits in any destination can also change. The socially optimum number of tourist visits is not etched in stone. If tourism can be made to make a larger contribution to the host community, residents would be happy to accept more tourists.

Public Policy Measures to Increase Economic Benefits from Tourism

DESTINATIONS CAN increase their net economic benefit from tourism by adopting appropriate tax measures and other policies. Because tourists benefit from services provided by destination governments and from unpriced amenities such as wonderful weather and beautiful scenery, most destinations have an incentive to tax tourists to generate revenues for the benefit of the residents of the host community. Yet, University of Toronto economist Richard Bird notes that ". . . many tourist countries seem to undertax their tourist exports." [30] Tourist destinations can increase their benefit–cost ratio from tourism in several ways.

A community may decide to levy adequate entry fees and user charges for the use of public resources (such as parks and wildlife reserves) and facilities where feasible. [31] It is also appropriate to charge residents less than full admission fees for their use of the same resources and facilities, on the grounds that residents already pay through their regular taxes or that they are entitled to enjoy the amenities of their community without additional payment. [32] It is also fair to ask tourists to pay more because they have a greater ability to pay. [33] Nonetheless, residents could still be better off even if they also have to pay the admission fees, provided that the revenues collected from the fees are spent on services that benefit them. [34]

A tourist destination may choose to impose adequate taxes on tourism to pay for general government services that also benefit tourists [35] and to extract tourism's *economic rents*. [36] Economic rent is an excess return to an asset above the normal market rate of return. It is "the income received by [the] owner of a resource over and above the amount required to induce that owner to offer the resource for use." [37]

Economic rent arises because every destination has some market power in the provision of tourism services, because every destination possesses special amenities—natural (climate and scenery), human (friendly people), man-made (the pyramids of Egypt or the canals of Venice)—or it has the geographic proximity to a high-income tourist-generating country that makes it some-what unique. Market power enables destination suppliers to charge prices higher than their costs, thus generating excess profits, or *economic rent*.

"Economic rent" is a difficult economic concept to understand for many people. It can, however, be illustrated with a simple, common sense example. Imagine a group of tropical islands located near each other that are compet-ing for tourists. They possess similar amenities so that they are excellent sub-stitute resort destinations—except the island of Hui Nalu, which has far superior beaches. Because of its superior beaches, tourists are willing to pay a higher price to visit Hui Nalu than the other island resort destinations. The cost of providing tourist services, however, is the same in all the islands. Entrepreneurs in tourism on the other islands are able to earn a competitive (i.e., approximately "normal") rate of return on their investments. Because they are able to charge higher prices to willing tourists, entrepreneurs on Hui Nalu are able to earn a higher than normal return even though they would have been quite pleased with a lower return. Economists refer to the above normal rate of return as economic rent, or simply, rent.

To whom does the rent accrue? It accrues to the owners of the resources. If the entire island of Hui Nalu were owned by one person, then the entire rent would accrue to him. What if the superior beaches belong not to any one person but to the entire community—to everyone? Should not the rent then be shared with everyone in the community? Indeed, economists who study tourism generally agree that destination governments should tax away (that is, extract) the economic rent for the benefit of the general public.[38] Of course, developers can be expected to lobby lawmakers against any new tax, thus pit-ting the private self-interests of the developers against the public interests of the community.

What if the rent is not taxed away? Like the early bird that catches the worm, the early entrepreneurs initially get to reap the rent. In other words, they get to earn excess profits. But excess profits are sure to attract other entre-preneurs, and as more of them arrive, competition drives down prices until the rent is competed away. As well, more development may diminish the attractiveness of the destination and reduce the price tourists are willing to pay to visit. To make sure that the rent is not dissipated, the government may choose to restrict the entry of new competitors by requiring them to apply for hard-to-obtain licenses and then extract the excess profits by charging hefty license fees for them.[39] Alternatively, the government may tax tourist businesses more heavily than nontourist businesses.[40] For example, real property tax rates in Hawaii are generally higher on hotels than on residential and other commercial properties. Commodity taxes[41] and tourist entry and departure taxes[42] are other types of taxes that can be used to extract tourism's economic rent.

Tourism businesses, however, are often difficult to tax. In developing countries with weak systems of tax administration, it is easier to levy sales taxes and import and export duties than to tax profits and income. The prevalence of nonresident (multinational or transnational) firms in tourism that are able to "shift" accounting profits across tax boundaries[43] also complicates local income and profits tax collection.[44] Thus, the effective taxation of tourism invariably takes the form of selective sales or excise taxes levied on tourist purchases such as hotel accommodations, rental cars, and entertainment.

In addition to taxes, governments can also impose *development exactions* or *development agreements*[45] to extract rents from tourism. Development exactions are conditions imposed on a developer to turn over land, facilities, or money to the government in exchange for government approval to develop.[46] An example of a highly controversial development exaction was one proposed by the mayor of Honolulu in the early 1990s, which would require Japanese golf course developers in Honolulu to make a payment of $100 million for each golf course before government approval would be granted for the development.[47] In the United States, courts have set conditions on the timing and size of exactions that can be legally imposed on developers.[48]

Governments can also maximize the amount of economic rent they collect from tourism by not engaging in competition among destinations to provide tax and nontax incentives to potential investors in the tourist industry without first weighing the costs and benefits of such action. Governments in both high income and developing countries provide all kinds of financial and nonfinancial incentives to encourage private investment in tourism. These may include government-provided below-market interest loans, construction tax credits, income tax holidays, accelerated depreciation allowances, import duty exemption, property tax relief, employee training subsidies, provision of land and infrastructure, government guarantees on loans and repatriation of profits, equity participation by the government, and so on.[49] The record of such incentives in successfully stimulating private investment is mixed.[50]

A number of potential negative consequences can occur when governments grant tax incentives. First, such tax incentives reduce the tax base and result in less revenues available for government programs. Second, tax incentives distort resource allocation because some activities are favored over other activities because they were granted a tax advantage. Third, they encourage corruption.[51]

Should governments subsidize private investment in the tourist industry? Richard Bird argues that:

> The correct answer is almost certainly "no." If private investors are not willing to risk their own funds in the tourist business, it is not clear why public money should remove the risk and leave them the profit.[52]

Not everyone agrees with Bird. Stephen Wanhill[53] and Howell Zee, et al.,[54] reason that markets may not always provide just the right amount of specific goods and services that people want. In the absence of government incentives, some projects that may generate sizable spillover benefits to the community would not be built. One form of market failure relates to the distributional consequences of private development projects.[55] Private developers usually don't consider the distributional impacts of their projects on the local populations. Governments may want to encourage investment in low-income, high unemployment areas to reduce income disparity or to support projects in areas that would reduce congestion or pollution. Governments may also want to support projects that use advanced technologies that may spill over to the rest of the economy and enhance the technological capability of the country. Wanhill writes:

> The spillover benefits of tourism are well known, and more than any other industry, tourism deals with the use of natural and cultural resources. The lessons of the past indicate it is unwise for the state to abandon its ability to influence the direction of tourism development either through providing financing or enacting legislation.[56]

However, Zee, et al., advise that if tax incentives are used, "the preferred form of tax incentives are those that provide for faster recovery of investment costs."[57]

Concluding Observations

FRANCES BROWN writes that tourism can be both a blight and a blessing to host communities.[58] Many of tourism's impacts on host communities are difficult, and perhaps even impossible, to measure. Nonetheless, so that correct actions can be taken, surveys of residents can identify what some of these impacts are and how serious and pressing they are perceived to be by residents. At the end of the day, it is not the ability to calculate the benefits and costs of tourism to the last dollar that is critical; it is the realization that host communities hold the power to make changes that can make tourism work for them.

This chapter has suggested fiscal instruments such as taxation, user charges, and development exactions to increase the net economic benefit of tourism to host communities. But increasing tourism's benefit–cost ratio is more than simply getting tourists to pay more. Tourism affects local residents in many other ways in addition to their pocketbooks.

To illustrate, some years ago I was in Kosrae, a small, mid-Pacific tropical island in the Federated States of Micronesia, conducting a study of the Kosrae tax system for the state government. While there, I met a Caucasian American couple from Guam vacationing in Kosrae. I asked them if they were enjoying their vacation. They replied that they were not having a good time because they felt that the local residents were hostile to them. What the couple did not realize was that residents were offended by this couple wearing walking shorts in public.[59] For American tourists, wearing shorts while sightseeing in many tropic vacation destinations such as Hawaii is a common practice. The tourist couple did not intend to offend; they were simply ignorant of local mores. Had they been informed of the local custom, either through pamphlets issued through tour operators and travel agents or shown a video program on the airplane before they landed, the unpleasantness could have been avoided. Unfortunately, it turned out to be a lose-lose situation rather than a win-win situation. It is not essential to be able to calculate the social cost of this couple's behavior on the residents of Kosrae. It is more important to be aware that it could have been easily avoided. A little visitor and resident education about tourism could increase tourism's net benefit to Kosrae.

Many other ways exist to increase tourism's benefits and decrease its costs on host communities. Protecting local residents' access to prime recreational and historic areas and rejecting socially destructive forms of tourism such as "sex tourism" are just a couple of ways to make tourism work for the host community rather than against it.[60] Paul Wilkinson perhaps said it best when he wrote the following about tourism development in island microstates:

Tourism development need not be "folly" if it is carefully planned and integrated into the local system. This suggests that island micro-states need to act simultaneously on two fronts to maximize benefits and minimize environmental, economic, and sociocultural costs. First, they have to decide on the degree to which they will become involved in tourism decision making in order that priority can be placed on their own goals, rather than those of external actors. Second, they have to examine alternative forms of tourism development to avoid many of the problems which have plagued some destinations.[61]

He could have been writing about any tourist destination.

Finally, it is often suggested that tourist destinations can enhance their net economic benefits from tourism if measures are taken to improve linkages between tourism and other economic sectors, for example, by requiring tourism businesses to use locally produced food, building materials, furniture, and decorations and to hire local labor and local firms to provide contract services. Governments can also promote greater local participation in tourism businesses by requiring outside investors to form joint ventures with local partners and possibly to sell their interests to their local partners later when capital and local expertise become available. Governments may issue business licenses only to local owners of selected small-scale tourism businesses, such as taxi services and diving and snorkeling businesses, which do not require a lot of capital or managerial expertise.[62] To the extent that more of the tourist spending remains in the community, greater net benefit accrues to residents. However, local content rules and "protectionist" legislation can be counterproductive if these measures merely drive up prices, lower the quality of tourism services, and end up scaring away tourists.

CHAPTER 12

TAXING TOURISM

Taxes are what we pay for civilized society.

OLIVER WENDELL HOLMES, JR.[1]

TAXES LEVIED ON tourists and tourism businesses have proliferated around the world since the 1980s. In the United States, state and local governments in every state raised taxes or imposed new ones on hotel and car rentals, amusement and entertainment attractions, and meals and alcoholic beverages at bars and restaurants.[2] The most widely levied tourist tax is the hotel room ("bed") tax. In 2002, local governments ranging from New Orleans (Louisiana) and Halifax (Nova Scotia) to Tokyo (Japan) enacted new taxes on hotel room rentals, and many other localities are trying to increase theirs.[3]

As well, the growing number of taxes levied on air travel is incurring the wrath of many air travelers. For example, taxes imposed on an economy round-trip ticket between Sydney and London include A$38 for departure tax;[4] A$36.56 passenger service charge; A$10 for the "Ansett levy," to pay for ex-Ansett employee "entitlements" following the financial collapse of the domestic airline;[5] A$3.58 noise tax; and A$12.80 for insurance levies. These taxes, usually levied at a flat fee per person, can be particularly onerous on short-haul trips. The executive director of the Board of Airline Representatives of Australia noted that taxes add about A$100 on the ticket price from Australia to New Zealand, which can be 25 percent of the cost of the round-trip airfare. Passengers traveling out of airports other than Sydney must also pay a separate levy to defray the cost of additional security measures that airports have put in place after the September 11, 2001, terrorist attacks in the United States. In the United States, the Air Transportation Association reports that in 1972 taxes on a $200 airline ticket were $7; in 2002 taxes and fees on a $200 ticket totaled $51.[6]

Recently, the governments of travel destinations have found new ways to tax tourism. In 2002, Venice began imposing a "coach tax" of up to (euro) €250 per motor coach (depending on where they park) when they enter the city; the city of Florence had imposed a smaller (€100) coach tax earlier. In the same year, the Nelson City Council (New Zealand) imposed a new waste water charge based on the number of toilets, prompting the local motel association president to complain that the new tax was unfair to motel operators: "Just because you've got a pan doesn't mean to say you've got anyone sitting on it."[7] Beginning May 1, 2002, the 11 million annual visitors to the Balearic Islands of Majorca, Ibiza, Menorca, and Formentera must pay an "eco-tax" of €1 per person per night, and €2 for guests of five-star hotels (children under 12 and pensioners are exempt). The European Commission is currently recommending an European-wide environmental or "green" tax on all air tickets, to encourage airlines to reduce greenhouse gas emissions. Norway already imposes a carbon dioxide tax on domestic flights.

Although many of these taxes levied by the governments of tourist destinations are also paid by their local residents, some (e.g., the hotel and car rental taxes) fall mostly on nonresident tourists. Hence, they are often referred to as *tourist taxes*. The proliferation of taxes and user charges levied on tourism has prompted the World Travel and Tourism Council (WTTC) to complain that governments are ignoring the basic principles of "intelligent taxation."[8] The WTTC is particularly unhappy with user charges and "add on" taxes— such as applying a separate hotel room tax or daily car rental tax in addition to the local sales tax to the hotel and car rental bills. In the United States, hotel room sales are generally taxed more heavily in states that levy both the general sales tax and a separate hotel room tax.[9]

In this chapter, we examine the economic reasons for the taxation of tourism. We explain why governments often single out tourists for selective taxation and why they tax tourist purchases more heavily than other consumer purchases.

Political Economy of Taxing Tourism

IT IS widely believed among tourism industry officials that, because tourists don't vote in the destinations they visit, it is easy for them to be singled out for special taxation. As one travel industry executive explained, "The industry has been overtaxed on the theory that it is better not to tax the local citizen. The traveler is not a constituent, so state and local governments can jack up room taxes and admission taxes. Visitors can complain, but who cares; they'll be going back soon."[10]

However, this view is simplistic. Whereas nonresident tourists may not vote in the places they visit, local tourist businesses such as hotels, tour wholesalers, travel agents, souvenir merchants, cruise lines, restaurants and nightclubs, transportation companies, and labor groups constitute powerful political interest groups that can successfully lobby lawmakers to defeat efforts to levy new or increase existing taxes and user chargers on travel and tourism.[11] To illustrate, a $5 admission fee levied on tourists visiting Honolulu's Hanauma Bay Nature Preserve was rescinded in 1995 and later replaced by a smaller $3 admission fee because of what one political columnist described as "industrial-strength lobbying" by tour operators.[12] In Florida, an attempt to levy a surcharge on "tourist-related sales" to boost Florida's tourism promotion budget failed to pass in 1991 because of opposition from the Florida Restaurant Association, Walt Disney World, and Florida-based cruise lines.[13] Efforts to levy a bed tax in Nelson City (New Zealand) and to increase one in Anchorage, Alaska, in 2002 were unsuccessful.

More evidence of the industry's political clout: In 2002, the tourist industry in Wisconsin successfully lobbied the state legislature to pass a law prohibiting the state's public schools from starting their fall terms until after Labor Day (September 2 in 2002), unless they obtained special waivers. Supporters of the new law explained that a later start of the school year would encourage more people to take vacation trips and thus stimulate business in the state.[14]

In the early 1990s, the leaders of the tourism industries became so alarmed over the proliferation of tourist taxes around the world that the WTTC—a global coalition of chief executive officers from all sectors of travel and tourism—with the sponsorship of the American Express Company, established the World Travel & Tourism Tax Policy Center at Michigan State

University in October 1993 to "track and monitor the status of taxes imposed on travelers and travel and tourism companies around the world. . . . Its aim is to provide timely information and analysis of tax policy issues and considerations to government policy makers, industry leaders, and the general public."[15] The WTTC has become one of the most influential private tourism advocacy groups in the world. In 1995, the Center inaugurated the World Travel & Tourism Tax Barometer, an annual series of rankings, beginning in 1994, and based on the (U.S.) dollar amounts of the most common taxes—meal, lodging, car rental, and airport arrival and departure taxes—paid by a traveler on a hypothetical trip at fifty-two of the most popular tourist cities around the world.

The WTTC Tax Barometer

THE WTTC Tax Barometer provides three separate rankings:

1. A composite index showing changes in hotel, car rental, meal, and air passenger taxes and user charges for a hypothetical trip since June 1994. The hypothetical trip includes purchases of four nights of lodging, five days' car rental, twelve meals, and one set of international arrival and departure airport charges. The total amount of taxes on the purchases in local currencies is calculated and converted to U.S. dollars and finally into an index, using 1994 as the base year (i.e., 1994 = 100). The average value of the indices for all fifty-two cities in June 2002 was 117, meaning that on average tourists paid 17 percent more in tourist taxes in 2002 than they did for the same trip in 1994, or an average annual increase (compounded) of less than 2 percent. The individual indices for the fifty-two cities are not adjusted for changes in the prices of the items purchased. Sydney scored the highest composite index value (1212), meaning that the amount of travel taxes paid by a tourist visiting Sydney on the WTTC hypothetical trip in 2002 was more than 12 times the amount she paid for the same trip in 1994. Mumbai had the lowest composite index (64), meaning that the tourist paid 36 percent less in travel taxes in 2002 than in 1994.

2. A ranking based on the estimated dollar amounts of travel taxes paid in each of the fifty-two cities. In 2002, the tourist on the hypothetical trip to Buenos Aires, Argentina, paid $345.79 in travel taxes; by comparison,

she would have paid only about $12 in travel taxes had she visited Beijing, China, instead. The average amount of travel taxes paid on the same trip among the fifty-two cities was $170.87.

3. A ranking based on the amount of taxes paid as a percent of the total bill, or the *tax effort*.[16] The tax effort for all fifty-two cities, for 2002, is reproduced in Table 12-1. The average tax effort among the fifty-two cities in 2002 was 13.95 percent; that is, travel taxes were equivalent to nearly 14

TABLE 12-1

TAX EFFORT AMONG
LEADING TOURIST DESTINATIONS: 2002

Destination	Tax Effort (%)	Destination	Tax Effort (%)
Copenhagen	25.25	Amsterdam	15.16
London	21.66	Toronto	15.09
Vienna	20.65	Rio de Janeiro	14.79
Brussels	20.17	Paris	14.46
Miami	19.51	Sao Paulo	14.03
Johannesburg	18.76	Mumbai	13.90
Buenos Aires	18.73	Auckland	13.39
Chicago	18.23	New Delhi	13.18
Stockholm	17.99	Rome	13.11
Frankfurt	17.94	Cairo	12.50
Tel Aviv	17.77	Madrid	11.17
Istanbul	17.71	Jakarta	10.72
Montreal	17.63	Barcelona	10.69
Munich	17.45	Manila	10.49
Los Angeles	17.16	Prague	10.20
Santiago	17.11	Seoul	10.14
Boston	17.08	Zurich	9.98
San Francisco	16.81	Geneva	9.45
Nairobi	16.80	Bangkok	7.80
Sydney	16.65	Kuala Lumpur	6.46
Vancouver	16.64	Tokyo	6.27
Athens	16.59	Osaka	6.21
Mexico City	16.33	Taipei	5.54
Helsinki	16.32	Singapore	4.98
New York City	15.62	Hong Kong	2.18
Honolulu	15.51	Beijing	0.97

Source: WTTC Tax Barometer at http://www.traveltax.msu.edu

percent of the total bill (including taxes) for the four items in the hypothetical trip. Copenhagen had the highest tax effort at 24.25 percent,
whereas Beijing had the lowest tax effort at less than 1 (.97) percent.
Twenty-one destinations had tax efforts that were below the average tax
effort of 13.95 percent, and thirty-one destinations had above average tax
efforts. The median tax effort was about 15 percent (Amsterdam and
Toronto).

Of the three rankings, only the ranking based on the tax effort is easily
interpreted for policy purposes. If, for the same trip, tourist taxes represent
24 percent of the cost of the trip in Copenhagen and less than 1 percent
in Beijing, a reasonable explanation of their difference is that national and
local governments in Denmark make a bigger effort to tax tourism than their
counterparts in China.[17] Clearly, huge differences exist in the tax effort among
tourist destinations.

To ascertain whether governments have changed their tax policies toward
tourism requires information on the trends in their tax effort over time. The
Tax Policy Center has not published indices showing which destinations have
increased their tax effort or by how much, and which have not.[18]

The other two WTTC Tax Barometer rankings are not easily interpreted.
Consider, for example, the barometer's overall tax index. In June 2002, London's overall index had a value of 126, an increase of 26 percent since June
15, 1994. But it is difficult to figure out how to use this information other
than to regard it as perhaps an interesting factoid. Because the amount of
travel taxes paid is the product of the *tax base* (i.e., the hotel, car rental, and
restaurant bills) and the *tax rate* (say, 10 percent on the hotel room bill, 5 percent on the car rental bill, and so on), then:

$$\text{Total Taxes} = \text{Tax Base} \times \text{Tax Rate}$$

The amount of tourist taxes actually paid could have increased either
because the tax base (i.e., prices of tourist purchases) has increased, the tax
rate has increased, or some combination of the two has occurred. It is impossible to tell by looking only at the index whether the 26 percent increase in
the amount of taxes paid for a visit to London was caused by increases in the
prices of hotel rooms, car rentals, and meals or whether tax rates on these
items have increased.[19]

A similar problem plagues the city rankings on the actual amounts of taxes paid for the same hypothetical trip. The five-day trip to Buenos Aires cost $345.79 in tourist taxes in 2002, but one to New York City cost only $228.00—a difference of $117.79.[20] The Tax Policy Center rankings indicate that Buenos Aires is the least competitive travel destination, based on the actual dollar amounts of tourist taxes paid on the same hypothetical trip. But is the taxman to blame? Are taxes so much higher in Buenos Aires than in New York because the prices of hotel room rentals, car rentals, and meals are much higher there, or are tax rates higher there because Buenos Aires is a less tax friendly destination?[21]

A Primer on Sales/Excise Taxes and User Charges

GOVERNMENTS TRADITIONALLY perform three economic functions: (1) maintain employment, price stability, and economic growth; (2) distribute income and resources among residents; and (3) ensure that specific goods and services are produced in the desired quantities.[22] The conventional wisdom is that stabilizing the economy, promoting its growth, and distributing incomes and economic resources are best performed by national or central governments. The main function of subnational (local) governments is to ensure that residents are provided local government services that they want, such as police and fire protection, in the right quantities and at the lowest costs.[23] If the desired services cannot be supplied by private markets, local governments must ensure that they are adequately provided through the intervention of the government. It may come as a surprise to some people that governments may be able to do a better job than the market or the private sector in making sure that the right amounts of certain goods and services are provided. To illustrate, we shall see later in this chapter why government intervention is usually necessary to ensure adequate funding for destination tourism promotion.

Carrying out the economic responsibilities of governments requires money. Governments get most of their revenues from taxes. As much as we don't like to pay them, taxes are a "necessary evil."

Taxes

Economists make a distinction between *taxes* and *user charges* (or *user fees*). A tax is an involuntary payment to the government that does not entitle the payer to receive a direct benefit of equivalent value in return.[24] For example, an income tax is a tax because you have to pay it whether you want to or not, and there is no guarantee that you will get your money's worth in services in return for your tax payment.

Taxes can be *direct taxes* or *indirect taxes*. Direct taxes are levied on persons,[25] whereas indirect taxes—also referred to as *commodity taxes*—are levied on goods and services. Thus, the income tax is a direct tax and a sales or excise tax is an indirect tax.[26] When it comes to taxing tourism among state and local governments in the United States, sales and excise taxes are the most widely used taxes.[27] The most widely employed sales tax used in the world is a national sales tax referred to as the *value-added tax*, or VAT.[28] However, it is important to keep in mind that people ultimately bear the burden of the taxes, whether the taxes are levied on individuals or businesses or levied on income or goods. A business may "pay" taxes to the tax collector, but a business is only an organization; the burden of the taxes it pays will ultimately be borne either by the buyers of its product, the owners of the business, or its employees.

Who Bears the Burden of Excise Taxes?

One of the most important economic lessons from taxation is that the person (or business) who writes the check to the tax collector may not be the person who actually bears the tax burden. The tourist who pays the tax itemized on her hotel bill may not be the person who actually pays it because some of the tax may have been shifted to someone else. The tax may also be borne partly by the owner of the hotel in lower net (after-tax) revenues and profits and partly by the hotel's employees in lower wages and salaries.

To illustrate, suppose the local government decides to levy an excise tax on hotels of $3 per night on their room rentals.[29] Many people believe that a hotel operator will simply pass the tax on to the hotel guests. Obviously, the hotel operator would like to do that if he could. Indeed, if he did pass the tax onto the guest, the hotel bill would show the same room rate as before, but now a $3 per night tax is added to the bill, and the guest ends up paying $3 more for each night of her stay in the same room. The hotel blames the higher hotel bill on the new tax. The guest, however, doesn't really care whether the higher bill is due to the tax; what matters is that she has to pay $3 more for each night of her stay. If she balks at paying $3 more per night for her room and decides instead to rent a cheaper (lower quality) room at some other hotel, or reduce the duration of her trip, or even cancel her trip altogether, then the hotelier faces the possibility of losing substantial business.

Reluctantly, he decides to reduce his room rate—but not necessarily by $3 per night. The guest bill still shows a $3 per night room tax, the government receives $3 from the hotel operator, but that tax was not entirely borne by the guest. Part of the tax burden was borne by the hotel operator when he reduced his room rate.[30] The $3 nightly room tax created a "wedge" between the tax-inclusive price of the room paid by the guest and the net after-tax price received by the hotelier. The difference between the two "prices" is the amount of tax revenue going to the government. In this example, the hotel operator was unable to pass the entire tax on to the guest. The conventional wisdom is that, generally, an increase in the excise tax will show up partly as an increase in the price to the consumer and partly in the lower price received by the seller.[31] If tax increases could easily be shifted to buyers, businesses probably would not fight so vigorously against them.

What factors determine the share of the tax burden passed *forward* to the consumer or shifted *backward* to the seller? The most important factor is who can most readily change their behavior in response to the tax increase.[32] The burden will fall most heavily on those who are least able to change their plans. In the example of the hotel excise tax increase, if hotel guests have few or no other options and must stay, then they are not likely to be very price sensitive. Therefore, the hotel operators will find it much easier to pass the tax on to the guests. In the extreme case, in which the guests are not price sensitive at all, the entire tax will be forward shifted to the guests. By this reasoning, lawmakers in destinations that are visited mostly by business travelers rather than tourists (such as Columbus, Ohio) have the incentive to levy higher tax rates on hotel room rentals because business travelers are generally less price sensitive.

If hotel operators can respond to the tax increase more readily than their guests by adjusting (i.e., reducing) the supply of hotel rooms available, then the lion's share of the tax increase will again be borne by hotel guests. Why? If absorbing the tax means lower net revenues to the hotel operator, and he now sees that it is more lucrative to rent his rooms to long-term renters and thus free himself from the burden of the hotel room tax, the available supply of hotel rooms for short-term rentals may fall quickly in response to the tax increase.[33] As the supply of available hotel rooms shrinks, hoteliers will be less willing to reduce their room rates.

It is clear from the examples above that the lion's share of the tax burden will be borne by those who are least able to adjust to the tax increase. Studies have shown that excise taxes levied on hotel room rentals are largely borne by hotel guests.[34] By contrast, amusements taxes in the United States are only partially or not forward shifted at all.[35]

Should Sales/Excise Taxes Have Uniform Rates?

An optimal sales or excise tax structure does not require that tax rates be the same on all goods and services. Indeed, abstracting from the cost of administrating different tax rates, uniform sales or excise tax rates are usually "not optimal."[36] Because sales taxes usually increase the tax-inclusive prices of goods and services, they change people's buying decisions; consumers may now decide to buy less and switch to goods and services that are not taxed. Ideally, taxes should interfere as little as possible with what consumers choose to buy, except by design.[37] The best way to achieve this is to levy the highest tax rates on the most price-insensitive goods.[38] If a higher tax rate is imposed on a good that is price inelastic in demand, consumers won't reduce their consumption of that good by very much; thus, its effect on consumer buying decisions is minimized. It is not surprising that in the United States, the highest tax rates in tourism are usually levied on hotel accommodations.

Tax Exporting

Getting nonresidents to pay your taxes is referred to as *tax exporting*.[39] Every state in the United States exports some of its taxes to nonresidents,[40] and some of them do it by design.[41] Indeed, most state and local taxes can be exported to some degree.[42] Successful tax exporting of an excise tax requires that sellers must be able to pass most or all of the tax on to the buyers[43] *and* the buyers must be nonresidents. In designing a tax system to tax tourists, *selective* sales taxes, which target a single or a narrow group of commodities mostly purchased by tourists, are excellent instruments to generate revenues to pay for local government services because they are highly exportable.

Not all local commodity taxes are readily exportable. A broad-based tax, such as the general sales tax, is not a highly exportable tax because it tends to fall more heavily on local residents than on tourists, as does an excise tax on restaurant meals.[44] A new (2002) Seattle law imposing a 10-cents per cup tax on espresso-based coffees—the "espresso tax"—will no doubt generate more revenue from locals than from tourists; hence, it is not a very exportable tax. Not many tax instruments target mostly nonresident tourists. Not surprisingly, taxes on hotel and car rentals, admission to tourist attractions, tickets for sightseeing tours, and airport entry and departure taxes are among the most widely used tourist taxes.

User Charges

User charges are prices charged by governments to users to pay for specific government services or privileges.[45] Admission fees to public parks, game reserves, and airport facilities and security charges are examples of user charges in tourism.[46] User charges, like prices in private markets, are not involuntary payments because only the users of specific public services must pay them.

User charges are an appropriate way to finance public services when most or all of the benefits go to identifiable users, and nonpayers can be excluded from using the services at a reasonable cost. Some public services, such as park upkeep and hiking trail maintenance, yield direct benefits to tourists, and user charges are an appropriate way to make them pay for the benefits they receive because they don't pay the local income or property taxes.

Besides raising money to pay for specific public services, user charges are often employed to ration the use of scarce resources. For example, when crowding at beaches, parks, and other recreation sites impose congestion costs on other users and diminish their enjoyment, user charges are an appropriate way to ration the use of these scarce resources.[47] Besides generating revenue for the public treasury, the new "coach tax" levied in Venice is ostensibly an attempt by the city to reduce the number of motor coaches coming into the congested city. User charges used for such purpose are most effective when demand is price elastic.

Economic Reasons for Taxing Tourism

WE ALL take for granted that we have to pay taxes if we want to have public services, but some other economic reasons for taxation are less obvious. The governments of tourist destinations tax tourism for at least four other reasons:

- To diversify their sources of revenue
- To export taxes to nonresident tourists
- To tax excess profits or economic rents from tourism to benefit local residents
- To correct for market failure.

Revenue Diversification

Taxing tourism enables the governments of tourist destinations to diversify their sources of revenue. Tourism is a growth industry. Including tourist taxes in the local tax structure contributes to the system's overall revenue elasticity. As long as tourism continues to grow at a faster pace than the (nations' and the world's) economy, tourist taxes promise to become an increasingly important source of government revenues in the future.

Tax Exporting

Tax exporting occurs when taxes levied by one jurisdiction are shifted (exported) to taxpayers of another jurisdiction.[48] When taxes levied on tourists exceed the cost of providing services to them, a net gain is realized by local residents. Residents can either consume more services or the same level of services at a lower out-of-pocket cost to themselves. For residents, tax exporting is ostensibly a good thing. The main problem with this "beggaring one's neighbor" tax policy is that residents may think that the cost of the public services they consume is cheaper than they actually are; residents may end up spending more money on public services than they should under careful benefit–cost scrutiny.[49]

No such spending distortion occurs when taxes paid by tourists only cover the costs of providing public services to them.[50] The U.S. Advisory Commission on Intergovernmental Relations (ACIR) notes that:

> Nonresidents, or visitors, may be major beneficiaries from certain services provided by a local or state government. In such cases, the interests of an efficient allocation of resources to those public services can be furthered by the use of taxes that—by virtue of their exportability—make it possible to collect an appropriate share of the costs of those services from the nonresident beneficiaries.[51]

Likewise, *impact fees* levied on developers are an excellent way to finance the additional costs of public infrastructure, such as roads and sidewalks, schools, water and sewage treatment facilities, and even low-income housing associated with the development of hotels, attractions, and other tourist facilities.[52] These charges are referred to as *impact fees* because they are specific charges levied on developers to defray the off-site public infrastructure costs stemming from the impacts of private land development.

Taxing Excess Profits/Economic Rents

Often, the best attractions of a destination—scenery, weather, people—are unpriced. Businesses are able to exploit these touristic assets for their own profit. Residents also can lay claim to the "rents." It is appropriate for governments to tax tourism to extract some of the rents for the benefit of their constituents, as long as the taxes don't scare too many tourists away.

Tourism can be overtaxed! For example, in 1990, the New York state legislature enacted a 5 percent hotel occupancy tax on hotel rooms priced at $100 or more per night, in addition to any existing state or local sales taxes. In New York City, the combined hotel room tax rose to 19.25 percent plus $2 per night on rooms priced at $100 or more. Nearly half the hotel room nights sold in New York City were priced at $100 or more.[53] As a result of the new add-on tax, overall tourist business apparently declined, thus prompting the State to rescind the tax in 1994.

New York's experience with the state's add-on hotel room tax provides another important lesson on the economics of tourist taxes: Tourists might not be very price sensitive to a modest tax increase when the current tax rate is low; but if the tax rate is increased repeatedly, the tax-inclusive price of the commodity purchased eventually becomes very expensive, and buyers become price sensitive. In sum, demand elasticities generally vary at different price levels and rise in tandem with increases in the price of a commodity. A low demand elasticity does not imply that there is no limit to how high taxes can be raised.

Correcting for Market Failure: The Case of Destination Travel Promotion

Many people believe that private markets can supply the goods and services we want more efficiently than governments, but that is not always true. When markets provide either too much or too little of the specific goods and services we desire, *market failure* occurs.

Environmental pollution is a good example of market failure. In the absence of government intervention, we may live with too many environmental pollutants. We examine the relationship between tourism and the natural environment in the next chapter. In this chapter, we examine another case of market failure in tourism, namely, the inability of tourism businesses to collectively promote their own tourist destinations.

Governments almost everywhere spend tax revenues to actively promote travel to their destinations.[54] Promotional activities include the maintenance of travel information offices at home and abroad, maintenance of Internet websites, publication of travel brochures and literature, mass media advertising and direct marketing, sponsorship of travel fairs and exhibits, and so on. Although governments also promote their other exports, their direct involvement in tourism promotion occurs at a much higher level.[55]

Government involvement in destination tourism promotion is not without public controversy. Many people object on ideological grounds, in that they believe governments should not interfere in private business. Instead, tourism promotion should best be left in the hands of the industry. In 1993, voters in Colorado abolished the state's tourism board.[56] In Ottawa (Canada), the Ontario provincial government recently refused a request by the Ottawa Tourism and Convention Authority to levy a hotel room tax to expand the convention center and increase and stabilize tourism marketing funds, arguing that the 400-member authority should levy its own internal fees on hotel room rentals instead.[57] By contrast, a Hong Kong-based tourist publication observed that "In Asia Pacific, the visitor industry is still regarded as a national virility symbol...privatization [of their national tourist offices] will not happen quickly in this region."[58]

Other critics of government-funded tourism promotion decry the paucity of evidence on its effectiveness.[59] For example, a dramatic increase in the Hawaii Tourism Authority's budget in recent years produced no apparent increase in tourist visits to Hawaii (Figure 12-1). Larry Dwyer and Peter Forsyth, however, argue that a country as a whole can benefit as a result of government-sponsored tourism promotion.[60]

This chapter does not attempt to evaluate the costs and benefits of government involvement in destination tourism promotion. Rather, we try to understand why it is such a prevalent practice. Specifically, we want to understand why the industry can't promote itself. After all, growers of Florida oranges, Washington State apples and cherries, and Hawaii papayas are able to get together among themselves to promote their products using their own money.

The ultimate economic objective of advertising and promotion is to change the demand faced by suppliers. If successful, a promotional campaign for any commodity increases demand and causes demand to be more price inelastic.

A distinction exists between *selective* and *primary* or *generic* advertising and promotion. Selective advertising is composed of the effort of a seller to influence sales for a specific brand or firm.[61] By contrast, primary advertising

Tourism Marketing Budget: 1997-2002

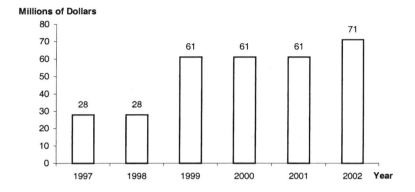

Visitor Arrivals

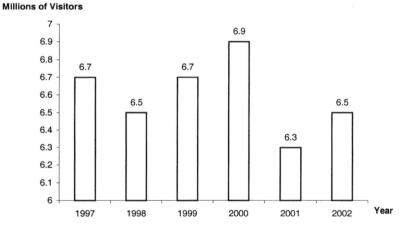

Note: Fiscal years are used for tourism marketing budget chart; and calendar years for visitor arrivals charts.

Source: Hawai`i Tourism Authority, published in *Honolulu Advertiser*, June 2, 2002.

FIGURE 12-1. Is there a relationship between tourism marketing and tourist arrivals?

promotes a generic product. For example, advertising by Sheraton Hotels to promote its own brand of lodging is selective advertising, whereas the collective effort of Florida orange growers to promote their orange juice is generic advertising. Advertising by government tourist bureaus to promote travel to their destinations is also generic advertising.

The main problem with the collective promotion of a generic product is that, if the promotional expenses are paid for by voluntary contributions, the incentive exists for individual firms not to contribute to expenses and, instead, free-ride on other firms' contributions. The reason is obvious: It is inherent in the nature of generic advertising that, once it is paid for, it benefits all sellers of the product, regardless of whether some of them contributed to its funding.[62] Those who pay can't exclude those who don't pay from benefiting from the advertising expenditures.[63] Hence, the incentive for an individual seller is to not contribute. Although everyone in the tourist industry complains that not enough money is being spent to promote their destination, the reality is that many will not contribute to a collective promotion budget. Henry Mok estimated that in 1986, 78 percent of the airlines, 66 percent of the hotels, 24 percent of the restaurants, and only 4 percent of all retail establishments in Hawaii belonged to (i.e., contributed to) the Hawaii Visitors Bureau (HVB).[64] Moreover, each year between 12 and 15 percent of the contributing members do not renew their contributions.[65] In 1995, voluntary contributions by individuals and businesses made up less than 5 percent of the Bureau's budget. The state government made up the rest. The inability of the tourist industry to organize and adequately fund destination promotion is a classic example of market failure. Without government intervention, not enough money is spent on promoting the destination.

When can private collective action succeed? Mancur Olson argues that successful private, group action will occur only if the group can mete out penalties to noncontributors or reward those who do.[66] It won't succeed if contributions are strictly voluntary. Collective action is also more likely to occur if sellers sell a homogeneous product like orange juice, and more difficult if they sell heterogeneous products like tourism. Sellers of heterogeneous products find it more difficult to agree on their common interest and how much money should be spent on generic advertising.

The success of agricultural grower associations to fund collective promotion is explained by government coercion through state and federal legislation that requires growers to contribute to an industry-administered fund to pay for generic product promotion. With the law behind the grower associations, it is easy to determine who is, say, an apple grower and who is not. Those who are must pay based on some well-defined formula—for example, a percentage of the gross receipts or so many cents per pound of output. This largely eliminates the free-rider problem. The money collected comes from the growers and "belongs" to the grower associations to be used for a clearly defined purpose.

The problem is not as simple when it comes to tourism. When Colorado voters voted, in 1993, to close their state-funded tourism board, efforts by the tourist industry to collect voluntary contributions to fund tourism promotion could not generate the same amount of money they had previously received from the state treasury. It soon became apparent that the model of private, collective action employed in agriculture can't easily be adapted for use in tourism. For example, it is not easy to determine which businesses belong to the tourist industry and should be compelled to pay.

How to minimize the free-rider problem in tourism promotion? One solution is for the government to tax the industry to pay for tourism promotion. In some instances, tourist businesses have sought the help of lawmakers to levy a special tourism promotion tax, with the revenues earmarked to fund destination promotion.[67] Most frequently, the tax is levied on hotel room rentals. Taxing tourism to pay for destination tourism promotion enhances economic efficiency in that it increases tourism promotion to the level desired by the industry. In this model of funding, the money generated, net of tax collection costs, and earmarked for tourism promotion comes from the industry and "belongs" to the industry.

Actually, in most destinations, revenues used by governments to fund tourism promotion come from their general funds and not from special taxes levied on tourism.[68] Where this occurs, the government funding of tourism promotion amounts to a subsidy from the public treasury to tourists and the tourist industry. For example, as a result of continuing weakness in foreign travel to the United States following the September 11, 2001, terrorist attacks, the U.S. Congress appropriated $50 million in 2003 to promote foreign travel to the United States. This appropriation amounts to a subsidy given to the tourism industry.

Concluding Observations

FISCAL SYSTEMS are judged by their efficiency and equity. A widespread perception exists among tourism industry officials that tourism is improperly and over taxed. They argue that taxes that target tourists and impose higher rates on their purchases violate sound principles of taxation because they distort consumer behavior and are unfair.

In this chapter, we learned that sound economic reasons exist for why destinations may want to levy taxes that fall largely on nonresident tourists. Moreover, imposing higher tax rates on tourist purchases is not inconsistent with attaining economic efficiency.

On the issue of equity, people, as expected, hold different opinions on what is fair and unfair. Some people adhere to the *benefit principle of equity*. That is, the burden of taxes should be equal to the benefits that people receive from government spending.[69] If the amount of taxes you pay is equal to the service benefits you receive from your government, that tax system is fair.

A few destinations—such as Hawaii and Delaware—have conducted detailed studies comparing the amounts of state and local taxes generated from tourists against the cost of public services incurred on their behalf. In those studies, it was found that tourists paid more taxes than the cost of public services they received.[70] By the benefit principle of equity, tourists and tourist businesses in Hawaii and Delaware paid more than their fair share of the cost of government. Indeed, industry officials argued that lawmakers should not burden the tourist industry with new taxes.

Although some people still view tax equity as balancing taxes paid against services received, this is not the only view. If it were, our progressive income tax system would be judged to be unfair. Likewise, taxing goods at higher tax rates (e.g., cigarettes) and exempting certain "necessity goods," such as food and medical care, would also be considered unfair. The dominant view of equity in taxation today is the *ability-to-pay principle* that requires that tax burdens depend on the ability of the people to pay them.[71] In the real world, it is impractical to charge different tax rates to different people at the point of sale based on their ability to pay. An alternative strategy is to charge different tax rates on different categories of goods. Because tourism is a luxury good, it would not be deemed unfair to tax tourism goods more heavily.[72]

Finally, in designing a fiscal system for tourist destinations, one must be mindful of potential intergovernmental mismatches in fiscal responsibilities. Some localities are blessed with superior touristic amenities, and these attract more tourists. More tourists, however, mean a higher cost of local government. Where the power to tax is centralized, but expenditure responsibilities are decentralized, a potential mismatch in tax and spending responsibilities can occur. This mismatch is a common occurrence. Ideally, the responsibility to raise revenues should go hand-in-hand with the responsibility to spend.[73] Unfortunately, that does not always occur. To illustrate, in Hawaii's centralized fiscal system, the state government reaps the lion's share of tourism-generated tax dollars, but the counties bear the larger share of the costs of providing public services to tourists. Unless the counties are granted their own taxing powers to tax tourism or a mechanism is developed to allocate resources from one level of government (the state) to another (the counties), the development of tourism could be impaired. The economy would not be operating efficiently because it is not able to achieve its potential. Hawaii's "problem" also applies to countries that rely on national sales taxes (i.e., the VAT) to tax tourism.[74] These considerations make a strong case for fiscal decentralization.

CHAPTER 13

TOURISM AND THE
NATURAL ENVIRONMENT

Take nothing but pictures. Leave nothing but footprints. Kill
nothing but time.

TOURIST MOTTO

TOURISM AND THE environment are interdependent. The U.S. National
Park Service reports that, in 2001, the number of national park visits had
increased to nearly 425 million, of which 280 million were recreational visits.[1] In 2001, 24 percent of the nearly 13.4 million overseas tourists to the
United States visited the national parks, 5 percent went hiking or camping,
and 4 percent took "environmental/ecological excursions."[2]

Around the world, so many people want to go back to nature that the secretary general of the World Tourism Organization (WTO) recently surmised
that ecotourism[3] is growing at "maybe double, even triple" the rate of the rest
of the industry.[4] Costa Rica has been the most successful country in promoting itself as an ecotourism destination, with nearly three-quarters of its visitors visiting at least one park during their stay.[5] To underscore the growing
importance of the natural environment to tourism, in May 2002, 1,100 del-
egates from more than 130 countries convened a special United Nations conference in Quebec, Canada, to celebrate the International Year of Ecotourism.[6]

Because of tourism's economic importance, the governments and residents of tourist destinations have an economic incentive to protect their own
environment to ensure the sustainability of tourism. A decrease in the quality
of the environment can decrease the appeal that the destination has for

tourists and cause the number of tourists to the destination to fall. In Negril, Jamaica, unrestricted dumping of garbage and untreated wastewater and sewage into the sea severely curtailed diving and resulted in a drastic reduction in the number of tourist visits.[7]

By contrast, protecting nature's resource base can pay economic dividends. A recent (2002) study found, for example, that Hawaii's 410,000 acres of coral reefs generate $360 million annually in net revenues and are valued at an estimated $10 billion to residents and tourists.[8] Hawaii's residents have an incentive to protect their coral reefs for their own present and future economic livelihood and recreational enjoyment. In Guilin, China, the local government threatened to close down factories that did not comply with air and water pollution standards to protect its valuable tourist industry. Costa Rica is using its lush rainforests for ecotourism instead of cutting them down to produce timber.

Businesses in travel and tourism also have an incentive to protect the environment to ensure their own sustainability. In 2000, the Conference Board and the World Travel and Tourism Council formed the Business Enterprises for Sustainable Travel (BEST)[9] to document those travel and tourism practices that promote sustainable tourism development.

Although tourism is dependent on the environment, the state of the environment can also be affected by tourism. Tourism can have positive environmental impacts by generating funds for environmental preservation, conservation of wildlife, and the creation and maintenance of parks and reserves. For example, game reserves in Africa are sustained by tourist spending. In Uganda, a gorilla viewing fee of $250 per day subsidized all of its national parks in the late 1990s.[10] In 2000, the National Zoo in Washington, D.C., paid $10 million for panda conservation projects in China and agreed to spend additional millions of dollars for panda research and a new panda exhibit at the zoo in return for the loan of two giant pandas from China.[11] An American tour operator established the Galapagos Conservation Fund to help preserve the archipelago's fragile ecosystem.[12]

Tourism can also foster an appreciation of the environment and thus encourage people to act responsibly when they interact with nature while on their vacation trips. Why should individual tourists care? After all, they are only temporary residents, and they'll be gone before the destination is spoiled. But many apparently do care. A recent study funded by the National Geographic Society revealed that 71 percent of the American traveling public indicated that it was important to them that their visits to a destination not damage the local environment.[13] When tourists were asked to make voluntary donations to support the Hanauma Bay Nature Preserve in Honolulu in 1996, most did contribute.[14]

In sum, the demand for a cleaner environment in general, and environmentally responsible or *green tourism* in particular, is greater today than ever before. Part of the reason is because, as we become more prosperous, one of the "goods" we value more highly is a higher-quality environment, and we are willing and more able to pay for it. Another reason is that as we become more aware of how our behavior affects the environment, we are better able to take actions to lessen our negative impacts.

But if tourism development is not managed properly, it can also create environmental problems and ultimately harm the natural environment. Oliver Hillel of the United Nations Environment Programme (UNEP) notes that "Tourism is not a smokestack-free industry. It is exactly as polluting as any other major industry."[15]

Tourism can affect the environment in several ways. First, tourists and tourism suppliers consume natural resources, such as water and energy. Tourists in Grenada consume seven times as much water as residents; moreover, foreign-owned hotels get preference over locals when there is a drought.[16] Residents of the Maldives, a group of small islands in the Indian Ocean, face water shortages because the number of tourists has increased from 1,000 in 1972 to almost half a million by 2000.[17] Directly and indirectly, tourism accounts for 40 percent of total energy consumed in Hawaii, although on average only one out of every eight people in Hawaii is a tourist on any given day.[18] Himalayan campers and hikers have cut down so many trees for their campfires that parts of Nepal are becoming deforested.[19]

Second, tourists and suppliers can pollute the environment by discharging waste and harmful substances into land, water, and air. In St. Lucia, tourists generate twice the amount of waste per person per day as residents.[20] The U.N. Environment Programme estimates that the average tourist produces about 2.2 pounds of solid waste and litter each day.[21] In the Caribbean, hotels were found to have discharged 80 to 90 percent of their sewage without adequate treatment into coastal waters, on beaches and around hotels, coral reefs, and mangrove swamps.[22] Years of garbage and equipment discarded by climbers litter the slopes of Mount Everest.[23] Fertilizers and pesticides used on golf courses can contaminate nearby watersheds. Snowmobiles in Yellowstone National Park create noise and air pollution, and ugly roadside advertisements and poorly planned and designed tourist facilities create visual pollution. Rapid tourism development can lead to massive population in-migration and urban sprawl. Urban sprawl consumes fringe areas, thus causing losses in agricultural and ecological benefits, traffic congestion, and visual and air pollution.[24]

Finally, tourists engage in recreational activities that can directly harm the environment through ecological disruption and damage to natural areas. Tourists can unintentionally trample native plants while hiking. Scuba divers and snorkelers can damage coral reefs by touching or standing on them or by accidentally kicking them with their fins. At Hanauma Bay Nature Preserve in Honolulu, tourists feeding the fish population changed the biodiversity of the bay's ecosystem by increasing the stock of fish significantly, particularly the aggressive varieties. As a result, crustaceans and seaweed have disappeared.[25] Cigarette smokers turn popular beaches into giant smelly ashtrays. Tourism can pose a threat to a destination's ecosystem by bringing in alien species in the ships and planes carrying tourists and goods to the destinations.[26] Visitors can also help to spread plant and fruit pests, as well as animal and human infectious diseases.

Tourism's environmental impacts can vary a great deal depending on the kind of tourist activity. In some cases, the activities themselves—such as snowmobiling in Yellowstone National Park—create the environmental externality, in this example, noise and air pollution. In other cases, the tourist activity—such as bird watching—produces little negative environmental impact; the largest impacts occur while tourists are traveling to and returning from their destinations. Studies have shown that as much as 90 percent of the energy consumed by tourists is in getting to and from their destinations.[27] John Dixon et al. note that "The magnitude of the threats posed by environmental damage due to tourism ranges from minor inconveniences to threats so severe that entire classes of resources become unusable."[28]

In this chapter, we examine the relationship between tourism and the natural environment from an economic perspective. We first develop a schematic model of tourism's relationship with the economy and the environment. We then examine how economics can offer policy-makers additional policy tools to deal with tourism's environmental problems.

Tourism, the Economy, and the Environment

TOURISM ENCOMPASSES both the activities of tourists (consumption) as well as the activities of tourism suppliers (production). Each can affect the environment in its own way. Figure 13-1 depicts a simple relationship between tourism, the economy, and the natural environment.

The economy consists of tourism and other suppliers who produce and sell to tourists and other consumers and to each other. Suppliers use primary inputs from the natural environment such as fuel, water, nonfuel minerals, and the like, in tandem with other kinds of inputs (e.g., labor and capital) to produce the goods and services demanded by tourists. Tourists also use inputs directly from the natural environment when they engage in recreational activities such as skiing, hiking, sightseeing, and swimming. Tourism can also

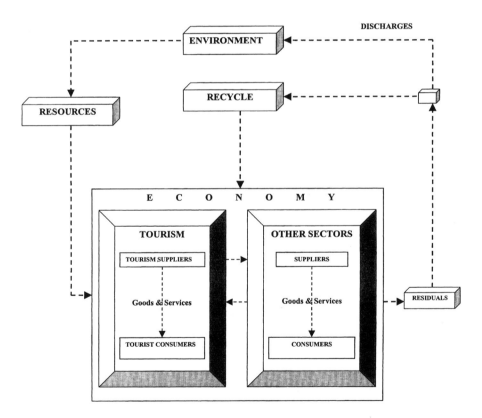

Source: Adapted from Field and Field (2002), p. 27, and Briassoulis (2000), p. 27.

FIGURE 13-1. Tourism, the economy, and the environment.

deplete nonrenewable environmental resources by damaging or destroying environmental resources important to tourism. Both suppliers and consumers generate residuals (i.e., leftovers), some of which are recycled; the rest is discharged into the environment. The discharges, or pollutants, include wastewater, solid waste, automobile emissions, heat, noise, and so on. Not shown in Figure 13-1 is that the state of the environment then feeds back to affect tourism in the future. A degradation of the natural environment reduces the demand for future tourist visits.

The model depicted in Figure 13-1 can be illustrated (Table 13-1) using selected environmental indicators developed by Abt Associates for the U.S. Environmental Protection Agency (EPA) for ten tourism and recreation activities in the United States.[29] Two resource inputs—water and energy use—are included; residuals/discharges include waste water discharge, municipal waste produced, and air emissions (converted into CO_2 equivalents).

TABLE 13-1

TOURISM, THE ECONOMY, AND THE ENVIRONMENT: U.S.

| | Tourism Suppliers | | | | Tourists | |
	Lodging	Restaurants	Retailing	Transportation	Activities*	Total
Resource Inputs						
Water Use (millions gals/yr)	150,000	33,000	6,500	—	59,000	248,500
Energy use (billions btu/yr)	190,000	36,000	16,000	2,700,000	18,000	2,996,000
Residual/Discharges						
Waste Water (tons/yr)						
Organic matter Released	15,000	21,000	340	—	240	36,580
Suspended Solids	8,700	3,600	270	—	200	12,700
Municipal Waste (tons/yr)	2,800,000	5,600,000	410,000	—	610,000	9,420,000
Air Emissions CO_2 equivalents (thousands tons/yr)	52,000	9,100	3,500	260,000	14,000	338,600

* Tourist and recreation activities include skiing, fishing, hunting, boating, golfing, casino gambling, amusement/theme parks, visits to historic places and museums, conventions and conferences, and waterside recreation (which includes any visits to freshwater or the coast for the primary purpose of being near the water, e.g., for swimming but not including fishing or boating).

Source: EPA, December 2000, Table 2, pp. 43–44.

An examination of Table 13-1 reveals that most of the natural resource inputs and residuals/discharges are attributable to tourism suppliers rather than directly to tourist activities. Transportation industries are the biggest users of energy, whereas hotels are the biggest water users. Hotels and restaurants are the biggest dischargers of wastewater and municipal waste, whereas transportation suppliers are the biggest dischargers of air emissions.

However, it would be a mistake to attribute the responsibility for pollution primarily to tourism suppliers. Although tourists may not directly be responsible for most of the tourism-generated pollutants in the environment, if they didn't have to travel to their destinations, the transportation industries would not be discharging 260 million tons of air emissions into the environment each year. By linking specific tourist activities to their suppliers, it is possible to get a more accurate picture of the environmental impacts of these activities. For example, convention attendees have the highest wastewater discharges per trip because of the higher percentage of attendees who stay in hotels, which are large dischargers of wastewater. Water-related recreational activities, such as swimming, use large amounts of energy and also generate large amounts of air emissions because participants tend to make multiple trips and travel long distances to enjoy such activities.

Figure 13-1 suggests three ways to reduce the environmental impact of tourism:

- We can reduce our use of natural resources by producing and consuming fewer tourism goods and services (for example, by reducing the demand for "goods intensive" types of tourism such as upscale tourism).
- We can reduce the amount of residuals generated from any given amount of tourism services produced/consumed. This can be done either by finding new production techniques and practices that use our environmental resources more efficiently (for example, by installing water conserving toilets and shower heads in hotels and using more fuel-efficient aircraft and automobiles) or switching to the production and consumption of those products that produce less residuals (for example, California requires oil companies to sell the more expensive "reformulated gasoline" that reduces the amount of automobile tailpipe emissions).
- We can encourage more recycling and reuse (such as converting waste cooking oil from restaurants into fuel and changing hotel bed linens and towels less frequently) and hence reduce the amount of resources used and discharged into the environment.

Why Do Tourists Harm the Environment?

TOURISTS OFTEN are not aware of the negative environmental consequences of their behavior. For example, they may not know that they can degrade the quality of the water if they go swimming right after they put suntan lotion on their bodies. Once tourists are properly educated, many opt to change their behavior. In Praia do Forte, Brazil, children have been teaching tourists about sea turtles and how to help in their conservation. As a result of tourists' increased awareness, fewer incidents of turtle harassment have occurred.[30]

Informed and rational individuals pollute the environment because they face incentives that encourage them to behave in a socially irresponsible manner. Barry and Martha Field explain that "People pollute because it is the cheapest way of solving a certain, very practical problem."[31] Campers and hikers may leave garbage along hiking trails and in forests to avoid the cost of carrying it back with them to the nearest trash bin. But a more complete explanation is that people weigh the expected marginal benefits and costs of their actions and engage in activities that give them positive net benefits, even if these activities harm the environment. For example, when tourists stay in hotels, they expect the bed sheets and bath towels in their rooms to be changed daily even if they do not change their sheets and towels daily at home. Why? Because the price they pay for the hotel room is the same whether or not the sheets and towels are changed everyday, but there is some benefit to the tourist from having clean sheets and towels. Hence, the incentive is to ask the maid to change them.

Tourism suppliers may place profits over environmental concerns. For example, snowmobile manufacturing and rental companies have vigorously opposed efforts by the George W. Bush administration to place restrictions on the number of snowmobiles operating in the Yellowstone National Park. Business owners in the town of West Yellowstone argue that allowing only 550 snowmobiles to pass through the West Yellowstone entrance each day would have a huge economic impact on the town. One opponent remarked, "How would you like it if someone came in and said 'we're taking half your money'?"[32]

On the other hand, tourist businesses will adopt environmentally friendly practices on their own when it is in their economic interest to do so. For example, a hotel in Mexico saved 20 percent of its energy bill by placing presence sensors in guest rooms to control air-conditioning and lighting.[33] A laundry and dry cleaning company in Honolulu uses recycled restaurant kitchen oil and grease for fuel and saves $3,000 per month in fuel bills.[34]

A major problem in tourism is that many of our natural resources are open to anyone who wants to use them. Economists refer to these resources as *open access resources.* Anyone can swim in the ocean or hike in the mountains. The tragedy of open access resources[35] is that their recreational amenity values are more likely to be degraded through excessive use and congestion than if the resources were privately owned and their owners charged access and user fees. For example, Terry Anderson and Peter Hill observed that before national park officials allowed automobiles into Yellowstone National Park, one vertically integrated railroad company effectively had a monopoly over rail service to the park, as well as lodging and in-park transportation services. Having an effective monopoly over park visits granted the rail company monopoly profits, but it also kept congestion down at the park because the company had the incentive to keep the price of visits high by reducing the number of visits. When park officials finally allowed automobiles into the park in 1915 (thus turning the park into an open access recreation resource) and regulated lodging prices at "depression levels," the number of visitations increased dramatically and diminished Yellowstone's recreational amenity value.[36]

How Much Pollution and Degradation Should Be Permitted?

SHOULD ANY amount of pollution be permitted? Some people take the view that if an activity pollutes and degrades the environment, that activity should cease altogether. This view does not take into account the benefits that are generated by activities that create pollution. Economists, instead, advocate that the amount of acceptable pollution should be determined by a careful comparison of incremental benefits and costs to the community. The optimum level of pollution is rarely zero pollution.

To illustrate, consider your own bedroom. You are responsible for keeping it clean. Even if you valued a pristine room, the actual condition of your room may not come close to being pristine. Why not? Because keeping a room in a pristine condition may not be worth the enormous effort required. But the alternative to a pristine room is not one that is buried under a mound of trash. Instead, you may opt for some intermediate state. Using the benefit–cost analysis described in Chapter 11, you compare the additional effort (i.e., marginal cost) that would be required to make your room just a little bit cleaner against the additional (marginal) benefit from having a somewhat cleaner room. When the room is quite messy, a little effort put into cleaning and tidying can produce substantial improvement and benefits. Beyond that, for each additional increment of cleanliness, the extra effort you must put into cleaning becomes greater and greater, but the marginal benefit becomes less and less. Finally, to get the last bit of dust in some hard-to-reach place requires a huge additional effort, but the marginal benefit is minuscule. Not surprisingly, few people make the required effort to maintain their own rooms in pristine condition. When do you stop cleaning? You stop when the marginal benefit from additional cleaning is equal to its marginal cost. Beyond that level of cleanliness, the marginal cost would exceed the marginal benefit, and it wouldn't be worth your effort to make your room any cleaner. Of course, different people perceive the marginal benefits and costs of having a clean room differently; after all, one person's rubbish is another person's treasure. Hence, one shouldn't be surprised if personal rooms vary greatly in their cleanliness and neatness.

But what if you're living with other people? The cleanliness of your room affects the well-being of others who live in the same house, and they may want you to keep a cleaner room. How do they persuade you to keep your room cleaner? One option is for them to pay you. The "bribe" increases the marginal benefit to you of keeping your room cleaner, and induces you to apply extra cleaning effort.[37] The bigger the bribe, the more cleaning effort you would be willing to put forth, and the cleaner your room. Another option is for them to levy a fine on you if you keep a dirty room or replace you with a cleaner housemate.

It doesn't matter whether the "carrot" or the "stick" approach is used to entice you to clean your room—both work! Which method is used depends on who has the right to a clean house. If the "right" belongs to everyone living in the house, then household members can promulgate a rule that establishes a minimum standard of cleanliness for every room in the house (including yours). If your room does not meet that standard, then you have to pay a fine.[38] On the other hand, if your room is your private property and no one else has any say about its condition, then you can demand that they bribe you to get your room cleaned. Once the *property right* is established, and if all the members of the household can readily reach an agreement on the incentive (or disincentive) structure, your room will be cleaner and a potential dispute between household members can be resolved among yourselves. City Hall doesn't have to get involved.[39]

Thus, one implication from this example is that we are going to have to live with some pollution. Another implication is that clarifying property rights and then allowing stakeholders to find their own solutions through private negotiations, or with the help of private conflict resolution specialists, may be one way to resolve some conflicts over tourism-generated environmental problems. For example, a hotel can negotiate with a nightclub next door to keep the level of noise down late at night for the benefit of its sleeping guests. On the other hand, finding an acceptable solution to an environmental problem that involves a lot of stakeholders often requires the intervention of the government because the large number of people makes the cost of reaching a private solution prohibitively expensive. When tourists are involved, a private solution is even more problematic because tourists aren't around long enough for residents to negotiate with them. Government involvement becomes even more critical when disputes involve stakeholders in different industries (e.g., tourism versus manufacturing) or different states and countries.

It may be a stretch to equate cleaning one's room with saving the Earth. But the underlying principle of keeping a house clean applies also to keeping the Earth green. Outlawing polluting activities altogether ignores the fact that a little pollution may produce little harm but large benefits. Almost all cruise ship–generated garbage is discharged at sea, thus polluting the ocean and coastal waters.[40] However, preventing a single piece of trash or a single gallon of wastewater from being discharged into the ocean may not be enforceable nor worth the cost to society even if it could be prevented. Preventing a large amount of such waste, however, is both enforceable and worthwhile.

Voluntary Initiatives and Self-Regulation

WHEN MAJORCAN authorities began levying a daily "eco-tax" on tourists beginning in May 2002, an irate British tourist complained that "Tourists aren't to blame for water shortages, traffic congestion, refuse-tipping, and decay—the Majorcan authorities are."[41] The tourist may well be right. Tourists contributed to those environmental problems, but the Majorcan authorities are to blame for not having solved them.

Sometimes industry self-regulation can be a useful approach to address environmental problems. For example, in June 2001, the sixteen members of the International Council of Cruise Lines (ICCL) adopted the first mandatory rules for waste management practices and procedures on cruise ships.[42] A certification program—Green Globe 21—awards Green Globe logos to resorts and destinations that voluntarily meet certain environmental standards. The program has awarded logos to some 500 companies and destinations in more than 100 countries.[43] A verification of compliance with the criteria is assigned to an independent international verification body, which also conducts regular audits to ascertain continued compliance. The European Blue Flag Campaign awards eco-labels to beaches and marinas for meeting environmental, sanitary, and safety standards.[44] Currently over 100 voluntary tourism certification and award programs exist around the world.[45] In 2001, about 7,000 tourist products were certified worldwide, of which about 6,000 were in Europe.[46] Like the well-known AAA Five Diamond award given to the best hotels and the Mobile Five Star award given to the best restaurants, these environmental certification programs enable recipients to market themselves as environmentally responsible suppliers and thus put competitive pressure on themselves to maintain and others to improve their environmental performance. The downside to the proliferation of these programs is that consumers may find it difficult to determine which are effective.

Industry self-regulation often doesn't work either because members cannot agree on an acceptable common criteria, or enforcement and penalty provisions are too weak. At Hanauma Bay Nature Preserve, a brief trial with industry self-regulation to decrease the number of tourist visits was judged to be a failure and was scrapped in favor of tougher government-imposed regulations.[47]

An intermediate solution between industry self-regulation and government regulation is a negotiated agreement between the industry and the government. For example, the illegal dumping of cruise ship waste in the ocean has been a major problem in the cruise industry.[48] Florida and Hawaii have signed "memoranda of understanding" (MOU) with cruise ship associations establishing environmental standards for cruise ships operating in their marine waters. The North West Cruise Ship Association MOU with the State of Hawaii addresses ship discharge, emissions, hazardous waste, and requests for ship records, among other things. Alaska, by contrast, elected to pass strict legislation in 2001 to regulate cruise ship dumping.[49] To date, it is the only state to have passed legislation to regulate the cruise ship industry. The advantage of negotiated agreements is that they are less costly to revise when both parties see an advantage to making a change; the disadvantage is that such agreements do not carry the weight or force of law. An environmentalist who helped write Alaska's cruise ship regulations remarked that Hawaii's MOU is a "worthless piece of paper" because it is self-policed by an industry "literally run amok since the 1970s."[50] Cruise owners, however, counter that violations of MOU would no doubt be reported in the media, and bad press can be a strong disincentive to behave irresponsibly.[51]

Command-and-Control versus Market-Based Remedies

GOVERNMENTS AROUND the world employ both *command-and-control* and *market-based* measures to address tourism induced environmental problems. Command-and-control measures rely on rules, standards, and regulation to control environmental externalities. "No littering," "no trespassing," and "no fishing" are examples of command-and-control instruments. Plenty of other tourism-related examples exist. A 1999 California law requires cruise ships arriving from international waters to dump their ballast water at least 200 miles off-shore.[52] The City and County banned smoking at Honolulu's Hanauma Bay Nature Reserve.[53] New Zealand controls access to its national parks by setting limits on the number of park visits.[54] In Australia, only a tiny fraction of the Great Barrier Reef is open to visitors. The little village of Zermatt, Switzerland, located at the foot of the majestic Matterhorn, is one of the world's great skiing and mountain climbing centers and proudly promotes itself as a village-without-cars. Tourists arriving at Zermatt in their automobiles must leave them in parking lots outside the village and use the village's "electro" buses and taxis, or they can ride in horse-drawn sleighs and carriages, or use bikes. For Zermatt, banning automobiles is a win-win situation because, although residents and tourists both benefit from reduced traffic congestion and air pollution, it also allows the village to accommodate more tourists.

Command-and-control measures are generally favored by environmental groups. They are also the instruments most commonly employed by governments to control pollution. They are expensive to police and often ineffective because of the institutional capacity of the local environmental regulatory agencies to enforce the rules and regulations.[55] The *80:20 rule* is regarded as a reasonable goal to achieve for an effective environmental regulatory program. The goal is to get 80 percent voluntary compliance, then an effective regulatory agency can go after the remaining 20 percent who don't comply.[56]

Increasingly, governments are turning to market-based measures to address environmental problems. These measures include imposing taxes or user fees on products that pollute when they are produced, consumed, or discharged, or levying charges on the emission of polluting substances. An environmental tax or fee can be viewed as a user charge for the use of the environment. The new eco-tax levied by Majorcan authorities is an example of a market-based tourism environmental tax. The European Commission's recommendation to impose a European-wide "green" tax on airline tickets is an example of using taxes as an incentive to induce airlines to reduce their greenhouse emissions. Economists have long argued for taxes and charges as an alternative to command-and-control measures to reduce waste, encourage reuse and recycling, and to generate revenues to pay for environmental programs. Market-based remedies often are able to achieve the same goals as regulation and in a shorter time.[57]

Although we tend to think of market-based remedies in terms of taxes and fees to discourage polluting activities, they also include economic incentives and deposit–refund systems. For example, in Barbados, the government grants tariff relief to hotels when they import environmental equipment to be used in the hotels.[58] In Yellowstone National Park, consumers are required to pay a bottle deposit, to be refunded when the empty bottles are returned. The goal of the deposit–refund system is to encourage less pollution and more recycling.

Even when market-based incentives are used, some people argue that the need for regulations and enforcement will always exist because the private sector responds most quickly when polluters are threatened with the potential loss of their licenses to operate.[59] Hence, market-based and command-and-control environmental remedies are seen as complements rather than as substitutes.

Congestion and Carrying Capacity at Popular Recreational Sites

THE GREATEST risk to the sustainability of many popular tourist attractions is the threat of their being overwhelmed by too many tourist visits, especially during the peak tourist season. For example, before the implementation of a new management plan (1990) at Honolulu's Hanauma Bay Nature Preserve to curb the number of visitors, 2.8 million visits were made to the preserve each year, averaging nearly 7,500 persons per day. By contrast, a planning consulting firm recommended an "optimal use level" of 1,363 persons per day.[60]

Mass tourism has increasingly drawn public attention to the environmental *carrying capacity* of unique and popular tourist attractions. The World Tourism Organization defines carrying capacity as "the level of visitor use an area can accommodate with high levels of satisfaction for visitors and few impacts on resources."[61] The main criticism of this definition is that it lacks workable precision because one visitor's satisfaction is different from another visitor's. Overcrowding at a tourist attraction may induce some visitors to quit coming to the area, only to be replaced by another group who finds the experience quite satisfactory. Indeed, some argue that the phrase "carrying capacity" should not be used at all.[62]

Many people interpret carrying capacity as establishing specific limits on the number of visits. Figure 13-2 demonstrates that the optimal number of visits to a tourist attraction is not etched in stone. The horizontal axis measures the number of visits to the attraction, which we assume to be the most important determinant of environmental stress on the site's ecosystem. 0N measures the impact of tourists on the site ecosystem. A is the present threshold level at which degradation of the site's ecosystems becomes clearly noticeable and the visitor experience begins to deteriorate. Hence, the number of visits that the site could accommodate without noticeable stress on the ecosystem—let's call it the "carrying capacity" of the site—is V_0. Absent any restrictions on site visits, the actual number of visits is at V_3.

The objective, then, is to reduce the number of visits from V_3 to V_0. However, V_0 is not an inflexible number of tourist visits the site can accommodate without placing undue stress on the ecosystem. If site managers implemented conservation management practices, such as requiring visitors to use trolleys provided by the attraction instead of personal automobiles, improving toilet and garbage collection facilities, and educating visitors on appropriate behavior, we can increase both the site's stress tolerance level (say, from A to B) and reduce the impact of visitor numbers on the site's ecosystem (say, from 0N to 0N'). The combination of improved management practices and visitor education can increase the number of visits to the site from V_0 to V_2 without additional deleterious effects on the ecosystem. Thus, the environmental carrying capacity of a recreational site is a flexible rather than a fixed target that depends on a lot of factors.

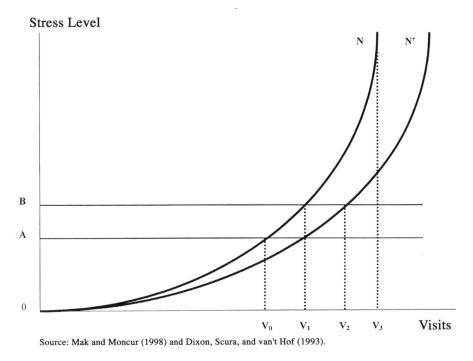

Source: Mak and Moncur (1998) and Dixon, Scura, and van't Hof (1993).

FIGURE 13-2. Relationship between improved park management, visitor education, and park protection.

Rationing Scarce Recreational Resources

How DO governments regulate the number of visits at popular tourist attractions? Governments use both price and nonprice rationing to regulate the use of scarce recreational resources. An example of price rationing is an admission fee; examples of nonprice rationing include first-come, first-served until a certain number of people have been admitted, and an advance reservation system.

The most frequently cited objection to an admission fee system is that it is regressive; that is, the burden of the fees falls relatively more heavily on lower income visitors.[63] But that is not always true. For example, visitors to Kakadu and Hinchinbrooke Island national parks in Australia are generally high-income visitors, and hence an admission fee would be progressive rather than regressive in its fiscal burden.[64] Another shortcoming of the admission fee system is that when the attraction is very popular or unique, demand for visits is very price inelastic,[65] and the admission fee would have to be raised so high to have a significant effect on visitations that it becomes politically unacceptable. In this case, nonprice rationing would have to be used in tandem with price rationing.[66] For example, at Hanauma Bay Nature Preserve, in addition to the $3 admission fee levied on nonresident visitors, park officials also close the road to the reserve when the 300 parking stalls are occupied.[67]

Nonetheless, significant advantages pertain to an admission fee system. First, it can help to control the number of visitors. Second, unlike the first-come, first-served system, an admission fee enables authorities to appropriate some of the economic rent from the scarce resource for the benefit of the public.[68] The revenue collected could be used to pay for upkeep.

For example, faced with decreasing international contributions to fund protected areas and a government budget crisis, in 1994, Costa Rica increased the admission fee charged to foreign tourists to its national parks from U.S.$1.50 to U.S.$15 per person. The number of visits decreased by one-third following the increase in fees, but the amount of revenues collected tripled. Fierce political opposition from the tourist industry persuaded the government to reduce the fee to $6 per person in 1996;[69] since then, the number of park visits have increased by an average of 10 percent each year.[70]

During the early 1990s, only about half of the world's protected areas charged admissions fees. Although the use of admission fees is spreading rapidly, nonetheless, fees remain generally quite modest and, in many places, are well below the amounts visitors are willing to pay.[71] To the extent that revenues generated are diverted to the general treasury rather than to protect the visitor attraction, the potential beneficial impact of the admission fees on the environment is diminished. Not surprisingly, a chronic shortage of money is available worldwide for conservation.

Visitors have their own preferences among rationing instruments. A survey of visitors at Hanauma Bay Nature Preserve found that nonresident tourists preferred the admission fee system, whereas local resident visitors to Hanauma Bay preferred the first-come, first-served system.[72]

Efthalia Dimara and Dimitris Skuras compared visitor preferences for three alternative rationing systems at Lake Cave in Greece: the first-come, first-served system, a variable admission fee system (with higher ticket prices on the weekends), and an advance reservation system.[73] They found that younger, less educated, and short-distance visitors prefer the first-come, first-served system. Older, higher income visitors who have to travel longer distances to reach the caves prefer the variable admission fee system. The advance reservation system was preferred by those who had planned their trips in advance and wanted to see as many attractions in the area as possible, and hence wanted to avoid the risk of possibly being turned away at the last minute.

Dimara and Skuras' findings are consistent with tourist and resident responses at Hanauma Bay. Higher income, but time-constrained, nonresident tourists prefer to pay an admission fee rather than wait in line and perhaps not get into the attraction. Residents, by contrast, typically have lower incomes than tourists, but are less time constrained and face lower travel costs, so they can return another day if they cannot get in today. Not surprisingly, residents prefer the first-come, first-served system.

The different responses from residents and tourists make it politically difficult to design an admission fee structure unless it features a two-tiered price system, with residents paying a lower (or, zero) admission fee to the attraction than tourists. In July 2001, a California tourist sued the City and County of Honolulu, alleging that the discriminatory admission fee structure at Hanauma Bay Nature Preserve of $3 per nonresident visitor, but no charge for residents, was a violation of the U.S. Constitution because it unjustly discriminated against people on the basis of their place of residence. U.S. federal judge Alan Kay ruled (October 17, 2002) that because residents already pay taxes, which underwrite the cost of upkeep at the preserve, "it is appropriate to exempt or preclude them from being charged an admission fee."[74] The ruling sets an important legal precedent for the rest of the country on recreation site management policy.

Concluding Observations

A MUCH greater public awareness and appreciation of the value of a quality environment exists today, and more of us demand that we treat the environment responsibly. This greater environmental awareness extends to tourism as well. Tourism generates sizable economic benefits, but it can also cause massive environmental problems if it is not developed and managed properly.

Many people believe that to have a quality environment, we need to cease polluting activities. By contrast, the key message of this chapter is that the amount of pollution we accept should be determined after a careful comparison of marginal benefits and costs to the community. The optimal amount of pollution is rarely zero pollution. Economists emphasize that market forces exert powerful influences over people's behavior; thus, the search for solutions to environmental problems that ignore these forces risks the probability of failure.

In the debate over whether it is better to use price or nonprice rationing to keep visitations down at congested recreation sites, it is useful to keep in mind that whichever method—price or nonprice rationing—is used, the decision is usually arrived at in the political market place, which means that the outcome must also attain political equilibrium. A political equilibrium is reached when no group of stakeholders can improve its position by holding out for a different choice. Hence, no one will devote resources to change the outcome.[75] It doesn't mean that everyone agrees with or is happy with the outcome; it does mean that no one wants to make the effort to change it.

Lawmakers can choose among various management tools to protect fragile recreational resources. However, their choices depend on their evaluations of trade-offs among competing objectives. Lawmakers want to protect the environment, to appropriate economic rents, and to achieve political equilibrium so that they can get reelected. Protecting the environment and collecting rents may conflict with achieving political equilibrium. The outcome is often a second-best world where no one gets what they want, but everyone learns to accept it.

CHAPTER 14

SUSTAINABLE TOURISM

Our society will be defined not only by what we create,
but what we refuse to destroy.

JOHN C. SAWHILL[1]

IN A PROVOCATIVE book published in 1993, Auliana Poon proclaimed "The golden age of tourism is over."[2] Poon equates tourism's Golden Age with mass tourism. She argued that the days of mass tourism, characterized by standardized, often rigidly packaged holidays, produced and consumed "en masse in a similar, robotlike and routine manner, with a lack of consideration for the norms, culture, and environment of host countries visited," are numbered and will give way to a "new tourism" that is sustainable in the long run.[3]

According to the World Tourism Organization (WTO), the current model of mass tourism is unsustainable because it does not take into account the importance of conservation, generally ignores the qualitative aspects of tourism while emphasizing quantitative growth, does not highlight the cultural and social amenities of destinations as selling points, and emphasizes short-term gain over long-term sustainability.[4] As a result, in the future, both tourists and residents of tourist destinations will be worse off. The WTO rallied forces to support sustainable tourism development. In the 1990s, "sustainable tourism" became a buzzword. It is currently endorsed by governments, the tourist industry, and NGOs[5] as the guiding principle in tourism planning and development.

Origin of Sustainable Tourism

THE ORIGIN of sustainable tourism can be traced to the 1987 Brundtland Report by the World Commission on Environment and Development (WCED). The report was an effort by the governments of several industrialized nations to embrace developmental strategies that balance the need for economic growth against the growing public demand to protect the environment from the increasing threat of industrialization.[6] In it, the WCED defined sustainable development as "progress that meets the needs of the present without compromising the ability of future generations to meet their own needs." The report highlights the three pillars of sustainable development: economic growth, environmental protection, and social equity.[7] The World Bank states succinctly that "sustainable development is about enhancing human well-being through time."[8]

The WTO has actively promoted sustainable development in tourism since the Rio Earth Summit in 1992. In April 1995, the World Conference on Sustainable Tourism, organized by the WTO and UNESCO, adopted the charter for sustainable tourism, which declared "sustainable tourism development" as:

> . . . any form of development, provision of amenities, or tourist activity that emphasizes respect for and long-term preservation of natural, cultural, and social resources and makes a positive and equitable contribution to the economic development and fulfillment of people living, working, or staying in these areas.[9]

The charter proposed a value-based model for future tourism development that emphasizes the protection of natural, social, and cultural resources.

Definition and Meaning of Sustainable Tourism

ALTHOUGH QUITE a few definitions of sustainable tourism exist,[10] the WTO currently defines sustainable tourism as development which:

> . . . meets the needs of present tourists and host regions while protecting and enhancing opportunities for the future. It is envisaged as leading to management of all resources in such a way that economic, social, and aesthetic needs can be fulfilled while maintaining cultural integrity, essential ecological processes, biological diversity, and life support systems.[11]

Thus, sustainable tourism is neither only about "greening" the tourist industry nor is it about ensuring the financial viability of tourist firms.

According to the WTO, achieving sustainable tourism requires that:

- The natural, historical, cultural, and other resources for tourism are conserved for continuous use in the future, while still bringing benefits to the present society.
- Tourism development is planned and managed so that it does not generate serious environmental or socio-cultural problems in the tourism area.
- The overall environmental quality of tourism areas is maintained and improved where needed.
- A high level of tourist satisfaction is maintained so that tourist destinations will retain their marketability and popularity.
- The benefits of tourism are widely spread throughout society.[12]

Well-being of Future Generations

CENTRAL TO the concept of sustainable tourism is the notion of *intergenerational equity*. Intergenerational equity means that a balance must exist between the interests of present and future generations.[13] Specifically, it requires future generations to be able to enjoy at least as good a quality of life[14] as that enjoyed by the current generation.[15]

The well-being of future generations depends, in part, on the capital assets or resources that will be passed on to them by the current generation. Capital assets, very broadly defined,[16] include manmade resources, human resources, cultural resources, and natural resources (see Figure 14-1). Natural resources can either be *renewable* or *nonrenewable*. Nonrenewable resources, such as coal, are depleted as they are used; renewable resources such as solar energy, water, fish, animals, and forests can be maintained forever through natural replenishment. A country's resources—manmade, human, or natural—can be complements or substitutes in the provision of the tourism product.

A way to make sure that the conditions faced by the next generation are not made worse by our activities today is to pass on to the next generation a stock of capital assets that is no less than we now have. The tough question is: Does the composition of the capital assets matter? Is it acceptable to degrade the natural environment and substitute a manmade asset instead? Put

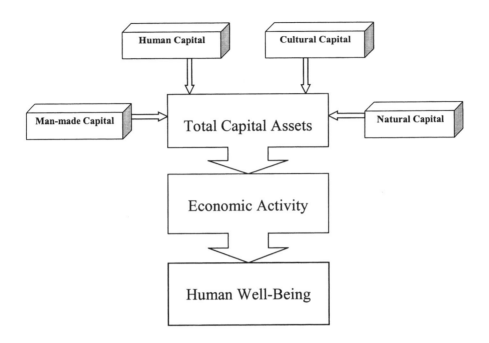

Source: Adapted from Fayall and Garrod (1997), p. 56.

FIGURE 14-1. Capital assets and human well-being.

another way, will the well-being of future generations be diminished if we ruin Hanauma Bay Nature Preserve by mismanaging it and pass on to the next generation a casino as a substitute? Or, can a personal visit to the Grand Canyon in Arizona be satisfactorily replaced by a virtual tour?

Environmental economists make a distinction between *weak sustainability* and *strong sustainability*.[17] Under weak sustainability, it is assumed that all resource inputs are fully substitutable. Strong sustainability requires no decrease in the natural capital.[18] Some people further identify "very weak" and "very strong" sustainability, implying that different degrees of substitutability exist among capital assets.[19] Environmentalists and limits-to-growth advocates typically take the strong sustainability position and argue that many of the natural resources are unique and cannot be substituted with manmade assets without significantly reducing the well-being of current and future generations; hence, these resources must be preserved.

The degree of substitutability between natural and manmade resources often depends on how they are actually used. If the resources are used in the production of some other produced output, the opportunities for substitution are likely to be high. For example, steel, plastic, or concrete can be used in place of wood in construction. Technology can replace labor in the production of many services. Sometimes, manmade resources can replace natural resources, but only at a very high cost.[20] In the long run, the law of diminishing returns[21] suggests that limits exist to the extent to which manmade resources can replace natural resources. For example, once a fishery is overfished, you cannot catch more fish, regardless of how many fishing lines you set out. Thus, even when substitution is possible, rarely are resources perfect substitutes.

By contrast, if resources are consumed directly in their untransformed state, it is likely that the specific attributes of the assets are important to consumers, thus implying less chance of finding suitable substitutes. In the case of nature-based tourism, tourists want to experience nature itself and would not regard a manmade replica as a good substitute for nature's amenities. Thus, the conservation and maintenance of natural resources employed in tourism are essential where a satisfying vacation experience may well be determined by a destination's natural amenities.

History shows that we have not been very good at preserving our natural resource amenities. Humans have put many of the world's ecosystems at risk, primarily because we have not been very successful at convincing decisionmakers that conserving the environment can yield net positive social benefits. Jeffrey Krautkraemer argues that one way to make environmental protection more attractive to decision makers is to make sure that all the amenity values generated by natural resources are properly counted.[22] Resources that are valued in the production of tourism services may also yield other benefits. For example, preserving a forest and not cutting it down for a housing development ensures that it continues to provide future recreational benefits; but a forest can also filter water, prevent run-off, and contribute to flood control. Counting only the benefits of saving the forest for its recreational amenities may relegate it to a second-best choice, after a new housing subdivision. The conservation of the forestland becomes more attractive if all the potential future benefits are included in the benefit–cost analysis, and not just those benefits that accrue to tourism. Krautkraemer concludes by noting that:

The first step in protecting the availability of natural resource amenities is to correct the institutional failures that result in undervaluation of these goods and services. This step is necessary whether one views sustainability as an efficiency or equity issue, and it is a tremendous task in itself.[23]

What is the value of a wildlife habitat? Is it valuable enough to convince decision makers to save it? The U.S. Fish and Wildlife Service recently proposed to designate almost 4,000 acres on the island of Kauai, Hawaii, as a critical habitat for two underground creatures of the lava tubes, cracks, and caves.[24] Lost income by not commercially developing the property was estimated by the consulting firm that prepared the study at between $547.7 million to $1.5 billion over the 2003–2020 period.[25] But no estimate was produced for the potential benefit from leaving the land in open space. The Fish and Wildlife Service cited the value of open space, preservation of the nearby coastline, reduced traffic, potential eco-tourism revenues, earnings from managing the conservation area, and the value of not losing the species as arguments in support of conservation. An attorney with the Earthjustice Legal Defense Fund remarked that "These are priceless."[26] The "priceless" tag, however, may not be adequate evidence to persuade decision makers to set aside the property for conservation. Valuing environmental amenities, especially those provided by unpriced (open access) resources, may be a challenging task, but it is not impossible.[27]

The Value of Environmental Amenities

VALUING RESOURCE amenities can be a relatively easy task when the services are bought and sold commercially, and data on prices and quantities transacted are available. It is more difficult to estimate their values when they are not transacted in normal markets. Economists have devised a number of techniques to quantify the values of unpriced, natural resource amenities.[28]

Resources can yield both *use* and *nonuse values*. Use values are derived from current use; nonuse values stem from the desire to preserve the resources for future use.[29]

Two of the most widely used environmental valuation techniques are the *travel cost* (TC) method and the *contingent valuation* (CV) method.[30] Both try to ascertain how much people are willing to pay to enjoy a resource amenity, even when they don't actually make a direct payment to enjoy it. The amount they are willing to pay is regarded as an estimate of the value of the amenity.

The *travel cost* method measures the value of environmental amenities by using the cost of travel to an attraction as a proxy for visitors' willingness-to-pay. Even when visitors don't have to pay to visit a state park or a beach, they have to travel to get there. The time and money cost they incur to get there is used to derive an approximate value of how much they are willing to pay.

The *contingent valuation* method takes a more direct approach by simply asking people what they are willing to pay to enjoy the amenity.[31] The contingent valuation method has been used in numerous studies to value environmental assets, including air quality, the recreational value of beaches, the value of saving wildlife and coral reefs, and so on.[32]

Neither the travel cost nor the contingency valuation method guarantees precise benefit estimates.[33] For example, when respondents are asked to give an estimate of what they are willing to pay to visit a wilderness area, they are not placed in a real situation and may nonchalantly toss out a hypothetical answer. There is no penalty for giving a "wrong" answer. But it is not always necessary to measure the amenity value precisely.

For example, during the 1970s, a big controversy arose over a proposal to build a dam on the Snake River, which winds through Hell's Canyon, the deepest canyon in North America.[34] The canyon offers spectacular views and excellent recreational amenities; it also provides a natural habitat for a diversity of wildlife. Because of its uniqueness, Hell's Canyon has few substitutes. But it is also an excellent location to build a dam to generate electricity. Should Congress allow a dam to be built there or leave it in its natural state? Economists from the Resources for the Future, Inc., were able to demonstrate to members of the U.S. Congress that the net current and future value of this unique site would be greater if it is kept in its natural state. Electricity, by contrast, could be generated in other ways. The researchers noted that, although the current benefits of preservation were estimated to be less than if a dam were built over the site, as demand for recreation continues to rise very rapidly, its potential future recreational value as a wilderness preserve was far greater. The data on which their estimates were based were "not very solid." Nonetheless, their benefit estimate for preservation was more than ten times higher than the alternate estimate from building a dam. Their estimated benefit from site preservation is unlikely to be ten times off the mark from the "true" value, even if the true value were known. Congress was convinced and voted to prohibit further development of this section of the river.

Alleviating Poverty to Improve Social Equity

THE CONCEPT of sustainable tourism is still in flux. At the global level, priority has shifted from "eco-" to "socio-" concerns in recent years. The WTO states that of the three pillars of sustainability—environmental, economic, and social—the social dimension is now "the uppermost."[35] (Of course, priorities may differ among individual countries.) Following the United Nations' Millennium Declaration to reduce global poverty during the twenty-first century, the WTO has expressed its commitment to reducing global poverty through tourism. The WTO notes that in the world's least developed countries, tourism is "almost universally the leading source of economic growth, foreign exchange, investment, and job creation."[36] Nonetheless, despite recent decades of impressive global economic growth, about 1.2 billion people in the world still live in extreme poverty (defined as living on less than $1 per person per day), and between 2.5 and 3 billion people live on less than $2 per person per day.[37] In its *World Development Report 2003*, the World Bank stresses the pressing need to reduce global poverty:

> When the poor lack voice and a stake in society, social assets (such as trust) and environmental assets (on which the poor depend) are eroded, stability is undermined, and the ability to solve economic, social, and environmental problems (that require collective action) dissipates. . . . As the world comes to resemble a single community, these lessons may apply even at the global level. . . . That is why ending global poverty is much more than a moral imperative—it is the cornerstone of a sustainable world.[38]

Tourism potentially is an important agent in the alleviation of global poverty. Currently, 80 percent of the world's extreme poor live in twelve countries.[39] In eleven of these countries, tourism is a significant and growing economic activity.[40] In June 2002, the WTO and the United Nations Conference on Trade and Development (UNCTAD) agreed to pool their efforts to reduce global poverty through tourism.[41] The joint project, named *Sustainable Tourism—Eliminating Poverty* (ST-EP), was launched during the 2002 World Summit on Sustainable Development in Johannesburg, South Africa, and aims to bring development and jobs to the world's poorest people, especially those living in Africa.

The conventional approach to alleviating poverty is to promote durable economic growth and then wait for income and jobs to "trickle down" to the poor. Recent research by David Dollar and Aart Kraay, tracking ninety-two countries over four decades, found that economic growth has led to poverty reduction.[42] They conclude that the traditional "growth-enhancing policies of good rule of law, fiscal discipline, and openness to international trade should be at the center of successful poverty reduction strategies."[43] Seiji Naya notes that, whereas the evidence available indicates that absolute poverty decreases with increases in per capita income, "much less certain is the degree or extent of poverty reduction that follows income growth."[44] Thus, counting on per capita income growth alone may not be enough to reduce poverty. During the nineteenth century, migration was an expedient way out of poverty for millions of people. Today, it is no longer a politically viable solution. The World Tourism Organization and UNCTAD aim to find more direct ways to reduce global poverty by bringing tourism to the people with the greatest needs.[45]

Balancing Objectives

GIVEN ITS multiple objectives, sustainable tourism often entails balancing conflicting objectives. For example, which is more important: Saving the environment or reducing poverty? Currently, one-quarter of the people (or, 1.3 billion people) in developing countries live on fragile lands.[46] They comprise a sizable percentage of the world's extreme poor. Fragile lands are those lands generally not well suited for agricultural production.[47] These lands include dryland, mountains, and poor soil quality land. Mountains, for example, supply fresh water for most of the world's population; they also contain over half of the world's biodiversity and a wide range of cultures at different elevations.[48] Obviously, bringing tourism to people living on fragile lands to alleviate poverty will put these ecosystems under greater environmental stress.

Sustainable tourism also entails making choices between current and future well-being. We can overexploit the environment for short-term economic gain, but in the long run a degraded environment reduces our future well-being. Because some people are more shortsighted than others, they prefer to live it up now and pay later.[49] And some may not give much thought to the next generation. Choosing between short-term versus long-term well-being requires balancing the interests of people who attach very different values to time.

How do we rank the different objectives of sustainable tourism? Despite the WTO's current emphasis on global poverty alleviation, within individual destinations, rankings of priorities will depend on the specific circumstances in those communities and which goals are deemed to be more pressing.[50] Economists would argue that no pre-set ranking exists, because each community must weigh the potential benefits and costs stemming from choices available to it. In sum, there is no "cookie cutter" solution. At the end of the day, durable outcomes are those which yield net positive social benefits and are also widely supported. It should come as no surprise that the most successful sustainable tourism development initiatives and projects involve community involvement and cooperation among the stakeholders.[51]

Monitoring Progress

IT IS one thing to profess a commitment to sustainability; it is quite another to live up to the promise. M. Thea Sinclair and Mike Stabler believe that much of the professed commitment to sustainable tourism is no more than "lip-service."[52] Hence, accountability is essential. Accountability entails taking inventory of our assets and developing indicators to show how well these assets are being used. Since the Brundtland Report, there have been many efforts to develop indicators of sustainable development. The most successful efforts have been in developing economic and environmental indicators. By contrast, it has been a struggle to develop social indicators of sustainability; one reason may be because we are still debating what social sustainability means and how to measure it.[53]

If developing indicators of sustainable development for an entire country is a difficult task, imagine how difficult it is to develop indicators of sustainability for only one sector—tourism. A major obstacle to progress in this arena is how to separate tourism's impacts from all other impacts. The WTO's suggestions for site-specific indicators of sustainable tourism for local communities appear in Table 14-1.

Some of the indicators in Table 14-1 are difficult to interpret. For example, the social impact of tourism is represented by a single indicator—the ratio of tourists to the local population. If the indicator value rises, is that good or bad for local residents? Could it not be both good and bad? Then, imagine that the ratio of tourists to the local population remains unchanged, but there is an improvement in the social well-being of the residents caused by an aggressive campaign to reduce tourism-related crime in the community. How is that improvement captured by the indicator? Obviously,

TABLE 14-1

CORE INDICATORS OF SUSTAINABLE TOURISM

Indicator	Specific Measures
Site Protection	Category of site protection according to IUCN* index.
Stress	Tourist numbers visiting site (annum/peak month)
Use Intensity	Intensity of use—peak period (persons/hectare)
Social Impact	Ratio of tourists to locals (peak period and over time)
Developing Control	Existence of environmental review procedure or formal controls over development of site and use densities.
Waste Management	Percentage of sewage from site receiving treatment (additional indicators may include structural limits of other infrastructure capacity on site such as water supply)
Planning Process	Existence of organized regional plan for tourist destination region (including tourism component)
Critical Ecosystems	Number of rare/endangered species
Visitor Satisfaction	Level of satisfaction by visitors (questionnaire based)
Local Satisfaction	Level of satisfaction by locals (questionnaire based)
Tourism Contribution to Local Community	Proportion of total economic activity generated by tourism only.

* International Union for Conservation of Nature and Natural Resources.
Source: World Tourism Organization (1998).

a lot of work remains to be done to develop indicators that are able to measure how well we use our natural, cultural, social, and manmade resources in tourism and, at the same time, satisfy the wants of tourists and residents. Indicators can be designed to measure progress for individual sites or for the entire destination. It is essential work if real progress is to be made on sustainable tourism development.

Concluding Observations

SUSTAINABLE TOURISM has both local and global dimensions, because tourism's impacts are not always confined locally. Tourists flying from one country to another contribute to global air pollution and climate change. Tourists consume resources that impact the world's ecosystems. Hence, sustainability must be examined from both local and global perspectives. It is not enough just to "think globally and act locally"; truly sustainable tourism requires that we act globally as well. That is why we need both local (destination, state, and local) and global institutions (United Nations and World Tourism Organization) to address the problems of tourism sustainability.

A cynical view of sustainable tourism contends that it is a notion developed in the developed countries and imposed on the less well-to-do countries to deny them the opportunity to improve their standard of living through tourism development.[54] Another cynical view contends that sustainable tourism is an idea exploited by the tourist industry to lobby for policies that would ensure the long-term viability and profitability of tourism businesses.[55] One critic complains that it is taking the fun out of tourism.[56] The optimistic view, on the other hand, argues that sustainable tourism conveys the important message that our environmental assets—natural, manmade, cultural, and social—should be maintained in a state that will sustain a flow of benefits to be enjoyed by present and future generations. Optimists, however, can disagree on how to achieve sustainable development.

The concept of sustainable tourism is easy to embrace, but it is not easy to implement. Economics can make valuable contributions to the debate over the best strategies to attain sustainable tourism. Economics emphasizes the need to use benefit–cost analysis in evaluating policy options. Economists have developed useful techniques to value environmental amenities so that a stronger case can be made for their conservation.

Brian Goodall and Mike Stabler argue that truly sustainable tourism is an unattainable goal for the foreseeable future.[57] But goals are not always set to be achieved. Even if the finish line is distant, it should not prevent us from taking steps to improve tourism's environmental and socio-economic performance. It is also essential to develop indicators that can show us how much progress toward sustainability we have made.

CHAPTER 15

TOURISM IN THE
POST–SEPTEMBER 11 WORLD

I'd rather be vague than precisely wrong.

J. M. KEYNES [1]

THE TRAVEL AND tourism industry in the United States was among the first casualties of the terrorist attacks of September 11, 2001, in New York City and Washington, D.C. That's because terrorists used commercial airliners as weapons of destruction. Four commercial airliners were destroyed in the attacks, and several hundred innocent lives on those planes and an additional 3,000 on the ground were lost. Immediately after, the nation's air transportation system was shut down for four days. In the first full week after flights resumed, the number of passengers fell by nearly 45 percent, from 9 million passengers in the week before September 11 to 5 million.[2] Cancellations poured into hotel reservation lines and travel agencies. The hotel industry was estimated to have suffered $700 million in lost revenue during those four days following the attacks; the U.S. airline industry lost nearly $5 billion dollars in passenger and freight revenues in the month of September alone.[3] It was widely feared that half the jobs in the travel and tourism industry in the United States would be lost.[4] The terrorist attacks occurred when travel and travel spending were already in decline because the U.S. economy was in recession.[5]

Fortunately, timely and sound economic crisis management by the Federal Reserve, the nation's central bank, kept the financial system operating almost seamlessly, and emergency spending appropriations by the U.S. Congress—including a $5 billion grant to the nation's airlines and $10 billion in loan guar-antees to keep them flying[6]—kept the short-run economic fall-out from escalating. As a result, the terrorist attacks of September 11 caused far less damage to the nation's economy than feared initially.[7] The stabilizing effects of the macroeconomic policy responses also helped the travel and tourism industry weather the initial storm from the attacks.

Under crisis, the travel and tourism industry proved to be far more resilient than had been expected, because recovery from the September 11 attacks began almost immediately. The nation's airline revenue passenger miles (RPM)[8]—although still in the negative territory—improved every month in the first six months after the September attacks, compared to the same months in the previous year:

Month	% Change in RPM
September 2001	-32
October	-23
November	-20
December	-14
January 2002	-13
February	-11
March	- 9

In response to lower demand, airlines cut seat capacity by 15 percent dur-ing the final three months of 2001.[9] They also cut fares.[10] Although cheap fares lured tourists back onto airplanes, the weak economy reduced business travel budgets and contributed to a slow recovery of business travel. Fear of flying and the hassles of getting through airport security also induced many people to switch to land modes of transportation (i.e., car, bus, and rail), espe-cially on shorter trips. In the United States, the number of people taking com-mercial flights for trips between 200 and 400 miles fell by 22 percent in the year after September 11.[11] The decline in the demand for air travel hit the metropolitan economies of the largest cities especially hard because large cities are more reliant on business travel, international tourists, and aviation.[12]

On the first anniversary of September 11, the travel and tourism in-dustry had not yet recovered to where it was before September 11. The Travel Industry Association of America (TIA) figured that domestic and international travel and tourism revenues in the United States in 2002 were 1.5 percent less than in 2001, and revenues in 2001 were 5.8 percent below those of 2000. Blame for the decline in travel and tourism revenues can be squarely directed at the decline in business and international travel, because the volume of domestic leisure travel was up 1.7 percent in 2002, following a 3.3 percent gain in 2001.[13]

The fall-out on travel and tourism from the September 11 terrorist attacks was also felt around the world.[14] The World Tourism Organization (WTO), however, noted with some satisfaction that international visitor arrivals around the world fell by less than 1 percent in 2001, from 696.7 million arrivals in 2000 to 692.7 million arrivals. The decline was only the second on record; the last occurred in 1982.[15] As in the United States, the WTO noted that the decline in international travel cannot be blamed entirely on the terrorist attacks, because international tourism growth was decelerating even before the attacks, because of a weak global economy. Indeed, in 2002, the number of international visitor arrivals rose to 714.6 million, or 19 million more than in 2000. The WTO concluded that "The economic situation in the world is a more powerful threat to international arrivals than fear of terrorism."[16] But, as in the United States, tourism employment did not fully recover. The United Nations International Labor Organization (ILO) reported that 6.6 million tourism employees—one out of every twelve—had lost their jobs between 2001 and 2002.[17]

Terrorism and the Future of Tourism

THE WORLD Tourism Organization reported that, in 2000, international visitor arrivals reached 697 million, a huge increase from the 25 million visitors who crossed international borders in 1950. Nonetheless, the average annual rate of growth in international visitor arrivals fell every decade between 1950 and 2000, and averaged 4.3 percent growth per year during the most recent decade (Figure 15-1). How will September 11 and the ensuing war on terrorism affect the future growth of international tourism? The WTO confidently predicted that "Liberty and the desire to travel will conquer the fear of terrorism."[18]

The tragic events of September 11 did not dissuade the WTO from holding its semiannual conference in Seoul, Korea, and Osaka, Japan, which began on September 23, 2001. At the conference, the WTO reiterated its

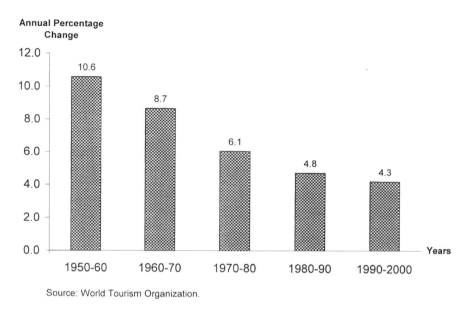

Source: World Tourism Organization.

FIGURE 15-1. Growth of international visitor arrivals.

long-term forecast of worldwide international tourist arrivals of 1 billion by 2010 and 1.5 billion by 2020.[19] Following a review of the damage from September 11 in November 2001, the WTO reaffirmed its earlier forecast that an average annual growth rate of 4.1 percent per year in international tourist arrivals until 2020 may be conservative.[20] It noted that the 4.3 percent average annual growth between 1990 and 2000 was achieved despite shocks from the first Gulf War, the disintegration of Yugoslavia, terrorist attacks on tourists at Luxor, Egypt, and the Asian financial crisis.

History informs us that tourism usually recovers quickly from terrorist attacks as consumers switch to destinations that are perceived to be safer, and the fear soon fades if the attacks are not repeated.[21] However, the current war on global terrorism is expected to be a long one, and it will be fought on many fronts. The nightclub bombings in Bali, Indonesia, in October 2002, and attacks on an Israeli-owned hotel and airline in Mombasa, Kenya, in November 2002, demonstrated that terrorists will retaliate. U.S. government and intelligence officials have repeatedly warned that further attacks by terrorists on tourist targets are highly likely. Persistent fear of more attacks, fanned by frequent government security alerts, diminishes people's enthusiasm for travel. The consulting firm PricewaterhouseCoopers noted that one week following each of the seven federal government terrorist alerts between

October 1, 2001, and November 2002, U.S. hotel occupancies fell by an average of 3.5 percent.[22]

Peter E. Tarlow, publisher of *Tourism Tidbits,* surmises that terrorists find tourism an attractive target because:

- An attack on tourism is an attack on that nation's economy.
- Terrorists crave media attention, and an attack on tourism will generate a lot of publicity.
- Tourist attractions represent "the spirit and essence" of a nation.
- Tourist attractions are visited mostly by strangers, hence terrorists can operate with relative anonymity.[23]

Tarlow argues that unless the industry can find ways to provide safe, secure, and convenient travel experiences, the twenty-first century may see the end of the global travel boom.

Indirectly, September 11 and the ensuing global war on terrorism will slow long-term economic growth around the world, as money spent on national defense and homeland security is diverted from other more profitable and productive private and public uses. Although the additional spending on defense and homeland security will initially boost economic growth, in the long run this spending will create a drag on the growth of the global economy.[24] The Paris-based Organization for Economic Cooperation and Development (OECD) noted that "[these effects are] more diffuse, so they tend not to feature so prominently in people's perceptions. But they could be felt like sand in the wheels [of the economy]."[25] Because demand for tourism is sensitive to economic growth, even a slightly slower growth of the world's economies will dampen somewhat the future growth of travel and tourism around the world.

Forces Shaping Tourism's Future

TOURISM'S FUTURE will be shaped by changes both on the demand side and the supply side of the tourism economy. On the demand side the most important factors, besides terrorism, include changes in consumer incomes, available leisure time, the relative cost of travel, demographics, and consumer taste. On the supply side, the most important factors include new information technology, changes in government tourism policies, and the environmental and social capacity of many tourist destinations to accommodate more tourism growth.[26]

Economic Growth

Pleasure travel is a luxury, especially travel to distant places. International tourist travel is still concentrated among the residents of a few countries. Among approximately 240 sovereign countries and territories in the world, the 15 largest tourist originating countries account for about 75 percent of the world's international tourists.[27] Figures 15-2 and 15-3 show that the propensity for international travel and spending vary widely among countries. For many countries with low propensities, the potential exists for significantly

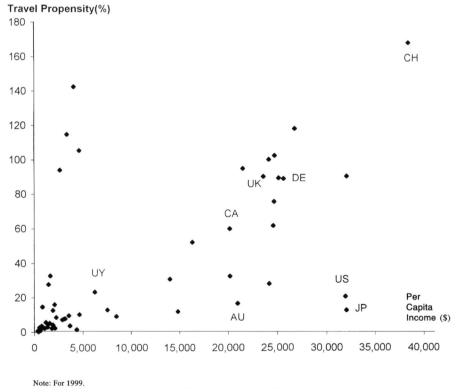

Note: For 1999.
Source: World Tourism Organization, *Compendium of Tourism Statistics 2001.*

FIGURE 15-2. Travel propensity abroad. Travel propensity equals number of trips divided by total population (trips abroad per capita). AU-Australia; CA-Canada; CH-Switzerland; DE-Germany; JP-Japan; UK-United Kingdom; US-United States; UY-Uruguay.

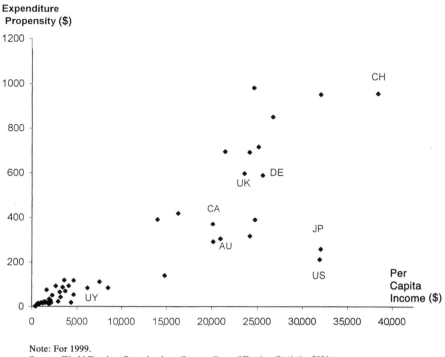

Note: For 1999.
Source: World Tourism Organization, *Compendium of Tourism Statistics 2001.*

FIGURE 15-3. Expenditure propensity for travel abroad. Expenditure propensity equals total spending abroad divided by total population (spending abroad per capita). AU-Australia; CA-Canada; CH-Switzerland; DE-Germany; JP-Japan; UK-United Kingdom; US-United States; UY-Uruguay.

more foreign travel and spending. In 1996, only 3.5 percent of the world's population had ever traveled abroad.[28]

Whether a person can go on a pleasure trip depends on whether he has the income and time to travel. Income is the most important determinant of the demand for travel. As the world's economies continue to grow, more people will have the financial means to travel for pleasure.[29] This increase in personal wealth is the main reason why tourism analysts believe that tourism will continue to grow well into the future.

The World Tourism Organization's *Tourism 2020 Vision* predicts that East Asia and the Pacific will likely become the second largest generator of international tourists by 2020, pushing the Americas into third place. China is expected to become the fourth largest tourist generating country in the world.

Leisure Time

Colin Clark observes that the increased competition stemming from global-ization is putting greater pressure on the amount of leisure time available to workers.[30] For many workers, reductions in working time have slowed, and working hours, especially for full-time skilled employees, have actually increased. He surmises that youth tourism will grow in the future as young people opt to travel before they embark on their careers. Once they begin full-time employment, it will be more difficult for them to take lengthy vacations. For time-pressed Americans, Clark sees a trend toward shorter, more frequent but more intensive (i.e., higher spending) vacations.[31] The trend toward shorter trips means that a higher percentage of the vacation trips will be domestic rather than foreign trips.

Tarlow envisions time-pressed consumers and businessmen will also be seeking convenience; this means avoiding shorter flights to minimize airport hassles and doing less shopping on vacation trips as airlines impose more stringent limits on baggage and carry-on items.[32] The demand for shopping tourism will also decline as nations open their markets and global goods become locally available.[33]

Travel Cost

The impressive growth of tourism in the post–World War II era was in no small part due to the sharp reduction in the relative cost of travel attributable to improvements in transportation. In the United States, the construction of the interstate highway system (now completed) facilitated long-distance travel. The introduction of commercial jet plane service in the late 1950s dramati-cally cut the time cost of travel, and subsequent increases in the size, range, and fuel economy of aircraft propelled a steady decline in the (real) cost per seat mile. This helped to stimulate long-distance travel—especially interna-tional travel. Improvements of a similar magnitude may be harder to come by in the future.

Indeed, mounting evidence shows that the relative cost of travel may be rising in some markets as air corridors, airport runways, and roads reach their capacities and efforts to expand them run into fierce political opposition from environmental and other local resident groups.[34] Adding to rising con-gestion costs are new environmental taxes and higher security and insurance fees following September 11. For some leisure travelers, recreational activities that do not require extensive travel may become an attractive substitute for travel.

Two areas remain where increases in productivity can be exploited to lower the relative cost of travel. First, there is clearly more room to exploit advances in information technology, either to integrate them into existing operations or to use them to develop new services. For example, the growing use of self-service computer kiosks at U.S. airports to check in passengers and print boarding tickets saves on employee costs for airlines and reduces check-in time for passengers. Another opportunity, especially in international aviation—and also domestic transportation in many countries—is deregulation or liberalization and subsequent exposure to the discipline of market competition. The U.S. Department of Commerce study of the relative economic performance of U.S. service industries between 1977 and 1993 found that deregulation and the application of new information technology were the two most common features of industries that enjoyed high productivity growth.[35]

Consumer Taste

Changes in consumer preferences will have a major impact on the future of tourist travel. Although sun-lust travel still dominates vacation travel, the growing numbers of experienced travelers are demanding more flexible and individualized vacations and unique experiences.[36] These tourists are more likely to travel independently rather than in large groups or on inclusive prepaid package tours.[37] The WTO predicts that the trendiest destinations of the future will be "the tops of the mountains, the depths of the oceans, and the ends of the earth."[38] Many of these places will be in the emerging destinations of less developed countries. The traditional dominance of Western Europe will gradually give way to destinations in Asia and Africa. In its *Tourism 2020 Vision*, the WTO predicts that, by 2020, the East Asia/Pacific region will overtake the Americas as the second most popular regional destination, after Europe. By then, China's National Tourism Administration predicts that China will become the world's largest tourist destination.[39]

Demographic Change

Demographic change will also have a big impact on the future of travel. The world's population is aging, and its growth rate is already in decline. Beyond 2040, there may be fewer people living on Planet Earth.[40] Nowhere is this more evident than in Japan, one of the leading tourist-generating countries in the world.[41] Japan's population, currently estimated at 127 million, is expected to reach its peak before 2010 and then decline gradually thereafter. Between 2000 and 2020, the number of Japanese under the age of 30—that is, the age group with the highest propensity to travel abroad—will decrease by 12 million, whereas the number of people aged 60 and older is expected to increase by more than 13 million. Population decline and aging will have negative effects on the demand for international travel. All else being equal, older people tend to travel less, even though they have more time and may have more money to travel than younger, working people. As well, a rapidly aging population, combined with slower—and soon negative—population growth, will retard Japan's economic growth in the future and significantly reduce the rate of growth of Japanese tourist travel abroad in the twenty-first century.[42] And among those who travel, a higher percentage of them will be grayer at the temples. On the positive side, the future generation of seniors will come from the current generation of highly traveled young people, and they are likely to travel more than their parents and grandparents at the same age. The elderly, or "silver" market, will exhibit very different patterns of demand for travel destinations and vacation goods and services. What is likely to happen in Japan could also happen in other industrialized countries.

Technology

The Internet and high speed computers are dramatically changing the way consumers search for travel information and purchase travel products. Indeed, this technology is revolutionizing the travel distribution business by enabling buyers and sellers to bypass the middleman—the traditional travel agents. Computers and the Internet also enable sellers to learn more about their customers quickly and cheaply, so that they can develop new products customized to satisfy their diverse tastes. The result will be the accelerated development of what Maggie Bergsma describes as *one-to-one marketing,* which "encompasses a set of marketing techniques aimed at selling to the individual.[43] Instead of selling one product to as many people as possible, it is about selling as many products and services as possible to one customer using databases and interactive communication."[44] Information technology that facilitates one-to-one marketing and consumer preferences for customization will reinforce each other in shaping the future development of tourism. It likely means less future demand for mass tourism in favor of more individualized and customized travel.

The trend toward one-to-one marketing also presents a whole new set of challenges for national/destination tourist offices (NTOs), which traditionally have operated on a model of mass media or wholesale (i.e., travel agent) marketing. In the new information technology age, in which the pace of technological development is accelerating and the number of information brokers increase exponentially, NTOs are challenged to stay flexible and competitive or become redundant.[45] Walter Leu notes that NTOs are searching to define their role now more than ever.[46] He nonetheless argues that an essential role remains for NTOs to play in "conceptual" destination marketing: Given that the tourism sector is a cross-section of a nation's industries, NTOs perform an important "umbrella function." But the days when NTOs merely served as public relations instruments for governments and politicians are over. The public will increasingly demand that they demonstrate their effectiveness.

New information technology also could have a significant impact on business travel. Tarlow surmises that new technologies in teleconferencing and interactive Web conferences will increasingly displace personal travel to meetings and conventions.[47] Not only will these new technologies save time and money, they also allay fears of kidnapping and terrorist attacks. Thus, communities that are economically dependent on meetings and conventions could be seriously hurt financially.

Government Policy

Lisa Mastny argues that tourism is one of the world's least regulated industries.[48] That surely isn't true of all the different industries that make up tourism.[49] Indeed, the transportation industry, arguably tourism's most important industry, is highly regulated everywhere. For safety reasons, common carriers will always be tightly regulated, but what matters to the future growth of tourism is government policies on economic regulation. To improve economic efficiency, governments around the world are clearly favoring less regulation and more competition in the transportation industries.

The governments of some countries still dictate to their own residents whether they can take pleasure trips abroad, to which destinations, and how much money they can spend, or what goods they can bring back. With peace and globalization, government barriers to travel are being dismantled, and travel has become freer in the past thirty years. As an internationally traded commodity, tourism is increasingly subject to fair trade principles, so that all nations can compete more equally on a level playing field.

Both regulatory reform in transportation and a more liberal political environment will have positive impacts on future travel. One caveat is whether a protracted war against global terrorism might slow the progress toward a more liberal travel environment.[50]

Will governments play a smaller role in tourism's future? Probably not, because governments are being asked to do more to protect the natural and social environments from the harmful spillovers of unrelenting tourism growth. Brian Goodall and Mike Stabler observe that "tourism is still an industry which contributes more to the creation of environmental problems than it does to their solution."[51] Already, in many places, the perceived problem is not too few, but too many, tourists. Solving tourism's negative spillovers will require more government intervention, not less.

Concluding Observations

A FAMOUS economist once joked that there are two kinds of forecasters, those who don't know, and those who don't know they don't know. Some of the most publicized predictions in history about mankind's future prospects have turned out to be duds.[52] Knowing the past and the present, and the technological possibilities just ahead,[53] may not be enough to accurately predict the future. Students of tourism agree that tourism will continue to increase. The prognosis is based on two premises: (1) that humans have a strong urge to travel, and (2) that more people will be able to afford to travel because the world's economies will continue to grow. Beyond that, opinions begin to differ on the precise details of changes to come. The future of tourism is not pre-ordained. It will be shaped by the choices that tourism's decision makers—consumers, suppliers, and destination residents through their governments—have yet to make. *Tourism and the Economy* emphasizes that economics can help decision makers evaluate the relative costs and benefits of the different options available to them. This book also has helped us to gain a better understanding of tourism and its latest trends and the forces that will bring about future changes in travel and tourism.

ENDNOTES

CHAPTER 1

1. Winner of 1992 Nobel Prize in economics.

2. World Tourism Organization (1993), p. 1.

3. World Tourism Organization (November 2001), p. 14.

4. Smith and Jenner (2000), p. 32.

5. This is the definition used by Hawaii and the U.S. Department of Commerce, Bureau of Economic Analysis. The terms "tourists" and "visitors" are frequently used interchangeably.

6. "Leisure" includes both tourism and recreation.

7. Starr (1981), p. 3.

8. Economists sometimes refer to them as "agents."

9. Economics recognizes that firms may value other objectives such as maximization of sales revenue, market share, or even output. One theory suggests that managers of for-profit firms merely attempt to achieve satisfactory, rather than maximum, results (Bull, 1991, pp. 54–58).

10. Brown (2000), p. 27.

11. Although the analyses in this book focus mainly on pleasure travel, by necessity the book uses tourism statistics and published studies that often include business, as well as other forms of, travel. However, the book does not make a separate effort to present analyses of the economics of business travel, religious tourism, edu-tourism, medical tourism, and so on.

CHAPTER 2

1. Bull (1991).

2. Ryan (1991).

3. Sinclair and Stabler (1997), p. 58.

4. Lofgren (1999), p. 284, fn # 4.

5. Ibid., p. 95.

6. Fisher (1996), pp. 146–151.

7. At www.nfow.com. Plog Research notes that the most satisfying vacation destinations typically share at least three of the following four attributes: beautiful outdoor scenery, warm weather, a variety of activities, and well-maintained lodgings and attractions. Hawaii topped the U.S. Delightful Dozen list for six straight years. The top international destinations ranked according to visitor satisfaction in 2002 were Ireland, Australia, New Zealand, Scotland, and the English countryside/Wales.

8. See, for example, Fujii and Mak (1980).

9. Quote taken from Plog (1991), p. 75.

10. Plog (1991) and Plog (2001).

11. Gray (1974).

12. Crandall (1994), p. 416.

13. Butler (1980). See also Toh, Khan, and Koh (2001).

14. I thank my colleague Mark Hukill for emphasizing this point. For example, it is the information on an available seat on a particular flight (and reservation) that is important to the airline, the GDS (i.e., computer reservation system), the travel agent, and the consumer. The consumption of the service comes only after the economic decision to purchase based on available information.

15. Destinations, as used here, can be local or regional destinations or countries.

16. At www.twcrossroads.com (Article ID=35498), hereafter referred to as *Travel Weekly Daily Bulletin.*

17. *Travel Weekly Daily Bulletin,* Article ID=37088.

18. Mak and Miklius (1990).

19. But the government continues to support tourism research and policy analysis. After the September 11, 2001 terrorist attacks, Congress (in February 2003) appropriated $50 million to fund a tourism marketing campaign and established the U.S. Travel and Tourism Advisory Board to direct the effort. *Travel Weekly Daily Bulletin*, Article ID=36799.

20. But not at restaurants and in stores.

21. A survey of 500 North American visitors to Hawaii in 1999 found that 23 percent of the respondents were "annoyed by seeing things that are priced higher for tourists than for residents of Hawaii." By contrast, a similar survey of 600 Japanese visitors found that 56 percent of the respondents were annoyed by the discriminatory pricing practice. Market Trends Pacific, Inc. (May 2000), p. 4. Some visitors argue that preferential prices given to local residents violate U.S. antitrust laws, specifically, the Robinson-Patman Act. However, the Act prohibits price discrimination if it has the potential to lessen competition. It is not obvious how preferential price discounts given to local residents harm competition. Price discrimination is a common business practice. Movie theaters, airlines, and amusement parks charge lower prices to children. Senior citizens, and sometimes students and military personnel, get discounts on many purchases. (Blair and Kaserman, 1985, pp. 261–262). Airlines routinely price discriminate between business and leisure travelers. Likewise, hotels also charge higher prices (referred to as "rack rates") to walk-in customers than to customers who call in to make reservations in advance.

22. Flinn (2002), p. C3.

23. The Japan Railpass entitles the holder ridership on the entire JR system, including its local trains, buses, and ferries.

24. Hence, money is not "capital" under this definition. In the world of finance, money is regarded as "financial capital." Economists also consider education, training and work experience as "human capital." Durable goods are those with useful lives of one year or more.

25. For the entire private business sector, structures represent about 62 percent of all capital employed and equipment comprises the remaining 38 percent.

26. McGuckin and Stiroh (2002), pp. 51–52.

27. See, for example, Mak and Moncur (2000).

28. Edgell (1990), p. 26; Bull (1991), p. 138; and Witt, Brooke, and Buckley (1995), p. 2.

29. De Kadt (1976), p. 38, and Diamond (1977), p. 549.

30. Market Trends Pacific, Inc. (May 2000), p. 4.

CHAPTER 3

1. *Time Magazine.*

2. Vogel (2001), p. xiii.

3. Lehmann (1981), p. 7. Today, only the Great Pyramid of Egypt remains of the seven manmade attractions.

4. Brown (2000), p. 9.

5. Lundberg (1985), p. 7.

6. Lofgren (1999), p. 110.

7. Lehmann (1981), p. 11. In the U.S. hotel porters were the first travel agents of the railway era.

8. Lofgren (1999), p. 77.

9. Ibid., p. 162.

10. Davis (1981), p. 23.

11. Plog (1991), p. 5.

12. Lofgren (1999), p. 63.

13. Aron (1999), p. 238. Aron notes (pp. 248–249) that the main impetus for the extension of paid vacations came not from the government but from employers who wanted, in part, to stall union organization of their companies.

14. Smith and Jenner (2000), p. 23.

15. Burkhart and Medlick (1974), p. 42, define mass tourism as "the participation of large numbers of people in tourism." Others define mass tourism as movements of a large number of people in group or prepaid package tours. See, for example, Vanhove (1997), pp. 50–51.

16. They are in order of spending, United States, Germany, U.K., Japan, France, Italy, Canada, Netherlands, China, Belgium/Luxembourg.

17. WTO (November 2001), p. 15.

18. Ibid.

19. Sinclair and Stabler (1997), p. 158; Tisdell (2001), p. 19.

20. Excluding international transportation payments. Travel Industry Association of America (March 12, 2002), p. 1; *Travel Industry World 2001 Yearbook* (2002), p. 6.

21. Smith and Jenner (2000), p. 207.

22. JTB News (January 9, 2003) at www.jtb.co.jp.

23. Brown (2000), pp. 102–103.

24. Ibid., p. 107.

25. Plog (1991), p. 8.

26. Ibid., p. 9.

27. Sinclair and Stabler (1997), pp. 21–26.

28. *Travel Industry World 2001 Yearbook* (2002), p. 81, and U.S. Census Bureau.

29. Demand is usually measured by the number of "trips"; sometimes demand is measured by the total amount of "spending" on pleasure trips.

30. Witt, Brooke, and Buckley (1995), pp. 53–54. They surmise that the strong pull of Italy may be due either to strong family ties or the influence of the Roman Catholic Church on American church members to visit Rome.

31. Goods of which the income elasticities of demand are greater than zero are considered *normal* goods; among normal goods, those with income elasticities close to zero are considered necessities. Although there is a difference between a good (which is tangible) and a service (which is intangible), for the sake of simplicity, economists often use the word "good" to refer to both.

32. Because quantity demanded and price are negatively related, a minus (-) sign always appears on the price elasticity of demand. For the sake of convenience, we ignore the minus (-) sign and concentrate only on the size of the number.

33. Another way of looking at it is that she has to give up $115.38 in purchases at home to purchase the Japanese dinner.

34. Crouch (1995). Data used in these studies typically come from the World Tourism Organization or the individual national tourist offices and hence include trips for all travel purposes, not only pleasure travel. The elasticities for pleasure travel only should differ somewhat from those in Table 3-1.

35. For technical reasons, these studies typically exclude travel time or costs of travel to competing destinations. For example, travel time is positively correlated with transportation costs, and empirical models are unable to isolate the separate effects of each on demand. As a result, the elasticities reported in Table 3-1 should be regarded as approximate values and not as precise estimates.

36. Studies often model the currency exchange rates separately from destination prices under the assumption that consumers are more aware of currency exchange rates and are likely to be more sensitive to the exchange rates when selecting their travel destinations than destination prices. Of course, the prices of some destination commodities are included in prepaid package tours. Research has shown that consumers are sensitive to prices of prepaid package tours.

37. Crouch (1994), p. 5.

38. Sakai, Brown, and Mak (2000).

39. Expressed as a percent. Because consumers can take more than one trip abroad per year, the average travel propensity for all residents of a country can be greater than 100 percent. Both the Netherlands and Germany had travel propensities that exceeded 100 percent in 1999, meaning that the number of trips taken abroad exceeded their populations. Smith and Jenner (2000), p. 22.

40. This is referred to as "ethnic tourism." World Tourism Organization (1994), p. 20.

41. This is referred to as "nostalgic tourism." Ibid., pp. 20–21.

42. *Newsweek International* (2002).

43. Smith and Jenner (2000), p. 13. By international standards, France and Italy do not have low travel propensities abroad. For example, the travel propensity for the United States in 1999 was 21 and for Japan, 13.

44. Pizam et al. (1997), p. 23.

45. Pizam and Tarlow (1999).

46. World Tourism Organization (1994), pp. 130–131.

47. Pizam and Fleischer (2002).

48. The National Capital Area Tourism Research Program (NCATRP) (August 30, 2002). However, room rates and room revenues had not fully recovered as a result of substantial price discounting.

49. *Honolulu Advertiser* (September 8, 2002), p. F3. A major reason for the slow recovery of Japanese visitors is the weakness of Japan's economy.

50. World Tourism Organization (1995).

51. World Tourism Organization (November 2001), p. 55.

52. Hamal (1996) shows that Australians consider domestic and international pleasure travel as viable substitutes. Indeed, he shows that a 1 percent increase in the price of overseas travel, all else being equal, increases demand for domestic holiday nights by .31 percent. Hence,

demand for domestic holiday travel in Australia is only slightly sensitive to changes in the price of foreign travel.

CHAPTER 4

1. Plog (1991).
2. Japanese travel magazine.
3. Lofgren (1999), p. 205.
4. *Travel Industry World 2002 Yearbook* (2003).
5. *Travel Journal Inc.* (2000), p. 48, and Japan Travel Bureau (1998). These exclude "group tours"—e.g., travel with a company or school group.
6. These are individual trips rather than individual travelers since a traveler could make more than one trip in a given year.
7. The NTA loosely defines a package trip as "any professionally arranged trip that includes at least two elements, like transportation and accommodation." Of the 144 million trips, 57 percent were for independent travel, whereas 43 percent were for group travel. *Travel Industry World 2001 Yearbook* (2002), p. 179.
8. Sheldon and Mak (1987), p. 13.
9. The terms "tour operators" and "tour wholesalers" are often used interchangeably. Tour wholesalers, however, may not operate their own tours at the destinations and function strictly as middlemen between suppliers and retail travel agents. Many tour wholesalers do operate their own tours and thus they serve both functions.
10. Sheldon and Mak (1987), p. 13.
11. Plog (1991), p. 89.
12. Ibid., pp. 92–94.
13. Of course, tour operators are aware of that and will take that into consideration in pricing the packages.
14. Up to some maximum.
15. Askari (1971) and Pyo (1989).
16. Sheldon (1986).
17. Japan Travel Bureau (1998).
18. *The Wall Street Journal* recently also found that package tours are not always cheaper than buying the individual components separately. *Honolulu Advertiser* (July 15, 2002), p. D4.
19. Varley (2000), p. 335.
20. Morris (1990).
21. Japan Travel Bureau (1998).
22. *Travel Industry World 2000 Yearbook* (2001), pp. 175–176.
23. Yamamoto and Gill (1999), p. 134.
24. Hawaii Department of Business, Economic Development and Tourism (DBEDT) (2002), p. 88.
25. Ibid.

CHAPTER 5

1. President, American Society of Travel Agents (ASTA).
2. *Travel Industry World 2002 Yearbook* (2003), p. 9.
3. *Travel Weekly* (August 24, 2000), p. 10.

4. *Travel Industry World 2002 Yearbook* (2003), p. 7.

5. Goeldner, et al. (2000), pp. 192–200.

6. Friedman (1992), pp. 208–210.

7. *Travel Weekly* (August 24, 2000), p. 14. "Fam" trips are free or discounted trips provided by travel destinations and suppliers to travel agents to promote a destination.

8. The program was established in 2001, because federal employee travelers complained that per diem allowances weren't sufficient to cover the cost of staying at a downtown hotel in many cities they visit. Staying at the FPLP hotels isn't required, but the General Services Administration (GSA) asks travelers to request a FPLP property when they call a travel agent to make their travel arrangements.

9. *Travel Weekly Daily Bulletin*, Article ID=36789.

10. The joint venture by the five largest U.S. airlines has raised concerns that it could reduce competition in the airline and airline distribution business. Office of Aviation & International Affairs (June 27, 2002).

11. *Travel Industry World 2002 Yearbook* (2003), p. 8. American Express is the largest U.S. travel agency. In 2001, its gross sales were $17.2 billion in the U.S. alone. However, the dot-com travel agencies were growing at a much faster rate. For example, in 1998, Travelocity.com had sales of only $285 million, and Expedia.com had sales of $250 million.

12. Stigler, (1962).

13. Morrison (December 1995), p. 29.

14. *Travel Weekly* (August 2000), p. 51.

15. Although most people contact their travel agents by phone.

16. *Travel Industry World 2001 Yearbook* (2002), pp. 177–178.

17. Koch and Cebula (2002).

18. *Travel Industry World 2002 Yearbook* (2003), p. 31

19. *Newsweek* (November 25, 2002), p. 60.

20. *Travel Industry World 2002 Yearbook* (2003), p. 9.

21. Office of Aviation & International Affairs (June 27, 2002), p. 18.

22. Shaw (2002), pp. E4–E5.

23. Although no one site is always the cheapest, "bot" search engines such as Qixo.com and SideStep.com search through all the major sites at once and list the highest to lowest prices for airfares, hotels, and car rentals; but you can't use them to make purchases.

24. Although disintermediation has not happened to the extent predicted by some because the complexity of the travel product often requires the assistance of a travel agent. Global Aviation Associates (2002), p. 7.

25. Ibid., p. 8.

26. Ibid., p. 10.

27. *Los Angeles Times* (March 10, 2002), p. L20.

28. Global Aviation Associates (2002), p. 5.

29. The same is occurring in the United Kingdom.

30. Commission rates on package tours and cruises remain at 10 percent or higher of the total price of a package. *Travel Industry World 2000 Yearbook* (2001), p. 175.

31. *Travel Industry World 2002 Yearbook* (2003), p. 7.

32. Rich (2002), p. F8.

33. *Travel Industry World 2002 Yearbook* (2003), p. 32.

34. Foss (2002), p. D1, and Harris (2002), p. F5.

35. However, Southwest Airlines, a discount airline, continues to pay a commission to travel agents. *Travel Weekly Daily Bulletin*, Article ID=36802.

36. Koch and Cebula (2002), p. 35.

37. *Travel Weekly Daily Bulletin*, Article ID=36817.

CHAPTER 6

1. Winner of the 1907 Nobel Prize for Literature.

2. Gronau (1970), p. 379.

3. Smith and Jenner (2000), pp. 70 and 177.

4. On p. 379. Bull (1991, pp. 46–47) takes a different approach whereby for any given trip duration, the traveler has a "preferred" travel distance. For example, a tourist who wants to go on a two-week vacation will travel farther from home than someone who only wants to go away for a weekend. In his approach, the cost of travel (i.e., the "preferred" distance) is determined by trip duration instead of the other way around.

5. A more technical exposition of these ideas can be found in Mak and Nishimura (1979).

6. State of Hawaii, DBEDT (2002), pp. 21 and 23.

7. Mak and Moncur (1980).

8. Lancaster (1966).

9. Mak and Moncur (1980) and Rugg (1973).

10. State of Hawaii, DBEDT (2002), p. 5.

11. Sakai, Brown, and Mak (2000).

12. Smith and Jenner (2000), p. 93.

13. *Travel Industry World 2002 Yearbook* (2003), p. 120.

14. However, tourist expenditure data are notorious for their poor quality. White and Walker (1982) and Sheldon (1990), p. 33.

15. Travel Industry Association (TIA) (March 12, 2002), p. 1.

16. Mak, Moncur, and Yonamine (1977).

17. The average lodging expenditures would be $52.50, $62.60, and $68.00, respectively, if we included all types of (commercial and noncommercial) lodging facilities used.

18. Sheldon (1990), p. 29.

19. *Travel Industry World 2002 Yearbook* (2003), p. 99.

20. For example, in March 2002, Smith Travel Research reports that average hotel room rates in Hawaii ($155.87 per day) were about twice that for the entire United States ($82.04). Of course, the U.S. average masks large differences in prices among cities.

21. See, for example, Sheldon (1990), pp. 34–43.

22. See, for example, *Mathematica* (1970), p. 28, and Mak, Moncur, and Yonamine (1977).

23. Kass and Okubo (2000), p. 11, and Falvey and Gemmell (1996).

24. Bonham, et al. (1992), p. 437; Hiemstra and Ismail (1992), pp. 45–56; Pyo, Uysal, and McClellan (1991), p. 450; Sakai (1985); and Mak (1988).

25. Fujii, et al. (1985), p. 170; Fujii, et al. (1987), p. 94; Sheldon (1990), p. 44; Pyo, Uysal, and McClellan (1991), p. 450.

26. Sheldon (1990), pp. 35–38. Government control over exchange rates may also have an impact on tourist spending abroad. (See Chapter 9.)

27. An appreciation of the yen also makes imported goods cheaper in Japan, thus inducing more Japanese to shop at home and reducing overall spending abroad. However, the sharp

appreciation of the yen against the dollar in the early 1990s did not translate into significantly lower consumer prices in Japan, thus further widening the disparity between the already high prices in Japan and the rest of the world and providing even stronger incentives for Japanese to buy abroad. Mak (1996).

28. This is clearly illustrated in the case of Japanese shopping abroad. Between 1990 and 1994, the Japanese yen appreciated in value against the U.S. dollar by 42 percent. The average amount spent abroad by Japanese visitors for shopping fell from 143,000 yen to 112,000 yen, a decline of 11 percent; the amount spent on shopping in dollars increased from $987 per trip to $1,096 per trip (Mak, 1996). Although Japanese bought more (or roughly the same amount of goods abroad), they spent less yen for them.

29. *Travel Industry World 2002 Yearbook* (2003), p. 99.

30. Thus, the value of the gift need not depend on the duration of the trip.

31. Nishiyama (1998).

32. Mak (1996) and *Japan Travel Blue Book* (1999/2000), p. 227. By contrast, Henthorne (2000, p. 249) notes that among cruise ship passengers in Jamaica, older visitors were more likely to shop than younger visitors.

33. *Japan Travel Blue Book* (2000), p. 231.

34. Yamanouchi (2003), p. C1.

35. Ibid., p. C2.

36. *Mathematica* (1970).

37. Travel Journal, Inc. (March 11, 2002).

38. The Hawaii Tourism Authority's (HTA) new strategic plan focuses on achieving visitor expenditure goals instead of visitor arrivals. The Authority's marketing campaign aims to target "active vacationers" who are believed to spend more money than tourists who spend most of their vacation just lounging on the beach. It also aims to attract more business travelers to the islands. Of course, different opinions exist on what constitutes "quality tourism." The World Tourism Organization defines quality tourism *from the supply side* as "the result of a process which implies the satisfaction of all the legitimate product and service needs, requirements and expectations of the consumer, at an acceptable price, in conformity with the underlying quality determinants such as safety and security, hygiene, accessibility, transparency, authenticity, and harmony of the tourism activity concerned with its human and natural environment." Others look at it from the *demand side*. For example, in July 2002, www.Expedia.co.uk., the United Kingdom's leading online travel agency, released results of a survey of tourist offices in seventeen of the most popular holiday destinations in the world to ascertain which nationals are the best tourists in the world. Among the questions asked were: who are "the best behaved," "the most polite," "speak the local language," "try the local delicacies," and "spend and tip the most." Overall, Germans were voted the world's best tourists, followed by Americans and Japanese. Germans were judged to be the "best behaved" and best at attempting to "speak the local language"; Italians were voted most likely to "try the local delicacies"; and Americans were considered the "most polite" and "spend and tip the most."

CHAPTER 7

1. Blair and Kaserman (1985).

2. See Chapter 6.

3. This is clearly illustrated in New York City following the September 11, 2001, terrorist attack on the World Trade Center. Lodging demand fell 8 percent in New York City in the

eleven months following the attack, but hotel room revenues fell by 24 percent as a result of sharp rate cuts by hoteliers. In Washington, D.C., the decline in room demand was greater (13 percent) following the attack on the Pentagon than in New York City, but because of smaller rate cuts, the decline in room revenue was much less than in New York City. National Capital Area Tourism Research Program (August 2002).

4. That is, assuming no agreement exists among the hotel operators not to cut their rates.

5. Caves (1987), p. 6.

6. At www.ntis.gov/naics. The numbers in parentheses are the numerical designations assigned to each of these industries, beginning with two-digit numbers for broad industrial sectors to detailed six-digit industry categories. Similarly, the United Nations maintains the global industry classification system known as the International Standard Industrial Classification System (ISIC). The NAICS was designed to provide comparability with the ISIC.

7. Although it is not one of 20 sectors in the NAICS.

8. The merger was called off in March 2002, because of disagreements over final details, but the two airlines received temporary antitrust immunity from the U.S. Department of Transportation after September 11, to enable them to allocate capacity and share revenues in the interisland market. As expected, fares increased and passengers found it more difficult to obtain seats.

9. *Travel Industry World 2001 Yearbook* (2002), p. 179.

10. Similarly, Japanese government regulators expressed concern that a proposed merger between Japan Airlines and Japan Air Systems, Japan's largest and third largest airlines, would hurt competition in Japan's domestic aviation markets. To allay concerns by regulators, the two airlines proposed to give up ten (or 5.5 percent) of their landing slots at Tokyo's Haneda Airport, to be reassigned to small competitor airlines. The two airlines did complete their merger. For a brief analysis of Japan's domestic airline industry, see La Croix and Mak (2001, pp. 218–222). By contrast, no alarm was sounded by U.S. regulators when American Airlines acquired TWA in 2001.

11. It doesn't have to be the largest firm that leads.

12. Schmeltzer (April 16, 2002), p. C1.

13. *Honolulu Star Bulletin* (March 20, 2002), p. C7.

14. An alternative measure of concentration is the Herfindahl-Hirschman Index (HHI)—sometimes simply referred to as the Herfindahl Index—which came into popular use in the 1980s. The HHI is the sum of the (mathematical) square of the market share of each firm in a market. For example, if four firms make up a market and their respective market shares are 40 percent, 30 percent, 20 percent, and 10 percent, the HHI would have a value of (40 x 40) + (30 x 30) + (20 x 20) + (10 x 10) = 3,000. HHI can range from nearly zero (perfect competition) to 10,000 (monopoly). A market with an HHI of less than 1,000 is considered unconcentrated; one that lies between 1,000 and 1,800 is moderately concentrated; and one with HHI above 1,800 is highly concentrated. The advantage of the HHI over the four-firm concentration ratio is that every firm's market share is included in the HHI; its disadvantage is that it requires information on each firm's market share, which may be difficult or impossible to obtain. Interestingly, a U.S. Department of Justice study of the actual size distribution of firms within markets indicates that the HHI levels of 1,000 and 1,800 roughly correspond to four-firm concentration ratios of 50 percent and 70 percent respectively. Blair and Kaserman (1985), p. 249.

15. *Travel Industry World 2000 Yearbook* (2001), pp.174–175.

16. *Travel Industry World 2001 Yearbook* (2002), pp. 188–189.

17. Shepherd (1982).

18. Sheldon (1986).

19. Morrison (1995), p. 36.

20. Lundberg, et al. (1995), p. 117.

21. Pizam and Knowles (1994), p. 284.

22. Competition forces sellers to set their prices at their (marginal) costs of production including a reasonable profit.

23. For a discussion of the other elements besides these two, see Caves (1987), Chapter 2.

24. They exclude the values of the companies' tangible assets and intangible assets other than the value of their brand names.

25. *Business Week* (August 5, 2002). The most valuable brand name in 2002 was Coca Cola at $69.64 billion, followed by Microsoft at $64.09 billion.

26. Disney, however, argues that its real competition is not another theme park but destinations like Las Vegas or Paris (Horn, 2002).

27. Hirsch (2003), p. E2.

28. Sheldon (1984 and 1986).

29. Blair and Kaserman (1985), p. 35.

30. *Travel Industry World 2002 Yearbook* (2003), p. 221. In 1997, Congress passed legislation granting Amtrak $2.3 billion in funding with the directive that the railroad achieve financial self-sufficiency by 2003; instead, Amtrak asked Congress for more than $1.8 billion each year for 2003 and 2004. *Travel Weekly Daily Bulletin,* Article ID=37423 and Article ID=37662.

31. Perez and Mitchner (2002), p. 26. It is noteworthy that, in recognition of the relevant geographic market, such a merger required approval—which was granted—from both U.S. and European regulators. P&O Princess Cruises accepted Carnival Corporation's merger offer. Although the merger did not affect the P&O Princess brands—which include Princess Cruises and P&O Cruises—and both remained separate legal entities, they are jointly operated by a single senior executive management team. In 2003, the combined companies offered nearly 100,000 berths.

32. Roberts (1998), p. 5.

33. Economists label that response the *cross elasticity of demand.* It is calculated as the percentage change in the demand for good Y divided by the percentage change in the price of good X.

34. Blair and Kaserman (1985), p. 227.

35. Roberts (1998), p. 8.

36. Observers note that the two cater to somewhat different markets: Avis caters more to business travelers, whereas Budget caters more to leisure and off-airport markets. *Travel Weekly Daily Bulletin,* Article ID=35785.

37. *The Honolulu Advertiser* (August 22, 2002), p. C1; and *Travel Weekly Daily Bulletin,* Article ID=35785.

38. In the United States, companies convicted of antitrust violations are required to compensate their rivals or consumers treble (three times the amount of) damages inflicted plus legal fees.

39. Dwyer et al. (1990), p. 9.

40. Blair and Kaserman (1985), p. 228.

41. Bull (1991), p. 74.

42. Burgess (April 20, 2002), p. C3.

43. *Travel Industry World 2001 Yearbook* (2002), p. 185.

44. *Travel Industry World 2002 Yearbook* (2003), p. 15. However, Hilton was only the sixth largest corporate hotel chain in the world. The largest corporate hotel chain in the world is Cendant Corporation, also based in the United States, which had 6,624 hotels and 553,771 hotel rooms in 2001.

45. Foreign direct investment involves part or whole ownership and management of a business abroad.

46. Prince Hotels also marketed its rooms to non-Japanese visitors as well.

47. Caves (1996), p. 12.

48. Ibid., p. 97.

49. Ibid.

50. Dwyer et al. (1990), p. 46.

51. U.S. Department of Transportation, Bureau of Transportation Statistics at www.bts.gov/.

52. Kahn (2000).

53. Buffett (1999).

54. U.S. General Accounting Office (1997).

CHAPTER 8

1. Cox and Love (1996).

2. Chairman, Tauck Tours.

3. Plassard (1995), pp. 93–129.

4. The U.S. Department of Transportation conducts a household survey of American travel every five to seven years. As of this writing, the latest available data are for 1995; the preliminary results of the latest (2001–2002) survey will be available sometime in 2003. In the 1995 survey, 29.3 percent of the household trips were business trips, 56.8 percent were pleasure trips, and 13.9 percent were personal business trips. For individual trips, the respective percentages were 22.5 percent, 62.9 percent, and 14.6 percent.

5. For household trips, the average (mean) round-trip distance was 872 miles; for person trips, 826 miles; the average distance for car trips was 555 miles. While not exactly comparable, the Travel Industry Association's Travel Scope Study estimates that, in 2001, approximately 1.018 billion domestic trips were taken that were at least 50 miles, one way. The volume of domestic leisure travel was 767 million person trips. Domestic leisure travel increased every year between 1999 and 2002.

6. In developing countries, road transportation can mean crowded buses or trucks rather than automobiles.

7. The reference to buses here does not include charter or tour buses, which cater to a different niche market: namely, the motorcoach tour business that operates in conjunction with bus tour operators.

8. Surveys in Switzerland find that rail travel also suffers from a "psychological deficiency"; in other words, it isn't "cool" to travel by rail. Kaspar (1995), pp. 70–71.

9. Plassard (1995), pp. 93–129.

10. The original intent of this Act was to strengthen national security, not to facilitate long-distance personal travel.

11. Cox and Love (1996).

12. Corsi and Harvey (1979).

13. Gentile (2002), p. D3.

14. Miller (2002), p. A3.

15. Miller, et al. (2001), p. 358. Indeed, at the 2003 Seatrade Cruise Shipping Convention held in Miami, Florida, one travel consultant tossed out the idea of "an ultimate cruise to nowhere," a noncruising cruise. The cruise ship would be docked during the entire "cruise." For people tired of the Caribbean, they would "have the ship experience, less the port of call." *Travel Weekly Daily Bulletin*, Article ID=37070.

16. The senior vice president of Carnival Cruise Lines observed that "We're really no different in passenger demographics than Las Vegas." (Newcott, 2003, p. 45). The average age of passengers vary among cruise lines; Disney Cruise Lines, not surprisingly, attracts younger adults with children, whereas the average age of a Crystal Cruise passenger is around 60.

17. *Travel Weekly Daily Bulletin*, Article ID=35828. The reality is that there are plenty of bargains out there. Travel writer Rudy Maxa opines that "The myth of cruising as a rich person's vacation is perpetuated, oddly enough, by the people who go on cruises. They return, tell about all the food and facilities and destinations, and naturally their friends think they secretly won the lottery." Newcott (2003), p. 46.

18. *Travel Industry 2001 World Yearbook* (2002), p. 193, and *Travel Industry World 2002 Yearbook* (2003), p. 24.

19. Lundberg et al. (1995), p. 117.

20. Chaplin (2001), p. F1.

21. *Travel Weekly Daily Bulletin*, Article ID=35139.

22. *Travel Industry World 2001 Yearbook* (2002), p. 193.

23. Batsell (1998). Norwegian Cruise Line began its Seattle–Alaska service in 2000.

24. Holland America also operates one-way cruises in the reverse direction from Alaska to Vancouver.

25. Lynch (2001), p. C1. In April 2003, Norwegian Cruise Line announced that it had purchased the *SS Independence* and the *SS United States* and planned to put them back into domestic service, but not in Hawaii. Yamanouchi (2003).

26. U.S. House of Representatives (1998).

27. Magin (2003), pp. A1 and A7.

28. Therefore, Pacific Southwest Airlines (PSA), a carrier that only operated within the State of California, was not subject to CAB regulation. It was, however, regulated by the California Public Utilities Commission.

29. For example, Western Airlines promoted free champagne on every Hawaii–U.S. mainland flight. United Airlines boasted that it flew more Boeing 747 jumbo jets to more U.S. mainland cities from Hawaii than any other airline.

30. The hub-and-spoke system was in use even before deregulation, induced by the rise in energy prices in the early 1970s. Deregulation made it easier for the airlines to expand this system because of eased entry.

31. Morrison and Winston (1995), pp. 8–9.

32. They defined "effective competition" as one divided by the Herfindahl Index (1/HHI) so that the higher the ratio the greater the degree of competition. (See Chapter 7, endnote 14, for a review of the HHI).

33. Koch and Cebula (2002), p. 34.

34. Kahn (May 2, 2000).

35. That is, adjusted for inflation.

36. Kahn (May 2, 2000).

37. Winston (1998), p. 101.

38. *Travel Weekly Daily Bulletin*, Article ID=37802.

39. GAO (1996).

40. Morrison (December 1995), p. 26.

41. Morrison and Winston (1995), p. 19.

42. GAO (1996).

43. Morrison and Winston (1995), p. 82.

44. This would not apply to business travelers because they don't pay their own fares. Morrison (December 1995, p. 27) suggests that "Frequent flyer programs for business travelers are an attempt to exploit the principal–agent problem: The agent (the business traveler) makes travel decisions that are not in the best interest of the principal (his or her employer).

45. Morrison (December 1995), p. 27.

46. A New River Media interview (circa 2002).

47. For example, in February 2003, Alaska Airlines cut its highest fares by nearly 50 percent and reduced the number of coach fares to as few as six: a walk-up, a three-day, two seven-days, and two fourteen-days.

48. Caves et al. (1987).

49. Bull (1991), pp. 64–65.

50. See, for example, *The Economist* (May 24, 2001), and LaCroix and Mak (2001).

51. Kellerhals, Jr. (1999).

52. U.S. International Trade Commission (1995), p. 5. Subsequently, the European Commission (EC) filed a lawsuit with the European Court of Justice arguing that individual agreements between the EU members and the United States are illegal because aviation deals with nonmember nations are trade agreements, and hence it alone had the authority to negotiate such deals. The EC hopes to negotiate an umbrella agreement that would cover all the EU members. In November 2002, the European Court ruled that parts of the individual open skies agreements between eight of the EU members and the United States are indeed illegal, and the deals must be amended. However, it did not rule that the European Commission had the exclusive right to negotiate such agreements. (Economist.com, November 6, 2002.) The ruling, however, will allow the EC to get involved in future aviation negotiations. This means protracted negotiations between the EC and member governments. The result is that it might take quite some time before airlines are free to fly to and from Europe and within Europe.

53. Kellerhals, Jr. (1999).

54. In 1998, the number of alliances, loosely defined, totaled 502 from simple code sharing agreements to joint purchasing agreements (Association of European Airlines, 1998, p. 4). The discussions of airline alliances, as in this chapter, focus on the limited number of agreements between major airlines in the United States and Europe.

55. Using their own airline flight numbers on their partner's flights, so that a flight operated by United Airlines may also be designated a Lufthansa Airlines' flight.

56. Association of European Airlines (1998).

57. U.S. Department of Transportation (December 1999); see also, Association of European Airlines (1998).

58. LaCroix and Wolff (1995), p. 35.

CHAPTER 9

1. Todd (2002).

2. At www.shr.aaas.org/rtt/report/two.htm.

3. For country by country entry formalities for U.S. visitors, see www.traveldocs.com/nations.htm#k.

4. The first country allowed into the initial four-year experimental program was Britain on July 1, 1988, followed by Japan on December 15, 1988. Edgell (1990), p. 57.

5. CNN.com, April 19, 2003. Likewise, in 2003, Indonesia scrapped visa-free entry to visitors from thirty-seven countries, including tourists from key markets such as Japan and Australia; it continues to grant visa waivers to residents of eleven nations that grant waivers to Indonesians.

6. Ascher and Edgell (1986), p. 5.

7. Mak and White (1998).

8. Some countries also impose limits on how much of its own currency foreign tourists may bring in.

9. Edgell (1990), pp.53–54.

10. Until 1987, foreign visitors were allowed into the country only for business purposes. In 1987, restrictions were relaxed to permit a limited number of foreign tourist visits. The stated purpose of the relaxation was to diversify the economy and reduce the country's dependence on oil exports. World Tourism Organization (1994), p. 87.

11. Ibid., pp. 106–107.

12. Witt and Moutinho (1994), p. 62.

13. Edgell (1990), p. 56, and Mak and White (1992), p. 19.

14. Brown (2000), p. 109.

15. Mak and White (1988), p. 140.

16. World Tourism Organization (2001), p. 100.

17. The exchange rate was approximately NT$32 for one U.S. dollar.

18. World Tourism Organization (2001), p. 181.

19. At www.publish.gio.gov.tw/FW/past/01113062.html.

20. JTB News, January 9, 2003, accessible at www.jtb.co.jp/soumu/english/press/jtb_news/.

21. *Travel Industry World 2001 Yearbook* (2002), p.6.

22. Mak and White (1992), pp. 17–19.

23. JTB Foundation, at www.jata-net.or.jp/english/materials/2002/materials0205.htm.

24. Zhang (1990), p. 5.

25. Foreign tourists from the former Soviet Union and Eastern European countries did visit China during the late 1950s and the early 1960s, but they numbered only a few thousand. Choy and Yao (1988), p. 28.

26. Tisdell (2001), pp. 230–231.

27. Choy and Gao (1988), p. 30.

28. Zhang (1990), pp. 3–5.

29. Ibid., pp. 2–9. China classified foreign tourists into three categories. It considered tourists from Taiwan, Macau, and Hong Kong as "compatriots"; Chinese from other countries as "overseas Chinese"; and non-Chinese visitors as "foreign tourists." For additional details on the development of tourism in China, see Tisdell (2001), pp. 220–281.

30. World Tourism Organization (2001), p. 42.

31. Swanson (2003), p. 18.

32. Smith and Jenner (2000), pp. 201–221.

33. Murphy (2002), p. 24. Murphy notes that Australia has ADS, and only .3 percent of Chinese visitors overstay their visits, compared to 5.1 percent of non-ADS visitors.

34. Ibid., p. 22.

35. Mak and White (1992), pp. 21–22. Their analysis also takes into consideration differences in income and population in those countries.

36. Mak and White (1988), p. 139.

37. Children under 12 pay half the amount. For those interested in minutiae, the Kansai airport passenger terminal, an architectural achievement and a tourist attraction itself, is the longest building in the world.

38. The lower allowance for returning Japanese visitors may be intended to protect the domestic tobacco industry. It is noteworthy that the Japanese government owns two-thirds of the outstanding shares of Japan Tobacco. LaCroix and Mak (2001), pp. 233–234.

39. Edgell (1990), p. 55.

40. Mak (1996), p. 27.

41. Estimates vary from 100 million to 200 million Mexicans who crossed into the United States by road on day trips in 1997.

42. Fisher (1996), p. 400.

43. Davila et al. (1999).

CHAPTER 10

1. World Tourism Organization.

2. Smith and Wilton (1997), p. 250.

3. Another way to put it is that we either have the wheat or the flour, but not both; thus, we don't count both goods when tallying what was actually produced in the economy.

4. Ignoring for the moment that there are also intermediate goods used in growing wheat.

5. Okubo and Planting (1998).

6. Kass and Okubo (2000).

7. The BEA produced a range of estimates: "high," "medium," and "low." Only the "medium" estimates are reported and discussed in this chapter.

8. U.S. households account for nearly 43 percent of *total* travel and tourism spending in the United States.

9. The TTSA estimates of tourism demand also exclude expenditures on consumer durables (e.g., automobiles and campers), imputed rents from vacation homes and time shares, skiing, health spas, financial services, and retail food (off-premises). Hence, the current TTSAs for the United States are still work in progress.

10. "Significant" in that "the industries' revenues and profits would be substantially affected if tourism ceased to exist." Okubo and Planting (1998).

11. Smith and Wilton (1997, p. 251) refer to goods and services "for which a significant portion of total demand comes from tourists" as "tourism commodities," and tourism commodities can be produced either by "tourism industries" or "nontourism industries."

12. U.S. Bureau of Economic Analysis (BEA), at www.bea.doc.gov/bea/dn2/gposhr.htm# 1994-2000.

13. The estimates of tourism employment do not include self-employment; hence, total employment in tourism is understated in the TTSAs.

14. Bull (1991), pp. 146–147, and Brown (2000), p. 57.

15. Ibid.

16. A brief primer on tourism multipliers is presented in the Appendix.

17. The WTTC also publishes tourism satellite accounts for selected (individual) countries, such as the United States.

18. One could argue that the inclusion of "indirect" or multiplier effects no longer entitles the WTTC tourism satellite accounts to be called an "account," because the estimates are no longer derived using accounting procedures. They are numbers generated, in part, from a model.

19. For critiques of the WTTC methodology, see Boskin (1996) and Smith and Wilton (1997).

20. Using the same methodology for the United States, the WTTC estimates that in 2000, travel and tourism spending by U.S. households, businesses, government, and international travelers totaled $1,001.9 billion or more than twice of that (i.e., $461 billion) estimated by the BEA for 1997. Consistently, WTTC produced higher estimates of travel and tourism's macroeconomic impacts than BEA. According to the WTTC, the travel and tourism industries (T&T Industry) accounted for (direct only) $496.4 billion, or 5.4 percent of the U.S. gross domestic product in 2000; including the indirect effects, the travel and tourism industries accounted for 9.6 percent of U.S. GDP. The WTTC estimates that the larger "tourism economy" accounted (direct and indirect) for nearly 12 percent of the U.S. gross domestic product in 2000. World Travel and Tourism Council, United States Travel & Tourism Satellite Account (2000), p. 1.

21. See, for example, Boskin (1996) and Smith and Wilton (1997).

22. Frechtling (1994), p. 362.

23. Mitchell (1970), p. 4.

24. Indirect taxes are taxes levied on transactions in goods and services, such as excise and sales taxes, and not directly on personal income.

25. Mitchell (1970), pp. 4–6.

26. The two most popular multiplier models in use today are *ad hoc* and *input-output* models (Fletcher, 1994, pp. 475–479). Ad hoc models are variants of the simple Keynesian multipliers first encountered by students in introductory macroeconomics courses. Because such models do not contain information on the flow of expenditures between industries and resource suppliers, they do not have the wealth of information contained in input-output models. An input-output (I-O) model is a mathematical representation of an economy depicting sales and purchases of goods and services among the producing industries, buyers, and resource owners (e.g., labor, capital, and land) (Fletcher, 1994, pp. 480–481). In this chapter, we focus on multipliers developed from input-output models of the economy.

27. Some of the blame must be assigned to authors who, in the interest of simplifying their explanations, make the mistake of using the well-known simple Keynesian multiplier to illustrate the concept of tourism multipliers. Unfortunately, the simple Keynesian multiplier does not distinguish between "output" and "income."

28. See, Fletcher (1994, pp. 480–481) for a brief description of input-output analysis.

29. Household earnings are defined as: wages and salaries + proprietors' income + director's fees + employer contributions to health insurance (personal contributions to social insurance). They are comprised largely of labor income. Thus, "household earnings" are different from the broader definition of "income" used earlier in this chapter.

30. Elliott (2002), p. 8.

CHAPTER 11

1. Brown (2000).

2. Of course, the decisions and actions of tourists can also affect (i.e., impose externalities on) other tourists. For example, adding a few more tourists to a crowded beach reduces the enjoyment of other beach-goers, and many of them may be other tourists.

3. Sandler (2001), p. 58.

4. Mitchell (1970), p.1, and World Tourism Organization (1994), p. 8.

5. On the other hand, an increase in a country's tourism exports also increases the demand for its currency abroad, thus resulting in the appreciation of its currency, all else being equal. The currency appreciation makes the country's other exports more expensive to foreign buyers. Thus, tourism's growth may retard the growth of a nation's other exports (Copeland, 1991). However, I am unaware of any empirical evidence showing that this "Dutch disease" effect has actually occurred in any country as a result of tourism development.

6. Dwyer, Findlay, and Forsyth (1990) and Heller and Heller (1973). Nonresident investment may not always increase the productive capacity of the local economy. Consider the case where a nonresident investor buys an existing hotel; a transfer of ownership occurs, but not a net increase in hotel capacity. Foreign direct investment in tourism yields net benefits if a net addition to investment and tourist flows occurs.

7. For example, since the 1960s, tourism and population have been growing faster in Hawaii's rural outer islands than in urban Honolulu, reversing the trend in urban population drift since the 1930s.

8. Cox, Fox, and Bowen (1995).

9. See, for example, Judd (2003).

10. Mitchell (1970); Dwyer, Findlay, and Forsyth (1970); and Archer (1977).

11. Frechtling (1994); State of Hawaii (1978), and Mathematica Inc. (1970).

12. A tariff is a tax on imports.

13. Gade and Adkins (1990).

14. Ebel (1990), Chapter 6.

15. Bird (1992), p.1155.

16. Mak (1991).

17. Mathematica (1970).

18. However, to the extent that goods purchased by tourists are also consumed in large quantities by locals, high prices also reduce the economic welfare of domestic consumers and thus impose a cost on the local economy .

19. For example, government-owned stores where essentially only foreigners may shop. Curiously, they were called "Friendship Stores."

20. If permitted, it could also induce labor immigration. For example, there are more foreign guest workers in Saipan (Commonwealth of the Northern Marianas) than there are local residents. Immigration dampens the upward wage pressure, reducing the net benefit of tourism to local labor.

21. Liu and Var (1986); Crandall (1994), pp. 414–417; and Mason and Cheyne (2000).

22. Brown (2000), pp. 56–59 and 66–78; Crandall (1994), p. 414–417; Pizam (1978); and Mason and Cheyne (2000).

23. However, tourism is not alone in generating these negative environmental spillover effects; other forms of development—such as extractive, agriculture, textile, and heavy manufacturing—may also produce undesirable side effects. Brown (2000), pp. 50–52.

24. See, for example, Pizam (1978); Liu and Var (1986); and State of Hawaii (1989).

25. *Newsweek International* (July 22/29, 2002), p. 46. In the United States, the guest capacity of a hotel is measured by the number of "rooms"; in Europe, and in many other countries, a hotel's guest capacity is measured by the number of "beds."

26. State of Hawaii (1989), p. 6.

27. The word "marginal" means "incremental" or "additional."

28. Why not stop at six? The answer is that you still received some satisfaction (1 util) from eating the sixth *sushi*, and you don't know that the next one will give you no more satisfaction until you've eaten it. So you eat the seventh *sushi*, after which you stop. Of course, you may not like *sushi* (i.e., the expected marginal benefit from the first one is negative) and thus choose not to eat any *sushi* at the party.

29. If you have to pay for the *sushi*, then the marginal cost is no longer zero, and you end up eating fewer *sushi*.

30. Bird, (1992), p. 1147.

31. It may not be feasible if collection costs are high.

32. Bird (1992), pp. 1151–1152.

33. See, for example, Dixon et al. (2000), and Chapter 12 for an explanation of this "fairness" rationale.

34. Clarke and Ng (1993).

35. Designing an appropriate access charge or user fee system for tourist access to public resources and facilities is different from designing a general tax system for tourism.

36. Bird (1992), p. 1147; Copeland (1989), p.1; Gray (1974), p. 393–394; and Dixon et al. (2001), p. 19.

37. Parkin (2000), p. G-2. Stigler (1966) defines economic rent as "the surplus of earnings of what can be earned in the next best alternative." Thus, if the next best alternative is a competitive (or, normal) rate of return, then economic rent is return in excess of the normal rate of return.

38. Bird (1992), Copeland (1989), Gray (1974), and Dixon et al. (2001).

39. The tourist industry may itself persuade the government to regulate entry, but would object to any new taxes that would transfer any rent to the government. For example, during the early 1970s, hotel operators on the Island of Hawaii called for the government to put a halt to additional hotel construction until the annual average islandwide hotel occupancy rate reached 80 percent; at the same time, hoteliers in Hawaii opposed an attempt to impose a hotel room tax. Ebel and Mak (1974), pp. 11–14.

40. Bird (1992), p. 1148.

41. Copeland (1989), and Clarke and Ng (1993).

42. Tisdell (1983), and Clarke and Ng (1993).

43. Using *transfer pricing*. Transfer price is the internal price between subsidiaries of a vertically integrated business (Newlon, 1999). For example, if a tour company owns hotels in a destination with high income/profits tax rates, the company's hotel subsidiary can reduce its tax liability by selling hotel rooms at below-market prices to its parent tour company, assuming that the tour company pays taxes in a lower tax jurisdiction. Through this internal pricing arrangement, profits from the hotel company are transferred from the high tax jurisdiction to the parent tour company that is located in a low tax jurisdiction.

44. To the extent that profits are reflected (i.e., capitalized) in the market values of businesses, Sakai and Mak (1991) suggest that one solution is to tax the capital gains when these tourist businesses are finally sold or transferred. However, this solution is not without problems.

45. Development agreements are agreements based on bargaining between the developer and the government, thus implying consent to pay on the part of the developer.

46. Frank and Rhodes (1987), pp. 47–48, and Mak (1993).

47. Callies (1992).

48. Callies and Grant (1991).

49. Fiscal incentives are also widely used by state and local governments in the United States to stimulate local investment. See Fisher (1996), pp. 619–623.

50. Zee et al. (2002).

51. Zee et al.(2002), pp. 2–3.

52. Bird (1992), p. 1155.

53. Wanhill (1995).

54. Zee et al. (2002).

55. Sinclair and Stabler (1997), pp. 178–179.

56. Wanhill (1995), p. 39.

57. Zee et al. (2002), p. 1.

58. Brown (2000).

59. By contrast, when a female member of my traveling group in Kosrae went swimming in the ocean, she wrapped a towel around her legs to hide them and only discarded it after she was in the water.

60. For other suggestions, see Vanhove (1997).

61. Wilkinson (1989).

62. World Tourism Organization (1994), p. 31, and *Newsweek International* (2002).

CHAPTER 12

1. U.S. Supreme Court Justice.

2. ACIR (1994).

3. Among them Poway (California), Del Mar (California), Lockport (New York), Martin County (Florida), Chattanooga (Tennessee), Converse County (Wyoming), and Osaka (Japan).

4. A$ refers to the Australia dollar.

5. The country's Tourism Task Force now wants to make the $10 Ansett levy permanent with money raised from the levy–around A$100 million—to be used to fund the Australian Tourism Commission and See Australia.

6. Fairbanks (2002), p. F6.

7. Accessed at www.traveltax.msu.edu/news/Stores/nelson3.htm.

8. World Travel and Tourism Council (1997), p. 20.

9. ACIR (1994), p. 12.

10. Loyacono and Mackey (1991), p. 22.

11. See, for example, Seiglie (1990).

12. Rees (1996), p. 5.

13. Loyacono and Mackey (1991).

14. National Public Radio (August 20, 2002). AAA reports that early school starts across the country were expected to cause a slight decline in travel during the Labor Day holiday.

15. Accessed at www.traveltax.msu.edu/.

16. Kenyon (1999), p. 363, defines *tax effort* as "the extent to which a government uses the potential receipts—generating capacity (tax or revenue bases) available to it."

17. Although it should be noted that tourists purchase more than just these four items.

Excluded from the WTTC Tax Barometer are sightseeing tours, entertainment, souvenir purchases, and so on.

18. It is possible to compute a trend for each city using annual information on the tax effort for the individual cities.

19. The problem is further complicated by differential changes in currency exchange rates over time, because prices and tax bills in local currencies are converted to U.S. dollars. For example, suppose total taxes for a trip to Tokyo was 12,000 yen in 1994 and stayed constant through 2002; if the yen–dollar exchange rate was 120 yen to the dollar in 1994, the tax bill, when converted to U.S. dollars, would have been $100. If the exchange rate in 2002 became 100 yen to the dollar (i.e., the yen appreciated against the U.S. dollar), the 12,000 yen tax bill would have been equivalent to $120. The dollar-denominated tax bill will have increased by 20 percent even though no increases in tax rates occurred in Japan.

20. There were no rental cars in Beijing; hence, neither the price of a rental car nor the tax on it is included in the Tax Barometer for that city.

21. It is possible to answer that question by analyzing the detailed information provided for each city. For example, by applying "what-if" analysis—what if prices in Buenos Aires for hotel rooms, car rentals, and meals were the same as in New York City—one could ascertain the portion of the difference in their travel taxes (i.e., $117.79 = $345.79 - $228) caused by differences in the prices of vacation goods and the portion due to differences in their tax rates. It turns out that the differences in their tax rates account for 69 percent of the difference in total taxes paid, and the difference in the tax base accounts for the remaining 31 percent. In sum, both higher prices (tax base) and higher tax rates account for the higher tax bill in Buenos Aires.

22. Fisher (1996), p. 31.

23. Of course, national governments also perform this important function just as subnational governments actively try to stabilize employment, promote economic growth, and redistribute income and resources within their jurisdictions.

24. Bruce (1998), p. 371.

25. A corporation is treated as an artificial person; hence the corporate income tax is a direct tax.

26. An excise tax is a tax levied on the purchase or sale of a good or service.

27. ACIR (1994).

28. Tait (1999), pp. 422–426. Ebrill et al. (2001) observed that 123 out of 180 countries in the world have adopted the VAT; only the United States and Australia, among industrialized countries, do not use a VAT. See Wanhill (1995) for the application of the VAT in tourism among the European Union countries. The VAT is a national sales tax. Unlike the sales tax in the United States, which is levied on sales at the retail stage, the VAT is levied on the value-added amount at each stage of production or sales; that is, it taxes the increase in the value of the goods and services as they go from one firm to another until they reach the final consumer. Because value added = sales – value of intermediate inputs, value added consists of wages and salaries, profits, rents, and interest paid (i.e., value added is essentially income). Although the VAT can be levied on income, in most cases it is levied on consumption. In a consumption-based VAT, for every taxable period, a vendor subtracts the VAT taxes he paid on his purchases from the VAT tax revenues he receives from his own sales, and the difference is his tax liability to the tax collector. In this way, the "value-added" is never actually calculated, even though it is called a value-added tax. The advantage of the VAT is that it largely eliminates tax pyramiding; that is, it would not be levied several times on the same good as it goes through different

stages of distribution. On the other hand, it induces a one-time jump in the prices of commodities (Tait, 1999, p. 423). Some countries (e.g., the EU countries) allow refunds on VAT paid by tourists on merchandise leaving the country.

29. In most travel destinations, the hotel room tax is an *ad valorem* tax; that is, the tax is stated as a percentage of the rental price of the room. The analysis of the burden of an ad valorem tax is essentially the same as that for a specific dollar tax (see Mak, 1988).

30. He may in turn pass it on to his employees by asking them to accept lower wage and salary increases than they would otherwise in the next round of wage and salary negotiations.

31. Bruce (1998), p. 420.

32. Bruce (1998), p. 417.

33. And in the long run, there may be fewer hotel rooms built. Even in the short-run, say within a year, the supply of "transient accommodations" in Honolulu, for example, is quite "elastic" as rooms—especially condominium rentals—move in and out of short-term rentals.

34. Fujii, Khaled, Mak (1985); Mak (1988); and Bonham et al., (1992).

35. Blair, Giarratani, and Spiro (1987).

36. Gentry (1999), p. 262.

37. Economists refer to this as the "neutrality principle."

38. Bruce (1998), pp. 459–460. Economists refer to this rule as the "inverse elasticity rule," which states that "the optimal commodity tax rate on each good is proportional to the inverse of its own price elasticity." (Bruce, 1998, pp. 459–460). That is, higher tax rates should be imposed on goods with lower price elasticities of demand.

39. Phares (1999), pp. 381–383.

40. Phares (1980).

41. Gade and Adkins (1990).

42. See, for example, Miklius, Moncur, and Leung (1989), vol. 2.

43. That is, the tax-inclusive price of the commodity must be higher than before the tax was levied.

44. Fujii, Khaled, and Mak (1985).

45. Fisher (1996), p. 174.

46. A distinction exists between benefit taxes and user charges. A benefit tax is an involuntary payment. In the United States, a good example of a benefit tax is the Social Security tax, which entitles the payer to a future benefit.

47. Fisher (1996), p. 183.

48. Phares (1999), p. 381.

49. ACIR (1989), p. 192.

50. Indeed, for this reason, Bill Fox (University of Tennessee–Knoxville) argues that *tax exporting* in tourism should be defined to apply only to taxes collected from tourists in excess of the cost of services provided to them.

51. ACIR (1989), p. 192.

52. Ulbrich (1999), pp. 188–190; Callies (1992), p. 170; and World Tourism Organization (1994), p. 44.

53. ACIR (1994) p. 30.

54. Recall from Chapter 2 that the United States has stopped funding destination tourism promotion; however, state and local governments in the United States still use public funds to promote tourism.

55. Diamond (1969), p. 53.

56. Bonham and Mak (1996), p. 3.

57. At www.traveltax.msu.edu/news/Stories/ottawacitizen8.htm.

58. *Travel Business Analyst* (1992), p. 9.

59. See, for example, Whitney (2002).

60. Dwyer and Forsyth (1993).

61. Selective advertising can also affect industry demand. For example, advertising and promotional expenditures by Coca Cola Company may increase consumer demand for all Coke soft drinks including those produced by Pepsi Cola as well as generic brands.

62. This is the "nonrival" feature of generic advertising.

63. This is the "nonexcludable" feature of generic advertising. Economists refer to goods that are "nonrival" and "nonexcludable" as "pure public goods."

64. Mok (1986).

65. Bonham and Mak (1996), pp.5–6.

66. Olson (1971 and 1982).

67. Bonham and Mak (1996), pp. 8–9.

68. Mak and Miklius (1990).

69. Bruce (1998), p. 461.

70. *Mathematica* (1970), State of Hawaii (1978), and U.S. Travel Data Center (1979).

71. Bruce (1998), p. 461.

72. Gentry (1999), p. 262.

73. In public finance, this is referred to as the "accountability principle." See ACIR (1989), pp. 142–143 and 190.

74. See, for example, Fox and Luna (2003).

CHAPTER 13

1. At www.nature.nps.gov/stats/.

2. *Travel Industry World 2002 Yearbook* (2003), p. 99.

3. There are many definitions of "ecotourism." Generally, it is agreed that ecotourism is nature-based and incorporates a desire to minimize negative impacts on the environment and society (The World Bank, 2002, p. 2). For a review of the various definitions and the policy issues surrounding ecotourism development, see Brandon (1996).

4. *Newsweek International* (2002), p. 42. Amaro (1999) notes that nature-based tourism has grown at an annual rate of 10 percent in the 1990s, or more than twice the rate of growth of international tourism.

5. Ecotourism Society (1998).

6. *Newsweek International* (2002), p. 43.

7. Dixon et al. (2001), p. xi.

8. Cesar et al. (2002).

9. At www.sustainabletravel.org.

10. Mastny (2002), p. 114.

11. Pianin (2002), p. 31. However, environmentalists are outraged by a proposal from Mandalay Bay Resort in Las Vegas to build a $10 million glass-enclosed panda exhibit next to its casinos that could generate as much as $50 million a year for panda conservation projects in China.

12. Seltzer (2002).

13. Ibid.

14. Mak and Moncur (1998), pp. 221–222.

15. *Newsweek International* (2002), p. 44.

16. Mastny (2002), p. 110.

17. Domroes (2001).

18. Tabatchnaia-Tamirisa et al. (1997), p. 390.

19. *Newsweek International* (2002), p. 43.

20. Dixon et al. (2001), p. xi. However, because tourists are not year-round residents, they contribute only 5 percent of the total waste; residents by far are the bigger waste generators. In countries that are less dependent on tourism than St. Lucia, residents pose far greater risks to the environment than tourists.

21. Mastny (2002), p. 110.

22. Ibid.

23. *Newsweek International* (2002), p. 43.

24. Field and Field (2002), p.16.

25. Mak and Moncur (1998), p. 218.

26. In 2002, environmentalists in California sued several cruise lines alleging that they violated a 1999 state law by illegally dumping ballast water from their cruise ships near shore, thus endangering ecosystems by introducing nonnative species. Davis (2002), p. C2.

27. Mastny (2002), p. 109.

28. Dixon et al. (2001), p. xi.

29. EPA (2000).

30. Vieitas et al. (1999).

31. Field and Field (2002), p. 5.

32. www.CNN.COM (November 12, 2002).

33. World Travel and Tourism Council et al. (2002), p. 65.

34. Shirkey (2002).

35. Economists refer to this tragedy as the "tragedy of the commons."

36. Anderson and Hill (1996).

37. And if you don't clean it, an "opportunity cost" of money lost occurs, because you won't be getting the bribe.

38. If the decision is made democratically, the median voter theorem states that the median voter will determine the cleanliness standard and it will not be an extreme one. Fisher (1996), p. 64.

39. This is a simple exposition of the famous Coase theorem in economics (see, e.g., Parkin, 2000, pp.435–436). The theorem demonstrates that not every market failure involving an externality requires government intervention to resolve.

40. Dixon et al. (2001), p. 16.

41. At www.traveltax.msu.edu/news/Stories/dailytelegraph9.htm.

42. World Travel & Tourism Council et al. (2002), pp. 49–50.

43. Mastny (2002), p. 121, and Dixon et al. (2001), p. 13.

44. Mastny (2002), p. 121.

45. World Tourism Organization (2002).

46. Ibid.

47. Mak and Moncur (1998).

48. In recent years, several major cruise lines were fined for illegal dumping and falsifying records. Adams (2002), pp. F1 and F2; see also Dawson (2002), p. 5.

49. Yamanouchi (October 25, 2002) and Dawson (2002), p. 5.

50. Dawson (2002), p. 5.

51. Hansen (2002).

52. Davis (2002), p. C2.

53. Mak and Moncur (1998).

54. Todd (2001), p. 16.

55. See, e.g., Dixon et al. (2001), p. 14, and International Monetary Fund et al. (2002), p. 32.

56. International Monetary Fund et al. (2002), p. 33.

57. International Monetary Fund (2002), p. 32.

58. Dixon et al. (2001), p. 14. On the other hand, removing a subsidy can also be effective in reducing pollution. For example, terminating the subsidy of electricity use could induce energy conservation and reduce air pollution (International Monetary Fund et al., 2002, pp. 20–23.) In the Republic of Belau, utility rates charged to hotels (and everyone else) are only a small fraction of the true cost of electricity generation (Mak, 1991).

59. International Monetary Fund et al. (2002), p. 32.

60. Mak and Moncur (1998), p. 217.

61. Lindberg et al. (2000), p. 557.

62. Ibid. (p. 559).

63. Wanhill (2000), p.567.

64. Knapman and Stoeckl (1995), pp. 5–15.

65. As with tourist visits to wild game reserves in Africa. The World Bank (2002).

66. Forsyth, Dwyer, and Clarke (1995).

67. Mak and Moncur (1998).

68. Suan (1989), however, suggests that when consumers have different preferences and valuations of their time, some visitors will no doubt be willing to pay more than the admission charge. Hence, not all the rent is likely to be appropriated by an admission charge.

69. Likewise, strong opposition from tour operators persuaded the Honolulu City Council to reduce nonresident tourist admission fees at Hanauma Bay Nature Reserve from $5 per person to $3 in 1996.

70. International Monetary Fund et al. (2002), p. 26.

71. International Monetary Fund et al. (2002), pp. 25–26, and Mastny (2002), p. 114.

72. Mak and Moncur (1995).

73. Dimara and Skuras (1998).

74. Waite (2002), pp. A1–A2.

75. Parkin (2000), p. 393.

CHAPTER 14

1. The Nature Conservancy.

2. Poon (1993), p.7.

3. Ibid., pp. 4–6.

4. Perez-Salom (2001).

5. NGOs are nongovernmental organizations. Examples of NGOs in the United States interested in the protection of the environment include the Nature Conservancy and the Sierra Club.

6. Briassoulis and van der Straaten (2000), p. 7, and Hunter and Green (1995), Chapter 3.

7. At www.doc.mmu.ac.uk/aric/eae/Sustainability/Older/Brundtland_Report.html.

8. The World Bank (2003), p. 13.

9. For a summary and chronology of actions taken by international organizations and conventions to promote sustainable tourism, see Perez-Salom (2001). In 1997, the members of the WTO signed the Mele Declaration, which called for ethics in tourism, the reduction of unsustainable patterns of consumption, and the conservation of natural and cultural diversity. Later in the same year, the WTO issued the Manila Declaration on the Social Impact of Tourism; the Manila Declaration identified ten principles of sustainable tourism, including the greater involvement of communities in planning, evaluation of tourism policies, improvement of people's standard of living through tourism, and the sensitization of visitors to local cultures.

10. See, for example, Perez-Salom (2001), p. 812, footnote # 54; Hunter and Green (1995), pp. 69–78; and Fyall and Garrod (1997), pp. 52–53.

11. WTO (2002).

12. Quoting from WTO (2002).

13. Of course, people's preferences can change over time, and balancing the interests of the current and future generations may not be as simple as might be suggested here.

14. That is, as high a level of "utility."

15. The World Bank (2003), p. 14.

16. The traditional, narrow definition of capital includes physical (e.g., buildings and equipment) and human capital (education, training, and work experience).

17. The World Bank (2003), pp. 14–15; Fyall and Garrod (1997), pp. 56–57, and Krautkraemer (2002), pp. 28–37.

18. Krautkraemer (2002), p. 36.

19. Fyall and Garrod (1997), p.57, and Hunter (1997), p. 853. Economists use the term "elasticity of substitution" to refer to different degrees of resource substitutability.

20. The World Bank (2003,) p. 25, and Krautkraemer (2001), p. 32.

21. The law of diminishing returns states that if you keep increasing one input and hold the other input(s) constant, the resulting increase in total output becomes smaller and smaller over time; eventually total output reaches a peak and then declines.

22. Krautkraemer (2002), pp. 33–34.

23. Ibid., p. 39.

24. The two creatures are the Kauai cave amphipod and the Kauai blind big-eyed wolf spider. The final amount set aside was 272 acres.

25. Industrial Economics, Inc. (2002).

26. TenBruggencate (2002), p. B1.

27. See, for example, Cesar et al. (2002), and Imber et al. (1991).

28. See, for example, Sinclair and Stabler (1997), pp. 187–198; Fyall and Garrod (1997), pp. 62–67; and Field and Field (2002), Chapter 7.

29. Tietenberg (1994), p. 55.

30. Field and Field (2002), pp. 150–156.

31. The word "contingent" is added because the CV method tries to get people to reveal what they would do in different, hypothetical (i.e., contingent) situations.

32. See, for example, Mitchell and Carson (1989).

33. See, for example, Field and Field (2001), pp. 155–158.

34. Tietenberg (1994), p. 58.

35. See www.world-tourism.org/sustainable/wssd/brochure-eng.htm. By contrast, Stabler (1997), p. 299, notes that "Sustainability and sustainable tourism is concerned with the human use of the environment."

36. At www.world-tourism.org/sustainable/wssd/brochure-eng.htm.

37. World Bank (2003), pp. 1 and 183. Of course, defining poverty is far more complex than simply drawing a minimum income line. For a discussion of the difficulties in defining poverty, see Naya (2002), pp. 68–69.

38. World Bank (2003), p. 184.

39. Asia is home to two-thirds of the world's poor.

40. WTO (2002), p. 10.

41. Ibid., pp. 14–15.

42. Dollar and Kraay (2001). In their study, the "poor" were defined as those in the lowest 20 percent of the income distribution.

43. Ibid., p. 32.

44. Naya (2002), pp. 68–69.

45. The ST-EP project, to date, has 3 components: (1) an international foundation to attract new, dedicated financing from business, philanthropic, and government sources; (2) a research base to identify linkages, principles, and model applications; and (3) an operational framework that provides incentives and promotes good practices among companies, consumers, and communities.

46. World Bank (2003), p. 59.

47. The terms "fragile lands" and "marginal agricultural lands" are often used interchangeably.

48. World Bank (2003), pp. 68–69.

49. "Shortsightedness" does not necessarily imply a character defect. Economists refer to shortsighted people as having "high personal discount rates." They value today more highly than tomorrow.

50. See, for example, World Bank (2003), pp. 23–26. A recent study released by the Pew Research Center for the People and the Press, which surveyed over 38,000 people in 44 countries, found that most people, in 2002, regarded the economy as their most important personal problem (p. 30). On global threats, a higher percentage of Canadians (44 percent) than Americans (23 percent) thought pollution and the environment posed greater danger to the world; in Africa, the leading concern is AIDS and infectious diseases.

51. World Tourism Organization (2000), p. 11.

52. Sinclair and Stabler (1997), p. 213.

53. World Bank (2003), p. 15.

54. Butcher (1997).

55. Stabler (1997), p. 14.

56. Butcher (1997).

57. Goodall and Stabler (1997), p. 298.

CHAPTER 15

1. Father of Keynesian economics.

2. Air Transportation Association at www.airlines.org.

3. Navarro and Spencer (2001), p. 22.

4. *Travel Industry World 2001 Yearbook* (2002), p. 4.

5. *Chicago Fed Letter* (February 2002). The National Bureau of Economic Research announced that the U.S. economy entered into recession in March 2001.

6. The Air Transportation Safety and System Stabilization Act of September 2001 pro-

vided $4.5 billion in grants to passenger carriers and $.5 billion to freight carriers. The law also limited third-party liability damage to $100 million per incident . Lenain et al. (2002), p. 19.

7. Ibid., pp. 13–16.

8. RPM is one fare paying passenger transported one mile.

9. Air Transport Association (March, 2002), p. 3.

10. The Air Transport Association reports that airlines began cutting their domestic airfares (relative to the same months in the previous year) in March 2001. In August 2001, the average domestic fare for the major carriers (excluding Southwest Airlines) was 12.6 percent lower than in the same month in 2000. In October, 2001, it was 19.2 percent lower than in 2000. Hence not all the fare cuts following September eleven can be attributed to the terrorist attacks.

11. Miller (2002), p. A3.

12. DRI-WEFA (2002).

13. At www.tia.org/Press/1R03_stateofindustry.asp.

14. *Travel Industry World 2001 Yearbook* (2002), pp. 5–6.

15. At www.world-tourism.org/newsroom/Releases/more_releases//june2002/data.htm.

16. At www.world-tourism.org/newsroom/Releases/2003/jan/numbers2002.htm.

17. *Travel Industry World 2002 Yearbook* (2003), p. 5.

18. WTO (November 2001), p. 7.

19. *Travel Industry World 2001 Yearbook* (2002), p. 6.

20. WTO (November, 2001), p. 12.

21. World Tourism Organization (November 2001) and Pizam and Fleischer (2002).

22. WSJ.com (February 24, 2003).

23. Tarlow (2002), pp. 48–49. To highlight this point, before and during the 2003 war in Iraq, the Federal Aviation Administration (FAA) imposed flight restrictions over Disney World and Disneyland.

24. For example, OECD estimates that an increase in public military-security spending by 1 percent of gross domestic product (GDP) and .5 percent of GDP in private security spending will reduce real GDP growth by .7 percent after five years. Lenain et al. (2002), p. 32.

25. Rhoads (2002), p. D1.

26. Global climate change has also been mentioned as a potentially significant influence on future tourism flows (Muller, 2001, pp. 62–63, and Lohman, 2001, pp. 286–288). For example, global warming could result in the inundation of coastal areas, rising snow lines, capricious weather, and more frequent natural disasters. It can also produce significant changes in major ecosystems that yield valuable service amenities in tourism. For example, coral reefs are highly sensitive and vulnerable to hot temperatures, because hot temperatures cause the corals to bleach and eventually die; indeed, Cornell University marine ecologist, Drew Harvell, remarked that "In a way, corals are the canaries in the coal mine for global warming" (Ten-Bruggencate, 2003). Wall and Badke (1994) argue that much more research needs to be done on the implications of global climate change on tourism. The World Tourism Organization (WTO) organized the first International Conference on Climate Change and Tourism in Djerba, Tunisia, April 9–11, 2003.

27. Todd (2002), p. 12.

28. *The UNESCO Courier* (1999), p. 27.

29. The World Bank predicts global income will grow at 3 percent per year for the next 50 years (World Bank, 2003, p. 4). It also predicts a record period of economic growth in developing countries over the next fifteen years (2003–2018), with China and India leading the way. World Bank (2003), p. 184.

30. Clark (2002), pp. 72–73.

31. For readers interested in minutiae, the United States is the only industrialized country in the world that has not yet legislated paid vacations. Kleiman (2003).

32. Tarlow (2002), pp. 49–50.

33. Mak (1996), and Tarlow (2002), p. 49.

34. Todd (2002), pp. 15–16.

35. U.S. Department of Commerce (1996).

36. *Newsweek International* (2002), and Mastny (2002), p. 103.

37. *Newsweek International* (2002), pp. 36–37.

38. WTO, 1998 news release.

39. CNN.com (October 8, 2002). In 2002, China was the fifth most popular international tourist destination after the United States, Spain, France, and Italy.

40. Eberstadt (2000).

41. Sakai, Brown, and Mak (2000).

42. Moffett (2003).

43. Bergsma (2002), p. 246.

44. A good example of one-to-one marketing is Amazon.com.

45. For example, the 17-year-old *Consumer Reports Travel Letter* published its last issue in January 2003, because it could not compete against the Internet. The executive director of the nonprofit Consumer Union that published the travel letter explained that so much travel information is now available for free on the Internet that people are unwilling to purchase printed material.

46. Leu (2002), p. 270.

47. Tarlow (2002), p. 49.

48. Mastny (2002), p.101.

49. Nor is it true in all destinations. See, for example, World Tourism Organization (1994).

50. There is growing concern that tighter travel restrictions imposed after September 11, 2001, may impede the flow of immigrant workers into the United States and result in a labor shortage in the travel industry. *Travel Weekly Daily Bulletin*, Article ID=37417.

51. Goodall and Stabler (1997), p. 299.

52. One of the most famous was Thomas Malthus' prediction during the late nineteenth century that population growth will outstrip growth in food supply, thus resulting in dire consequences for humankind. More recently, "limits to growth" warnings, first issued by the Club of Rome in 1972 and in sequels, have not come to pass. Lomborg and Rubin (2002), pp. 42–44.

53. Check out the April 2001 and November 2002 issues of the *Conde Nast Traveler* magazine for some of the anticipated innovations just ahead (in the next ten to fifteen years and beyond) in auto and air travel, ships, airports, hotels, and personal travel gadgets.

GLOSSARY OF ECONOMIC TERMS

Accountability Principle. The principle, in public finance, that the responsibility to raise revenue should go hand-in-hand with the responsibility to spend.

Agent. An individual (person or institution) authorized by another to act on its behalf. For example, a travel agent is authorized by the travel company, such as an airline, to sell its products.

Alliance. As in airline alliance, in which a group of airlines agrees to collaborate and coordinate their business activities, yet remain as separate companies.

Antitrust Laws. Laws that regulate monopolies and oligopolies and prohibit certain kinds of anticompetitive market behavior.

Appreciation. As in currency appreciation. If one currency appreciates in value against another currency, it has increased in value relative to the other currency. More units of the other currency must be given in exchange for one unit of this currency. Similarly, if one currency *depreciates* in value against another currency, it has decreased in value relative to the other currency.

Barriers to Entry. A legal or natural barrier that insulates a firm from its competitors.

Cabotage Law. Laws that protect domestic transportation suppliers, such as airlines, shipping companies, and cruise lines, from foreign competition by reserving domestic business for domestic firms.

Capital. Durable manmade goods such as the equipment, machinery, and buildings people use in the production of goods and service.

Cartel. A group of sellers acting together to restrict output to raise prices and profits.

Coase Theorem. The idea that if property rights are clearly defined, only a small number of parties are involved, and it is not very costly to engage in private negotiations, then private solutions to disputes are possible and efficient without the need for government intervention.

Collective Action. A group of people with a common interest acting jointly to achieve an objective.

Collusion. An agreement among competitors not to compete with each other, but instead, act jointly to restrict output in order to raise prices and profits.

Command-and-Control. Measures that rely on rules, standards, and regulation to direct people's activities.

Conglomerate Integration/Merger. The combination of companies that are in different lines of business.

Contestable Market. A market with low barriers to entry.

Contingent Valuation. A method to determine the value of an environmental amenity by asking people directly what they are willing to pay to enjoy that amenity.

Development Exaction. Conditions imposed on a developer to turn over land, facilities, or money to the government in exchange for government approval to develop. Also "development agreement," which implies mutual consent.

Direct Foreign Investment. Part or whole ownership and management of a business abroad.

Direct Tax. A tax levied on "persons." For example, the income tax is a direct tax.

Disintermediation. Action taken to bypass the middleman.

Dominant Firm. A term used by economist William Shepherd to describe a firm with 50 to 90 percent of total sales in a market.

Earmarked. Dedicated to. As in earmarking, or dedicating, the revenues from a tax for a specific purpose.

Economic Regulation. Government regulation and control over price, output, and entry and exit in industries and markets.

Economic Rent. The income received by an owner of a resource above the amount required to induce the owner to supply it. Also, an excess return to an asset above the normal (competitive) market rate of return.

Economics. The study of choices that people—consumers, businesses, and governments—make to allocate their scarce resources to satisfy their wants.

Economies of Scale. The decrease in the average cost of production as the firm increases the scale (size) of its operations.

Effective Competition. A term used by economist William Shepherd to describe a market that is not characterized either as a monopoly, a dominant firm, or a tight oligopoly. Describes a competitive market with low market concentration.

Efficiency. A situation where the goods and services provided are those that are most highly valued.

Equity. Fairness.

Excess or Monopoly Profits. Profits in excess of those expected in extremely competitive markets.

Excise Tax. A tax on the sale of a particular good or service.

Experience Goods. Goods and services whose attributes and qualities can be determined only after they are purchased and consumed.

External Benefits. Benefits that accrue to people other than the buyers of a good or service.

External Costs. Costs that are not borne by producers or sellers of a good but by other people.

Externalities. A cost or benefit from production or consumption that falls (or spills over) on someone besides the producer or consumer.

Foreign Exchange. Foreign currency.

Four-Firm Concentration Ratio. The percentage of the total sales of a product accounted for by the four largest firms in the market. The higher the percentage, the greater is the market "concentration."

Free Rider. Someone who benefits from an activity without paying for it. A freeloader.

Goods and Services. Things that people value and produce to satisfy their wants. Goods are physical things, whereas services are intangible, such as work performed for people.

Gross Domestic Product. Or, simply "GDP." The GDP is the value of all final goods and services produced in the economy during a specific time period, usually one year.

Herfindahl-Hirschman Index. The Herfindahl-Hirschman Index (sometimes referred to as the Herfindahl) is the sum of the (mathematical) square of the market share of each firm in a market. Like the four-firm concentration ratio, it is a measure of the degree of market concentration.

Heterogeneous Good. A commodity that has many different or diverse attributes. For example, tourism is often described as a heterogeneous good, meaning that it is made up of many different kinds of goods and services, like air transportation, lodging, food and drink, and so on.

Horizontal Integration. When two or more competing companies selling the same product consolidate or coordinate their business operations.

Horizontal Merger. When two or more competing companies selling the same product decide to become a single company.

Impact Fees. Fees levied on developers to pay for the additional costs of public infrastructure such as roads, water, sewage treatment facilities, schools, and other constructions associated with new developments.

Incentive. An inducement to entice someone to take some specific action.

Income Elasticity of Demand. Measures how consumers change their demand for a good or service when their incomes change while everything else remains the same. Demand is "income elastic" if a small percentage change in income results in a larger percentage change in the demand for a good or service. Similarly demand is "income inelastic" if a small percentage change in income results in an even smaller percentage change in the demand for that good.

Indirect Tax. Also often referred to as a "commodity tax." A tax levied on goods and services. Sales and excise taxes are examples of indirect taxes.

Industry. The sellers of a particular product. For example, the lodging industry is composed of the sellers of accommodations. An industry consists only of sellers and not buyers.

Intergenerational Equity. Fairness that balances the interests of present and future generations.

Intermediary. A middleman. For example, a travel agent is an intermediary or a middleman who arranges transactions between buyers and suppliers.

Intermediate Goods. Goods that go into the making of other goods.

Labor. The work time and effort people put into the production of goods and services.

Labor Intensive. As in a labor-intensive commodity; that is, a good whose production employs more labor relative to other factors of production, such as capital and land.

Land. Resources that are gifts of nature—such as land, forests, oceans, and minerals—that people use to produce goods and services.

Marginal. Additional or incremental, as in marginal cost and marginal benefit. Marginal cost is the cost of producing one more unit of a good or service. Marginal benefit is the benefit from consuming one more unit of a good or service.

Market. A group of buyers and sellers buying and selling a particular product.

Market-Based. Relying on the forces of demand and supply to influence economic behavior and outcome.

Market Failure. A situation in which the market does not use resources efficiently. Market failure results in either too much or too little of desired goods and services.

Market Structures. Refers to the four types of markets in which firms operate. The market types range from extremely competitive markets (perfect competition) to virtually no competition at all (monopoly).

Monopolistic Competition. A market in which many sellers compete, but each seller is somewhat insulated from its competitors because each sells a somewhat different product. In a monopolistically competitive market, it is relatively easy for firms to enter and exit.

Monopoly. A market in which there is only one seller selling a product for which no close substitutes exist.

Monopoly Power or Market Power. A firm is said to have "market power" if it is able to influence the market price by manipulating the quantity it offers for sale. It can also be thought of as "pricing power."

Multinational or Transnational Corporations. Corporations that do business in more than one country.

Natural Resources. Resources that are the gifts of nature, such as the air we breathe, beaches, rivers, forests, mountains, flora and fauna, the ocean, and so on.

Nonexcludable. A situation in which it is impossible or too costly to exclude some people from consuming a good or service.

Nonrenewable Resource. A resource that can be only used once and cannot be replaced once used.

Nonrival. The consumption of one good or service does not decrease the amount available to others.

Normal Good. A good for which demand increases when buyers' incomes rise.

Normal Profits. Profits that a business can expect to realize in an extremely competitive market.

Oligopoly. A market in which only a small number of sellers (oligopolists) compete, and it is not easy for a new competitor to enter the market.

Open Access Resource. A resource that is accessible to everyone.

Open Skies Agreements. Agreements among countries to permit open access to each other's aviation markets.

Opportunity Cost. Value of the next best thing you must give up to acquire something else.

Perfect Competition. A market of many atomistic sellers selling identical products so that no single seller has any influence over the market price. In a perfectly competitive market, the entry or exit of firms is easy.

Political Equilibrium. A situation in which no group of stakeholders can improve its position by holding out for a different choice.

Price Discrimination. The ability of a seller to charge different prices to different buyers for the same item, based on the buyers' willingness to pay.

Price Elasticity of Demand. Measures the price sensitivity of buyers to a (small) change in the price of a good while everything else remains the same. Demand is "price elastic" if a small percentage change in the price of the good results in a larger percentage change in the quantity demanded of that good. Buyers then are said to be price sensitive. By contrast, demand is "price inelastic" if a small percentage change in the price of the good results in an even smaller percentage change in the quantity demanded of that good. Buyers then are said to be not price sensitive.

Principal. The boss.

Product Differentiation. To make a product slightly different from the product offered by competitors. Differences can be actual or perceived.

Property Right. Legal right to the exclusive ownership, use, and disposal of a resource or asset.

Proprietary Asset. An asset that is exclusively one owner's to use and enjoy.

Public Good. Or "pure public good." A good or service that can be consumed by everyone at the same time without diminishing the amount available to each person, and no one can be excluded from consuming it.

Real. Adjusted for price changes. As in "real" airfare; that is, airfare adjusted for changes in the general price level in the economy over time.

Regulation. Government rules to limit people's activities.

Relative Price/Cost. The price/cost of one good relative to the price/cost of some other good(s).

Renewable Resource. A resource that can be used repeatedly.

Resources. Inputs, such as land, labor, and capital, used in the production of goods and services.

Strong Sustainability. The idea that some resources are unique and no good substitute for them exists; hence, these resources must be preserved in their original states.

Subsidy. A payment made by the government to a producer or seller.

Sustainable Development. Progress or development that meets the needs of the present without compromising the ability of future generations to meet their own needs. Sustainable development is about enhancing human well-being through time. Sustainable tourism development applies the ideas of sustainable development to tourism.

Tariff. A tax on imports.

Tax. An involuntary payment to the government that does not entitle the payer to receive a direct benefit of equivalent value in return.

Tax Base. The value upon which a tax is levied. Thus, the amount of total taxes collected = tax base × tax rate.

Tax Effort. The intensity level of taxation or the extent to which a government uses the potential tax or revenue base available to it.

Tax Exporting. Shifting taxes to nonresidents.

Tight Oligopoly. A term used by economist William Shepherd to describe a market in which the top four firms account for more than 60 percent of total sales in a market.

Travel and Tourism Satellite Accounts. Often referred to as the *tourism satellite accounts*, or *TTSA*. A quantitative technique to measure the economic contribution and size of tourism in the economy.

Travel Cost Method. A method of valuing unpriced environmental amenities based on the cost of travel to enjoy them. It is used as a proxy for a consumer's "willingness-to-pay" to enjoy an amenity.

Travel Propensity. The number of yearly trips divided by the total population. A country that has a high travel propensity means that the residents of that country tend to travel a lot.

Tourism Consumer Product. What consumers are looking for on their pleasure trips—a satisfying vacation experience.

Tourism Seller Product. Goods and services sold by tourism suppliers.

Unpriced Natural Resources. Natural resources that can be used by anyone without explicitly paying a price.

User Charge. (Often referred to as *user fees*.) A price charged by governments to users to pay for specific government services or privileges.

Utility. The satisfaction or benefit that a consumer derives from the consumption of a good or service.

Value Added. The incremental increase in the value of a commodity when it goes through another stage of production or sale. It is calculated by subtracting the cost of the intermediate goods used in the production from the sale price of the finished good.

Value-Added Tax. A national sales tax, or VAT, widely used around the world, except in the United States and Australia, among industrialized countries.

Vertical Integration/Merger. When a company acquires another company that either supplies inputs to it (*backward integration*) or purchases from it (*forward integration*).

Weak Sustainability. The idea that all resources are substitutable for each other.

CHAPTER REFERENCES

CHAPTER 1

Brown, Frances. 2000. *Tourism Reassessed, Blight or Blessing.* Boston: Butterworth Heinemann.

Bull, Adrian. 1991. *The Economics of Travel and Tourism.* Melbourne, Australia: Pitman Publishing.

Department of Business, Economic Development and Tourism (DBEDT). 2000. *Annual Visitor Research Report, 2000.* Honolulu: Department of Business, Economic Development and Tourism.

Goeldner, Charles R., J. R. Brent Ritchie, and Robert W. McIntosh. 2000. *Tourism: Principles, Practices, Philosophies,* 8th edition. New York: John Wiley & Sons, Inc.

Smith, Christine and Paul Jenner. October 2000. *The World's Leading Outbound Markets.* London: Travel & Tourism Intelligence.

Starr, Nona S. 1981. *Tourism for the Travel Agent.* Wellesley, Mass.: Institute of Certified Travel Agents.

World Tourism Organization (WTO). 1993. *Recommendations on Tourism Statistics.* Madrid: WTO.

_____. November 2001. *Tourism after 11 September 2001: Analysis, Remedial Actions and Prospects.* Special Report, Number 18. Madrid: WTO.

CHAPTER 2

Blair, Roger D. and David L. Kaserman. 1985. *Antitrust Economics.* Homewood, Ill.: Richard D. Irwin.

Brown, Frances. 2000. *Tourism Reassessed, Blight or Blessing.* Boston: Butterworth Heinemann.

Bull, Adrian. 1991. *The Economics of Travel and Tourism.* Melbourne, Australia: Pitman Publishing.

Butler, Richard W. 1980. "The Concept of the Tourist Area Cycle of Evolution: Implications for the Management of Resources," *Canadian Geographer,* vol. 24, pp. 5–12.

Crandall, Louise. 1994. "The Social Impact of Tourism on Developing Regions and Its Measurement." In: J. R. Brent Richie and Charles R. Goeldner (eds.), *Travel, Tourism and Hospitality Research, A Handbook for Managers and Researchers,* 2nd edition. New York: John Wiley & Sons Inc., pp. 413–423.

de Kadt, Emanuel. 1979. *Tourism, Passport to Development.* New York: Oxford University Press.

Diamond, J. 1977. "Tourism's Role in Economic Development: The Case Reexamined." *Economic Development and Cultural Change,* April, pp. 540–553.

Edgell, David, L. Sr. 1990. *International Tourism Policy.* New York: Van Nostrand Reinhold.

Fisher, Ronald C. 1996. *State and Local Public Finance*, 2nd edition. Chicago: Richard D. Irwin.

Flinn, John. 2002. "Two-tier pricing for tourists, locals rarely worth the worry." *San Francisco Chronicle*, Sunday, February 17, p. C3.

Fujii, Edwin and James Mak. 1980. "Tourism and Crime: Implications for Regional Development Policy." *Regional Studies,* vol. 14, pp. 27–36.

Goeldner, Charles R., J. R. Brent Ritchie, and Robert W. McIntosh. 2000. *Tourism, Principles, Practices, Philosophies,* 8th edition. New York: John Wiley & Sons.

Lofgren, Orvar. 1999. *On Holiday, A History of Vacationing.* Berkeley, Cal.: University of California Press.

Mak, James and Walter Miklius. 1990. "State Government Financing of Tourism Promotion in the U.S." In: *Proceedings of the National Tax Association and Tax Institute of America Meeting,* pp. 58–63.

Mak, James and James E. T. Moncur. 1998. "Political Economy of Protecting Unique Recreational Resources: Hanauma Bay, Hawaii." *Ambio,* May, vol. 27, no. 3, pp. 217–223.

Market Trends Pacific Inc. 2000. *North America Bulletin, May, 2000.* Honolulu: Market Trends Pacific Inc.

McGuckin, Robert H. and Kevin J. Stiroh. 2002. "Computers and Productivity: Are Aggregation Effects Important?" *Economic Inquiry,* January, vol. 40, no. 1, pp. 42–59.

Nelson, Philip. 1970. "Information and Consumer Behavior." *Journal of Political Economy,* March/April, LXXVIII, pp. 311–329.

Plog, Stanley C. 1991. *Leisure Travel: Making it a Growth Market...Again.* New York: John Wiley & Sons, Inc.

_____. 2001. "Why Destination Areas Rise and Fall in Popularity: An Update of a Cornell Quarterly Classic." *Cornell Hotel and Restaurant Administration Quarterly,* vol. 42, no. 3, June, pp. 13–24.

Roberts, Mark. 1998. "Home and Away." *The Economist,* January 10, pp. 3–16.

Ryan, Chris. 1991. *Recreational Tourism, A Social Science Perspective.* New York: Routledge.

Sinclair, M. Thea and Mike Stabler. 1997. *The Economics of Tourism.* New York: Routledge.

Smith, Stephen L. J. 1994. "The Tourism Product." *Annals of Tourism Research,* vol. 21, no. 3, pp. 582–595.

Toh, Rex S., Habibullah Khan, and Ai-Jin Koh. 2001. "A Travel Balance Approach for Examining Tourism Area Life Cycles: The Case of Singapore." *Journal of Travel Research,* May, vol. 39, no.4, pp. 426–432.

Witt, Stephen F., Michael Z. Brooke, and Peter J. Buckley. 1995. *The Management of International Tourism,* 2nd edition. New York: Routledge.

CHAPTER 3

Aron, Cindy S. 1999. *Working at Play, A History of Vacations in the United States.* New York: Oxford University Press.

Brown, Frances. 2000. *Tourism Reassessed, Blight or Blessing.* Boston: Butterworth and Heinemann.

Burkhart, A. J. and S. Medlik. 1974. *Tourism. Past, Present and Future.* London: Butterworth and Heinemann.

Crouch, Geoffrey I. 1994. "Demand Elasticities for Short-Haul versus Long-Haul Tourism." *Journal of Travel Research,* vol. 33, no. 2, Fall, pp. 2–7.

———. 1995. "A Meta-Analysis of Tourism Demand." *Annals of Tourism Research,* vol. 22, no. 1, pp. 103–118.

Davis, Bob. 1981. "How It All Began…" In: Nona S. Starr (ed.), *Tourism for the Travel Agent.* Wellesley, Mass.: Institute of Certified Travel Agents, pp. 23–25.

Dulles, Foster Rhea. 1965. *A History of Recreation, America Learns to Play,* 2nd ed. New York: Appleton-Century-Crofts.

Hamal, Krishna. 1996. "Substitutability between domestic and outbound travel in Australia," *Paper presented at the Australian Tourism and Hospitality Research Conference, Coffs Harbour, Australia 6–9 February, 1996,* BTR Conference Paper 96.6. Canberra, Australia.

Lehmann, Armin D. 1981. "A Brief History of Human Travel." In: Nona S. Starr (ed.), *Tourism for the Travel Agent.* Wellesley, Mass.: Institute of Certified Travel Agents, pp.7–16.

Lofgren, Orvar. 1999. *On Holiday, A History of Vacationing.* Berkeley, Cal.: University of California Press.

Lundberg, Donald E. 1985. *The Tourist Business,* 5th ed. New York: Van Nostrand Reinhold.

National Capital Area Tourism Research Program (NCATRP). 2002. *Catastrophe and Recovery: The Course of Lodging Demand in the Washington D. C. Metropolitan Area in the Year Since September 11, 2001.* NCATRP Report 2002-1. Washington, D.C.: George Washington University, International Institute of Tourism Studies.

"9-11-02: Hawaii's changing economy." 2002. *The Honolulu Advertiser,* September 8, pp. F1–F7.

Pizam, Abraham and Aliza Fleischer. 2002. "Severity versus Frequency of Acts of Terrorism: Which Has a Larger Impact on Tourism Demand?" *Journal of Travel Research,* vol. 40, no. 3, February, pp. 337–339.

Pizam, Abraham and Peter Tarlow (eds.). 1999. "Special Issue on War, Terrorism, Tourism: Times of Crisis and Recovery." *Journal of Travel Research,* vol. 38, no. 1, August.

Pizam, Abraham, Peter Tarlow, and Jonathan Bloom. 1997. "Making Tourists Feel Safe: Whose Responsibility Is It?" *Journal of Travel Research,* vol. 36, no. 1, Summer, pp. 23–28.

Plog, Stanley C. 1991. *Leisure Travel: Making it a Growth Market…Again!* New York: John Wiley & Sons, Inc.

Sakai, Marcia, Jeffrey Brown, and James Mak. 2000. "Population Aging and Japanese International Travel in the 21st Century." *Journal of Travel Research,* vol. 38, no. 3, February, pp. 212–220.

Sinclair, M. Thea and Mike Stabler. 1997. *The Economics of Tourism.* New York: Routledge.

Smith, Christine and Paul Jenner. 2000. *The World's Leading Outbound Markets.* London: Travel & Tourism Intelligence.

Swarbrooke, John and Susan Horner. 1999. *Consumer Behavior in Tourism.* Boston: Butterworth Heinemann.

"The Future of Travel." 2002. *Newsweek International,* July 22/July 29.

Tisdell, Clem. 2001. *Tourism, Economics, the Environment, and Development.* Northampton, Mass.: Edward Elgar Publishing Inc.

Towner, J. 1995. "What is tourism's history?" *Tourism Management,* vol. 4, pp. 339–343.

Travel Industry Association of America (TIA). 2002. *Travel Statistics and Trends.* At http://www.tia.org/Travel/EconImpact.asp. Accessed March 12, 2002.

Travel Industry World 2001 Yearbook—The Big Picture. 2002. Spencertown, N.Y.: Travel Industry Publishing Company Inc.

Vanhove, Norbert. 1997. "Mass Tourism, Benefits and Costs." In: Salab, Wahab and John J. Pigram (eds.), *Tourism, Development and Growth: The Challenge of Sustainability.* New York: Routledge, pp. 50–77.

Vogel, Harold L. 2001. *Travel Industry Economics, A Guide for Financial Analysts.* New York: Cambridge University Press.

Witt, Stephen F., Michael Z. Brooks, and Peter J. Buckley. 1995. *The Management of International Tourism,* 2nd ed. New York: Routledge.

World Tourism Organization (WTO). 1994. *National and Regional Planning: Methodologies and Case Studies.* New York: Routledge.

_____. 1995. *Global Tourism Forecasts to the Year 2000 and Beyond,* vol. 1. Madrid: WTO.

_____. 2001. *Tourism after 11 September 2001: Analysis, Remedial Actions and Prospects.* Madrid: WTO.

CHAPTER 4

Askari, Hossein. 1971. "Demand for Package Tours." *Journal of Transport Economics and Policy,* vol. 5, no. 1, January, pp. 40–51.

Hawaii Department of Business, Economic Development, and Tourism. 2002. *Annual Visitor Research Report, 2001.* Honolulu. Also *Annual Visitor Research Report,* 2000.

Japan Travel Bureau. 1998. *JTB Report, '98.* Tokyo: JTB Overseas Travel Department.

Kent, William E., Robert A. Meyer, and Thomas M. Reddam. 1987. "Reassessing Wholesaler Marketing Strategies: The Role of Travel Research." *Journal of Travel Research,* Winter, pp. 31–33.

Lofgren, Ovar. 1999. *On Holiday, A History of Vacationing.* Berkeley, Cal.: University of California Press.

Morris, Steven. 1990. *The Japanese Overseas Travel Market in the 1990s.* London: Economist Intelligence Unit.

"Package deals are flexible online." 2002. *The Honolulu Advertiser,* July 15, p. D4.

Plog, Stanley C. 1991. *Leisure Travel: Making it a Growth Market…Again!* New York: John Wiley & Sons, Inc.

Pyo, Sung Soo. 1989. *U.S. Tourism Demand: Seemingly Unrelated Regression Models.* Ph.D. thesis on the Department of Parks, Recreation and Tourism Management. Clemson, S.C.: Clemson University.

Sheldon, Pauline J. 1984. *Economics of Tour Packaging.* Ph.D. thesis in economics. Honolulu: University of Hawaii at Manoa.

_____. 1986. "The Tour Operator Industry, An Analysis." *Annals of Tourism Research,* vol. 13, pp. 349–365.

Sheldon, Pauline J. and James Mak. 1987. "The Demand for Package Tours: A Mode Choice Model." *Journal of Travel Research,* Winter, pp. 13–17.

Travel Industry World Yearbook, 2001—The Big Picture. 2002. Spencertown, N.Y.: Travel Industry Publishing Co.

Travel Journal International. 2000. *Japan Travel Blue Book, 1999/2000.* Tokyo: Travel Journal, Inc.

Varley, Paul. 2000. *Japanese Culture,* 4th edition. Honolulu: University of Hawaii Press.

Yamamoto, Daisaku and Alison M. Gill. 1999. "Emerging Trends in Japanese Package Tourism." *Journal of Travel Research,* vol. 38, no. 2, November, pp. 134–143.

CHAPTER 5

"British Airways Cuts Pay for U.K. Agents." 2002. At *Travel Weekly Daily Bulletin,* February 13.

Foss, Brad. 2002. "It's Adieu to Smaller Travel Agencies." *The Honolulu Advertiser,* March 22, pp. D1–D2.

Friedheim, Eric. 1992. *Travel Agents.* New York: Travel Agent Magazine Books.

Global Aviation Associates, Ltd. 2002. *The Economics of Travel Distribution in an Internet Driven Environment.* Washington, D.C.: Global Aviation Associates, Ltd.

Goeldner, Charles R., J. R. Brent Ritchie, and Robert W. McIntosh. 2000. *Tourism: Principles, Practices, Philosophies,* 8th edition. New York: John Wiley & Sons, Inc.

Harris, Bonnie. 2002. "Traditional Travel Agencies Succumb to Online's Grip." *The Honolulu Advertiser,* August 11, p. F5.

Hawaii Department of Business, Economic Development, and Tourism (DBEDT). 2002. Visitor Satisfaction Survey, January–June, 2001 (Special tabulation by Mr. Cy Feng, February 4, 2002).

Jouzaitis, Carol. 2002. "Letters." *Los Angeles Times,* March 10, p. L20.

Koch, James V. and Richard J. Cebula. 2002. "Price, Quality, and Service on the Internet: Sense and Nonsense." *Contemporary Economic Policy,* vol. 20, no. 1, January, pp. 25–37.

Lundberg, Donald E. 1980. *The Tourist Business,* 4th edition. Boston: CPI Publishing Company, Inc., Chapter 5.

Mak, James and James E. T. Moncur. 1980. "Demand for Travel Agents." *Journal of Transport Economics and Policy,* May, pp. 221–231.

Miller, Richard K., Terri C. Walker, and Ciji A. Fleming. 2001. *The 2001 Travel and Tourism Market Research Handbook,* 4th edition. Norcross, Ga.: Richard K. Miller & Associates, Inc.

Morrison, Steven. 1995. "The Effects of Airline Deregulation in the United States." In: *International Comparison of Privatization and Deregulation among the U.S.A., the U.K. and Japan—volume III: Airline and Trucking.* Tokyo: Government of Japan, Economic Research Institute, Economic Planning Agency, pp.15–48.

Office of Aviation & International Affairs. 2002. *Report to Congress, Efforts to Monitor Orbitz.* Pursuant to U.S. Department of Transportation Appropriations for FY 2002 Conference Report, House Report No. 107-308. Washington, D.C.: Government Printing Office.

"Put Yourself Here." 2002. *Newsweek,* November 25, pp. 60–61.

Rich, Motko. 2002. "Hotels Unlikely to Drop Commission Payments to Agents." *The Honolulu Advertiser,* June 9, p. F8.

Shaw, Russel. 2002. "Shopping for Online Travel Bargains." *The Honolulu Advertiser,* June 11, pp. E4–E5.

Stigler, George J. 1961. "Economics of Information." *Journal of Political Economy,* vol. 69, no. 3, June, pp. 213–228.

Travel Industry World 2002 Yearbook—The Big Picture. 2003. Spencertown, N.Y.: Travel Industry Publishing Co. Also, *Travel Industry World 2001 Yearbook.*

Travel Weekly. 2000. *U.S. Travel Agency Survey,* vol. 59, No. 68. Accessed August 24, 2000 at www.twcrossroads.com/.

U.S. Department of Commerce. 2002. *A Nation Online: How Americans Are Expanding Their Use of the Internet.* Washington, D.C.: Government Printing Office.

Vogel, Harold L. 2001. *Travel Industry Economics, A Guide for Financial Analysts.* New York: Cambridge University Press.

Weber, Karin and Wesley S. Roehl. 1999. "Profiling People Searching For and Purchasing Travel Products on the World Wide Web." *Journal of Travel Research,* vol. 37, no. 3, February, pp. 291–298.

CHAPTER 6

Bonham, Carl, Edwin Fujii, Eric Im, and James Mak. 1992. "The Impact of the Hotel Room Tax: An Interrupted Time Series Approach." *National Tax Journal,* vol. XLV, no. 4, December, pp. 433–442.

Bull, Adrian. 1991. *The Economics of Travel and Tourism.* Melbourne, Australia: Pitman Publishing.

Falvey, Rodney E. and Norman Gemmel. 1996. "Are Services Income Elastic: Some New Evidence." *The Review of Income and Wealth,* 42, September, pp. 257–269.

Fujii, Edwin T., Mohammed Khaled, and James Mak. 1985. "An Almost Ideal Demand System for Visitor Expenditure." *Journal of Transport Economics and Policy,* May, pp. 161–171.

———. 1987. "An Empirical Comparison of Systems of Demand Equations for Tourist Expenditures in Resort Destinations." *Philippine Review of Economics and Business,* vol. 24, Nos. 1 & 2, March/June, pp. 79–102.

Gronau, Reuben. 1970. "The Effect of Traveling Time on the Demand for Passenger Transportation." *Journal of Political Economy,* vol. 78, no. 2, March/April, pp. 377–394.

Hawaii Department of Business, Economic Development and Tourism (DBEDT). 2002. *Annual Visitor Research Report, 2001;* also *Annual Visitor Research Report, 2000.* Honolulu: DBEDT.

Hiemstra, Stephen J. and Joseph A. Ismail. 1992. "Analysis of Room Taxes Levied on the Lodging Industry." *Journal of Travel Research,* vol. 31, no. 1, Summer, pp. 42–49.

Henthorne, Tony L. 2000. "An Analysis of Expenditures by Cruise Ship Passengers in Jamaica." *Journal of Travel Research,* vol. 38, no. 3, February, pp. 246–250.

"How hotels are faring." 2002. *The Honolulu Advertiser,* April 5, p. D1.

Kass, David I. and Sumiye Okubo. 2000. "U.S. Travel and Tourism Satellite Accounts for 1996 and 1997." *Survey of Current Business,* July, pp. 8–24.

Lancaster, Kelvin J. 1966. "A New Approach to Consumer Theory." *Journal of Political Economy,* vol. LXXXIV, pp. 132–157.

Mak, James. 1988. "Taxing Hotel Room Rentals." *Journal of Travel Research,* Summer, pp. 10–15.

———. 1996. *The Future of Hawaii as a Tourist Shopping Destination.* Unpublished paper. Honolulu: Department of Economics, University of Hawaii at Manoa.

Mak, James and James E. T. Moncur. 1980. "The Choice of Journey Destinations and Lengths of Stay: A Micro Analysis." *The Review of Regional Studies,* vol. 10, no. 2, February, pp. 38–47.

Mak, James, James E. T. Moncur, and David Yonamine. 1977. "Determinants of Visitor Expenditures and Visitor Lengths of Stay: A Cross-Section Analysis of U.S. Visitors to Hawaii." *Journal of Travel Research,* vol. 15, no. 1, pp. 5–8.

Mak, James and Edward Nishimura. 1979. "The Economics of a Hotel Room Tax." *Journal of Travel Research,* vol. 17, no. 4, Spring, pp. 2–6.

Mathematica, Inc. 1970. *The Visitor Industry and Hawaii's Economy, A Cost-Benefit Analysis.* Princeton, N.J.: February 20.

Miller, Richard K., Terri C. Walker, and Ciji A. Fleming. 2001. *The 2001 Travel and Tourism Market Research Handbook,* 4th ed. Norcross, Ga: Richard K. Miller & Associates, Inc.

Nishiyama, Kazuo. "Why Are the Japanese Obsessed with Luxury Brand-Name Goods?" In: James Mak, Shyam Sunder, Shigeyuki Abe, and Kazuhiro Igawa (eds.). *Japan: Why It Works, Why It Doesn't.* 1998. Honolulu: University of Hawaii Press, pp. 39–44.

Pyo, Sung Soo, Muzaffer Uysal, and Robert W. McClellan. 1991. "A Linear Expenditure Model for Tourism Demand." *Annals of Tourism Research,* vol. 18, no. 3, pp. 443–454.

Sakai, Marcia. 1985. *A Micro-Analysis of Demand for Travel Goods: An Application to the Business Traveler.* Ph.D. thesis in economics. Honolulu: Department of Economics, University of Hawaii at Manoa.

Sakai, Marcia, Jeffrey Brown, and James Mak. 2000. "Population Aging and Japanese International Travel in the 21st Century." *Journal of Travel Research,* vol. 38, no. 3, February, pp. 212–220.

Sheldon, Pauline J. "A Review of Tourism Expenditure Research." In: C. P. Cooper (ed.). *Progress in Tourism, Recreation and Hospitality Management,* vol. 2. London: Belhaven Press, pp. 28–49.

Smith, Christine and Paul Jenner. 2000. *The World's Leading Outbound Markets.* London: Travel & Tourism Intelligence.

Travel Industry Association of America (TIA). 2002. *Travel Statistics & Trends.* Accessed March 12, 2002, at www.tia.org/Travel/EconImpact.asp.

Travel Industry Publishing Company Inc. 2003. *Travel Industry World 2002 Yearbook—The Big Picture.* Spencertown, N.Y.: Travel Industry Publishing Company, Inc. Also, *Travel Industry World 2001 Yearbook.*

Travel Journal Inc. 2000. *Japan Travel Blue Book, 1999/2000.* Tokyo: Travel Journal Inc.

————. 2002. *Trends and Tendencies of Major Brand Package Tours.* Accessed March 11, 2002, at www.tjnet.co.jp/int/news/020311/tji031102.html.

White, Kenneth J. and Mary B. Walker. 1982. "Trouble in the Travel Account." *Annals of Tourism Research,* vol. 9, pp. 37–57.

Yamanouchi, Kelly. 2003. "Better Tourism Data Requested." *The Honolulu Advertiser,* January 13, pp. C1–C2.

Chapter 7

"Airfare War Erupts over Business Travelers." 2002. *Honolulu Star-Bulletin,* March 20, p. C7.

Blair, Roger D. and David L. Kaserman. 1985. *Antitrust Economics.* Homewood, Ill.: Richard D. Irwin, Inc.

Buffett, Warren. 1999. At www.skygod.com/quotes/airline.html.

Bull, Adrian. 1991. *The Economics of Travel and Tourism.* Melbourne, Australia: Pitman Publishing.

Burgess, Robert. 2002. "Cendant Corp. Betting Big On Boom in Travel." *The Honolulu Advertiser,* April 20, pp. C1–C2.

Caves, Richard E. 1987. *American Industry: Structure, Conduct, Performance,* 6th edition. Englewood Cliffs, N.J.: Prentice-Hall, Inc.

————. 1996. *Multinational Enterprise and Economic Analysis,* 2nd edition. New York: Cambridge University Press.

"Cendant Agrees to Buy Budget Car Rental." 2002. *The Honolulu Advertiser,* August 22, p. C1.

Dwyer, Larry, Christopher Findlay, and Peter Forsyth. 1990. *Foreign Investment in Australian Tourism.* BTR Occasional Paper No. 6 (March). Canberra: Bureau of Tourism Research.

Hirsch, Jerry. 2003. "Two Disney Parks Boosting Ticket Prices." *The Honolulu Advertiser,* January 12, p. E2.

Horn, John. 2002. "The Battle for Orlando." *Newsweek,* vol. 140, issue 7, August 12, pp. 40–41.

Kahn, Alfred. 2000. *Statement of Alfred E. Kahn,* Testimony before the Subcommittee on Antitrust of the United States Senate Committee on the Judiciary, May 2.

La Croix, Sumner J. and James Mak. 2001. "Regulatory Reform in Japan: The Road Ahead." In: Magnus Blomstrom, Byron Gangnes, and Sumner LaCroix (eds.). *Japan's New Economy, Continuity and Change in the Twenty-First Century.* New York: Oxford University Press, pp. 215–244.

Lundberg, Donald E., M. Krishnamoorthy, and Mink H. Stavenga. 1995. *Tourism Economics.* New York: John Wiley & Sons, Inc.

Morrison, Steven. 1995. "The Effects of Airline Deregulation in the United States." In: *International Comparison of Privatization and Deregulation among the U.S.A., the U.K. and Japan—volume III: Airline and Trucking.* Tokyo: Economic Research Institute, Economic Planning Agency, December, pp.15–48.

National Capital Area Tourism Research Program (NCATRP). 2002. *Catastrophe and Recovery: The Course of Lodging Demand in the Washington D.C. Metropolitan Area in the Year Since September 11, 2001.* Washington, D.C.: George Washington University, International Institute of Tourism Studies.

Perez, Evan and Brandon Mitchner. 2002. "Carnival Looks to U.S. Regulators." *The Wall Street Journal,* July 25, p. D6.

Pizam A. and T. Knowles. 1994. "The European Hotel Industry." In: C. P. Cooper and A. Lockwoods (eds.). *Progress in Tourism, Recreation and Hospitality Management,* vol. 6. New York: John Wiley & Sons, pp. 281–295.

Roberts, Mark. 1998. "Home and Away." *The Economist,* January 10, pp. 3–16.

Schmeltzer, John. 2002. "Higher Airfares Flop as Northwest Balks." *The Honolulu Advertiser,* April 16, p. C1.

Sheldon, Pauline J. 1986. "The Tour Operator Industry, An Analysis." *Annals of Tourism Research,* vol. 13, pp. 349–365.

Shepherd, William G. 1982. "Causes of Increased Competition in the U.S. Economy, 1939–1980." *Review of Economics and Statistics,* vol. LXIV, November, pp. 613–626.

Sinclair, M. Thea and Mike Stabler. 2002. *The Economics of Tourism.* New York: Routledge.

"The 100 Top Brands." 2002. *Business Week,* August 5, pp. 95–99.

Travel Industry World 2002 Yearbook—The Big Picture. 2003. Also 2001 and 2000 Yearbooks. Spencertown, N.Y.: Travel Industry Publishing Company Inc.

U.S. General Accounting Office (GAO). 1997. *Airline Deregulation: Barriers to Entry Continue to Limit Competition in Several Key Domestic Markets.* Washington, D.C.: Government Printing Office.

U.S. Government, Bureau of Transportation Statistics. 2000. *National Transportation Statistics, 2000,* BTS01-01, accessible at www.bts.gov/.

U.S. Government, Office of Management and Budget. 1997. *North American Industry Classification System, United States, 1997.* Springfield, Va.: National Technical Information Service, accessible at www.ntis.gov/naics.

CHAPTER 8

"A Victory for Brussels, Sort Of." 2002. *Economist.com*, November 6.

Association of European Airlines. 1998. *Airline Alliances and Competition in Transatlantic Airline Markets*. Final report (August 21) at www. ea.be/Publications/FramePage_ pub. htm.

Batsell, Jack. 1998. "Cruise Line Looks to Drop Anchor in Seattle." *Seattle Times.com,* October 4.

Bull, Adrian. 1991. *The Economics of Travel and Tourism.* Melbourne, Australia: Pitman Publishing.

Caves, Douglas W., Laurits R. Christensen, Michael W. Tretheway, and Robert J. Windle. 1987. "An Assessment of the Efficiency Effects of U.S. Airline Deregulation via an International Comparison." In: Elizabeth Bailey (ed.), *Public Regulation: New Perspectives on Institutions and Policies.* Cambridge, Mass.: MIT Press.

Chaplin, Steve. 2001. "Ocean of Opportunity, Cruise Lines' Huge Array of Choices Allows Passengers to 'Taste Test' Adventures." *The Honolulu Advertiser,* October 7, pp. F1 and F5.

Corsi, Thomas M. and Milton E. Harvey. 1979. "Changes in Vacation Travel in Response to Motor Fuel Shortages and Higher Prices." *Journal of Travel Research,* vol. 17, No. 4, Spring, pp. 7–11.

Cox, Wendell and Jean Love. 1996. *40 Years of the U.S. Interstate Highway System, An Analysis.* Accessed at www.publicpurpose.com/freeway1.htm#intro.

Gentile, Gary. 2002. "Road-Trip Trend May Curtail Hawaii Visits." *The Honolulu Advertiser,* June 24, pp. D1 and D3.

Gronau, Reuben. 1970. "The Effect of Traveling Time on the Demand for Passenger Transportation." *Journal of Political Economy,* vol. 78, no. 2, March/April, pp. 377–394.

Kahn, Alfred. Circa 2000. New River Media. Interview at www.pbs.org/fmc/interviews/kahn.htm.

_____. 2000. *Statement of Alfred Kahn.* Testimony before U.S. Senate Subcommittee on Antitrust Legislation of the United States Senate Committee on the Judiciary, May 2, 2000 at www.judiciary.senate.gov/beta/oldsite/522000 aek.htm.

Kaspar, C. 1995. "For New Demands, New Services." In: The European Conference of Ministers of Transport (ECMT), *Why Do We Need Railways?* Paris: International Seminar, 19–20 January, pp. 61–92.

Kellerhals, Merle D. Jr. 1999. *Open Skies Aviation Agreements Cut Air Fares Substantially.* Accessed at www.usembassy.it/file9912/alia/9912060h.htm.

Koch, James V. and Richard J. Cebula. 2002. "Price, Quality, and Service on the Internet: Sense and Nonsense." *Contemporary Economic Policy,* vol. 20, no. 1, January, pp. 25–37.

La Croix, Sumner J. and David J. Wolff. 1995. *The Asia-Pacific Airline Industry: Economic Boom and Political Conflict.* East-West Center Special Reports, No. 4.Honolulu: East-West Center.

La Croix, Sumner, J. and James Mak. 2001. "Regulatory Reform in Japan: The Road Ahead." In: Blomstrom, Magnus, Byron Gangnes, and Sumner La Croix (eds.), *Japan's New Economy: Continuity and Change in the Twenty-First Century.* New York: Oxford University Press, pp. 215–241.

Lundberg, Donald E., M. Krishnamoorthy, and Mink H. Stavenga. 1995. *Tourism Economics.* New York: John Wiley & Sons, Inc.

Lynch, Russ. 2001. "Independence to Sail Into Sunset." *Honolulu Star-Bulletin,* October 30, pp. C1 and C4.

Magin, Janis L. 2003. "Congress OKs Cruise Exemption." *The Honolulu Advertiser,* February 14, pp. A1 and A7.

Miller, Leslie. 2002. "Airport Hassles, Not Just Fear, Have Many Travelers Preferring Road." *The Honolulu Advertiser,* October 21, p. A3.

Miller, Richard K., Terri C. Walker, and Ciji A. Fleming. 2001. *The 2001 Travel and Tourism Market Research Handbook,* 4th edition. Norcross, Ga.: Richard K. Miller & Associates.

Morrison, Steven. 1995. "The Effects of Airline Deregulation in the United States." In: *International Comparison of Privatization and Deregulation among the U.S.A., the U.K. and Japan—volume III: Airline and Trucking.* Tokyo: Government of Japan, Economic Research Institute, Economic Planning Agency, pp.15–48.

Morrison, Steven and Clifford Winston. 1995. *The Evolution of the Airline Industry.* Washington, D.C.: The Brookings Institute.

Newcott, William R. 2003. "Cruise Control." *Modern Maturity,* January/February, pp. 45–48.

Plassard, Francois, "For New Demands, New Services." In: The European Conference of Ministers of Transport (ECMT), *Why Do We Need Railways?* Paris: International Seminar, 19–20 January, pp. 93–129.

"The Squeeze on Europe's Air Fares." 2001. *The Economist,* May 24.

Travel Industry World 2002 Yearbook—The Big Picture. 2003. Also 2001 and 2000 *Yearbook.* Spencertown, N.Y.: Travel Industry Publishing Company Inc.

U.S. Department of Transportation, Bureau of Transportation Statistics. 1997. *1995 American Travel Survey Profile,* BTS/ATS95-US. Accessed at www.bts.gov/btsprod/nets/Ch1_web/1-33.htm.

U.S. Department of Transportation, Office of the Secretary. 1999. *International Aviation Developments: Global Deregulation Takes Off (First Report).* Washington, D.C.: Government Printing Office.

U.S. General Accounting Office (GAO). 1996. *Airline Deregulation: Changes in Airfares, Service and Safety at Small, Medium-sized, and Large Communities.* Washington, D.C.: Government Printing Office.

U.S. House of Representatives, Subcommittee on Coast Guard and Maritime Transportation, Committee on Transportation Infrastructure. 1998. *Effect of the Passenger Services Act on the Domestic Cruise Industry.* Accessed at http://commdocs.house.gov/committees/Trans/hpw105-65.000/hpw105-65_of.htm.

U.S. International Trade Commission. 1995. *The Economic Effects of Significant U.S. Import Restrictions: First Biannual Update,* Publication 2935. Washington, D.C.: Government Printing Office.

Winston, Clifford. 1998. "U.S. Industry Adjustment to Economic Deregulation." *Journal of Economic Perspectives,* vol. 12, September, pp. 89–110.

Yamanouchi, Kelly. 2003. "Cruise Co. Purchases 2 Ships." *The Honolulu Advertiser,* April 15, pp. C1 and C6.

CHAPTER 9

Ascher, Bernard and David L. Edgell. 1986. "Barriers to International Travel." *Travel & Tourism Analyst,* October, pp. 3–14.

Brown, Frances. 2000. *Tourism Reassessed, Blight or Blessing.* Boston: Butterworth Heinemann.

Choy, Dexter J. L. and Yao Yue Can. 1988. "The Development and Organization of Travel Services in China." *Journal of Travel Research,* vol. 27, no. 1, Summer, pp. 28–34.

Davila, Victor R., Nader Asgary, Gilberto de los Santos, and Vern Vincent. 1999. "The Effects of Government Restrictions on Outbound Tourist Expenditures." *Journal of Travel Research,* vol. 37, no. 3, February, pp. 285–290.

Edgell, David L. Sr. 1990. *International Tourism Policy.* New York: Van Nostrand Reinhold.

Fisher, Ronald C. 1996. *State and Local Public Finance.* Chicago: Richard D. Irwin.

Government of Japan. 1989. *Tourism in Japan, 1989.* Tokyo: Japan Ministry of Transportation.

La Croix, Sumner J. and James Mak. 2001. "Regulatory Reform in Japan: The Road Ahead." In: Magnus Blomstrom, Byron Gangnes, and Sumner La Croix (eds.), *Japan's New Economy: Continuity and Change in the Twenty-First Century.* New York: Oxford University Press, pp. 215–244.

Mak, James. 1996. *The Future of Hawaii as a Tourist Shopping Destination.* Unpublished paper. Honolulu: Department of Economics, University of Hawaii at Manoa.

Mak, James and Kenneth White. 1988. "Tourism in Asia and the Pacific." In: Chung H. Lee and Seiji Naya (eds.), *Trade and Investment in Services in the Asia-Pacific Region.* Boulder, Colo.: Westview Press, Inc., pp. 121–147.

———. 1992. "Comparative Tourism Development in Asia and the Pacific." *Journal of Travel Research,* vol. 31, no. 1, Summer, pp. 14–23.

Murphy, David. 2002. "Follow the Flags to Save Tourism." *Far Eastern Economic Review,* March 7, pp. 22–25.

Smith, Christine and Paul Jenner. 2000. *The World's Leading Outbound Markets.* London: Travel & Tourism Intelligence.

Swanson, David. 2003. "Way Beyond the Great Wall." *National Geographic Traveler,* January/February, p. 18.

Timothy, Dallen J. and Richard W. Butler. 1995. "Cross-Border Shopping, A North American Perspective." *Annals of Tourism Research,* vol. 22, no. 1, pp. 16–34.

Tisdell, Clem. 2001. *Tourism Economics, the Environment and Development.* Northampton, Mass.: Edward Elgar Publishing, Inc.

Travel Industry World 2001 Yearbook—The Big Picture. 2002. Spencertown, N.Y.: Travel Industry Publishing Company Inc.

Travel Journal International. 2000. *Japan Travel Blue Book, 1999/2000.* Tokyo: Travel Journal Inc.

Witt, Stephen F. and Luiz Moutinho (eds.). "Government Controls On and Support For Tourism." In: *Tourism Marketing and Management Handbook,* 2nd edition. New York: Prentice Hall, pp. 60–64.

World Tourism Organization (WTO). 1994. *National and Regional Planning: Methodologies and Case Studies.* New York: Routledge.

———. 2001. *Compendium of Tourism Statistics, 2001 Edition.* Madrid: WTO.

Zhang, Guangrui. 1990. *China's Tourism: Historical Review and Future Prospects.* Shanghai, China: Shanghai Academy of Social Sciences.

CHAPTER 10

Archer, Brian H. 1977. *Tourism Multipliers: The State of the Art.* Bangor Occasional Papers in Economics, No. 11. Bangor: University of Wales Press.

Boskin, Michael J. 1996. "National Satellite Accounting for Travel and Tourism: A Cold Review of the WTTC/WEFA Group Research." *Tourism Economics,* vol. 2, no. 1, March, pp. 3–12.

Brown, Frances. 2000. *Tourism Reassessed, Blight or Blessing.* Boston: Butterworth Heinemann.

Bull, Adrian. 1991. *The Economics of Travel and Tourism.* Melbourne: Pitman Press.

Elliott, Michael. 2002. "Must the Backpackers Stay Home?" *Time,* December 16, p. 8.

Fletcher, John E. 1994. "Economic and Forecasting Economic Impact." In: Stephen F. Witt and Luiz Moutinho (eds.), *Tourism Marketing and Management Handbook,* 2nd edition. New York: Prentice Hall, pp. 475–479.

———. 1994. "Input-Output Analysis." In: Stephen F. Witt and Luiz Moutinho (eds.), *Tourism Marketing and Management Handbook,* 2nd edition. New York: Prentice Hall, pp. 480–487.

Frechtling, Douglas C. 1994. "Assessing the Economic Impacts of Travel and Tourism—Introduction to Travel Economic Impact Estimation." In: J. R. Brent Ritchie and Charles R. Goeldner (eds.), *Travel, Tourism, and Hospitality Research, A Handbook for Managers and Researchers,* 2nd edition. New York: John Wiley & Sons, Inc., pp. 359–365.

Hawaii Department of Business, Economic Development and Tourism (DBEDT). 2002. *The Hawaii Input-Output Study, 1997 Benchmark Report.* Honolulu: Research and Economic Analysis Division.

Kass, David I. and Sumiye Okubo. 2000. "U.S. Travel and Tourism Satellite Accounts for 1996 and 1997." *Survey of Current Business* (July 2000). Accessed at www.bea.doc.gov/bea/ARTICLES/NATIONAL/Inputout/2000/0700tta.pdf.

Liu, Juanita C. and Turgut Var. 1982. "Differential Multipliers for the Accommodation Sector." *Tourism Management,* vol. 3, no. 3, September, pp. 177–187.

Mitchell, Frank, 1970. "The Value of Tourism in East Africa." *Eastern Africa Economic Review,* vol. 2, no. 1, June, pp. 1–21.

Office of Travel & Tourism Industries. 1998. *Description of the Travel and Tourism Satellite Account (TTSA) Program* (August 20, 1998). Accessed at www.tinet.ita.doc.gov/view/ttsa/.

Okubo, Sumiye and Mark A. Planting. 1998. "U.S. Travel and Tourism Satellite Accounts for 1992." *Survey of Current Business* (July 1998). Accessed at www.bea.doc.gov/bea/an/0798 ied/maintext.htm.

Smith, Stephen J. and David Wilton. 1997. "TSAs and the WTTC/WEFA Methodology: Different Satellites or Different Planets?" *Tourism Economics,* vol. 3, no. 3, pp. 249–264.

World Travel & Tourism Council (WTTC). 2000. *United States Travel & Tourism Satellite Account, Year 2000 Estimates.* Accessed at www.wttc.org/.

———. 2002. *The Impact of Travel & Tourism on Jobs and the Economy—2002, Executive Summary.* Accessed at www.wttc.org/.

CHAPTER 11

Archer, Brian. 1977. "The Economic Costs and Benefits of Tourism." In: Brian S. Duffield (ed.), *Tourism, A Tool for Regional Development.* Edinburgh: Leisure Studies Association Conference.

Bird, Richard M. 1992. "Taxing Tourism in Developing Countries." *World Development,* vol. 20, no. 8, pp. 1145–1158.

Brown, Frances. 2000. *Tourism Reassessed, Blight or Blessing.* Boston: Butterworth Heinemann.

Bruce, Neil. 1998. *Public Finance and the American Economy.* Reading, Mass.: Addison-Wesley.

Callies, David. 1992. "Development Fees." In: Randall W. Roth (ed.), *The Price of Paradise.* Honolulu: Mutual Publishing, pp. 169–172.

Callies, David and M. Grant. 1991. "Paying for Growth and Planning Gain: An Anglo-American Comparison of Development Conditions, Fees and Development Agreements." *The Urban Lawyer,* vol. 23, pp. 221–248.

Clarke, Harry R. and Yew-Kwang Ng. 1993. "Tourism, Economic Welfare and Efficient Pricing." *Annals of Tourism Research,* vol. 20, no. 4, pp. 613–632.

Copeland, Brian R. 1989. *Taxing Tourists: Optimal Commodity Taxation and Public Goods Provision in the Presence of International Tourism.* Unpublished paper. Vancouver, British Columbia: University of British Columbia.

———. 1991. "Tourism, Welfare and De-industrialization in a Small Open Economy." *Economica,* vol. 54, no. 4, pp. 515–529.

Cox, Linda, Morton Fox, and Richard L. Bowen. 1995. "Does Tourism Destroy Agriculture?" *Annals of Tourism Research,* vol. 22, no. 1, pp. 210–213.

Crandall, Louise. 1994. "The Social Impact of Tourism on Developing Regions and Its Measurement." In: J. R. Brent Ritchie and Charles R. Goeldner (eds.), *Travel, Tourism, and Hospitality Research, A Handbook for Managers and Researchers,* 2nd ed. New York: John Wiley & Sons, pp. 413–423.

Dixon, John, Kirk Hamilton, Stefano Pagiola, Lisa Segnestam. 2001. *Tourism and the Environment in the Caribbean: An Economic Framework.* Environment Department Papers No. 80. Washington, D.C.: Environment Department, World Bank.

Dwyer, Larry, Christopher Findlay, and Peter Forsyth. 1990. *Foreign Investment in Australian Tourism.* BTR Occasional Paper No. 6. Canberra: Bureau of Tourism Research.

Ebel, Robert (ed.). 1990. *A Fiscal Agenda for Nevada.* Reno: University of Nevada Press.

Ebel, Robert and James Mak. 1974. *Current Issues in Hawaii's Economy.* Honolulu: Crossroads Press Inc.

Fisher, Ronald C. 1996. *State and Local Public Finance.* Chicago: Richard D. Irwin Publishers.

Frank, James and R. Rhodes (eds.). 1987. *Development Exactions.* Washington, D.C.: Planners Press.

Frechtling, Douglas C. 1994. "Assessing the Impacts of Travel and Tourism—Measuring Economic Costs." In: J. R. Brent Ritchie and Charles R. Goeldner (eds.), *Travel, Tourism, and Hospitality Research, A Handbook for Managers and Researchers,* 2nd edition. New York: John Wiley & Sons, pp. 393–402.

"The Future of Travel." 2002. *Newsweek International,* July 22/July 29, pp. 34–65.

Gade, Mary N. and Lee C. Adkins. 1990. "Tax Exporting and State Revenue Structures." *National Tax Journal,* 43, March, pp. 39–52.

Gray, H. Peter. 1974. "Towards an Economic Analysis of Tourism Policy." *Social and Economic Studies,* vol. 23, no. 3, September, pp. 386–397.

Hawaii Department of Business and Economic Development. 1989. *1988 Statewide Tourism Impact Core Survey: Summary.* Honolulu: Department of Business and Economic Development, Tourism Branch.

Hawaii Office of Tourism. 1978. *State Tourism Study, Public Revenue-Cost Analysis.* Honolulu: Office of Tourism, Department of Planning and Economic Development.

Heller, H. Robert and Emily E. Heller. 1973. *The Economic and Social Impact of Foreign Investment in Hawaii.* Honolulu: Economic Research Center, University of Hawaii.

Judd, Dennis R. (ed.). 2003. *The Infrastructure of Play: Building the Tourist City.* Armonk, N.Y.: M.E. Sharpe.

Liu, Juanita and Turgut Var. 1986. "Resident Attitudes Toward Tourism Impacts in Hawaii." *Annals of Tourism Research,* vol. 13, no. 2, pp. 193–194.

Mak, James. 1991. *The Benefits and Costs of Tourism in Palau.* Foreign Investment and Tourism Conference, January 9–11, 1991, Koror, Republic of Palau. Honolulu: Department of Economics, University of Hawaii at Manoa.

———. 1993. "Exacting Resort Developers to Create Non-Tourism Jobs." *Annals of Tourism Research,* vol. 20, pp. 250–261.

Mason, Peter and Joanne Cheyne. 2000. "Residents' Attitudes to Proposed Tourism Development." *Annals of Tourism Research,* vol. 27, no. 2, pp. 391–411.

Mathematica, Inc. 1970. *The Visitor Industry and Hawaii's Economy: A Cost-Benefit Analysis.* Princeton, New Jersey: Mathematica, Inc.

Mitchell, Frank. 1970. "The Value of Tourism in East Africa." *Eastern Africa Economic Review,* vol. 2, no. 1, June, pp. 1–21.

Newlon, T. Scott. 1999. "Transfer Pricing, Federal." In: Joseph J. Cordes, Robert D. Ebel, and Jane G. Gravelle (eds.), *Encyclopedia of Taxation and Tax Policy.* Washington, D.C.: The Urban Institute Press, pp. 408–411.

Pizam, Abraham. 1978. "Tourism's Impacts: The Social Costs to the Destination Community as Perceived by Its Residents." *Journal of Travel Research,* vol. 16, Spring, pp. 8–12.

Sakai, Marcia and James Mak. 1991. "A State Perspective on Taxing Foreign Investments in the U.S." *Intergovernmental Perspective,* vol. 17, no. 3, Summer, pp. 31–34.

Sandler, Todd. 2001. *Economic Concepts for the Social Sciences.* New York: Cambridge University Press.

Sinclair, M. Thea and Mike Stabler. 1997. *The Economics of Tourism.* New York: Routledge.

Stigler, George. 1966. *The Theory of Price,* 3rd edition. New York: MacMillan Press.

Tisdell, Clem A. 1983. "Public Finance and the Appropriation of Gains from International Tourists: Some Theory with ASEAN and Australian Illustrations." *Singapore Economic Review,* vol. 28, pp. 3–20.

Vanhove, Norbert. 1997. "Mass Tourism, Benefits and Costs." In: Wahab, Salah and John J. Pigram (eds.), *Tourism, Development and Growth, The Challenge of Sustainability.* New York: Routledge, pp. 50–77.

Wanhill, Stephen R. C. 1994. "Evaluating the Worth of Investment Incentives." *Journal of Travel Research,* vol. 33, no. 2, Fall, pp. 33–39.

Wilkinson, Paul. 1989. "Strategies for Tourism in Island Microstates." *Annals of Tourism Research,* vol. 16, pp. 153–177.

World Tourism Organization (WTO). *National and Regional Tourism Planning, Methodologies and Case Studies.* New York: Routledge.

Zee, Howell H., Janet G. Stotsky, and Eduardo Ley. 2002. *Tax Incentives for Business Investment: a Primer for Policy Makers in Developing Countries.* Washington, D.C.: International Monetary Fund.

CHAPTER 12

Blair, Andrew R., Frank Giarratani, and Michael H. Spiro. 1987. "Incidence of the Amusement Tax." *National Tax Journal,* vol. XL, no. 1, March, pp. 61–69.

Bonham, Carl, Edwin Fujii, Eric Im, and James Mak. 1992. "The Impact of the Hotel Room Tax: An Interrupted Time Series Approach." *National Tax Journal,* vol. XLV, no. 4, December, pp. 433–442.

Bonham, Carl and James Mak. 1996. "Private versus Public Financing of State Destination Promotion." *Journal of Travel Research,* vol. XXXV, no. 2, Fall, pp. 3–10.

Bruce, Neil. 1998. *Public Finance and the American Economy.* Reading, Mass.: Addison-Wesley.

Callies, David L. 1992. "Development Fees." In: Randall Roth (ed.), *The Price of Paradise.* (Honolulu: Mutual Publishing Co., pp. 169–172.

Cordes, Joseph J., Robert D. Ebel, and Jane G. Gravelle (eds.). 1999. *The Encyclopedia of Taxation and Tax Policy.* Washington, D.C.: The Urban Institute Press.

Diamond, Peter. 1969. "On the Economics of Tourism." *Eastern Africa Economic Review,* vol. 1, no. 2, December, pp. 53–62.

Dwyer, Larry and Peter Forsyth. 1993. "Government Support for Inbound Tourism Promotion: Some Neglected Issues." *Australian Economic Papers,* vol. 32 no. 61, December, pp. 355–74.

Ebrill, Liam, et al. 2001. *The Modern VAT.* Washington, D.C.: International Monetary Fund.

Fairbanks, Katie. 2002. "Airfare, Minus Inflation, Actually Down." *The Honolulu Advertiser,* August 25, p. F6.

Fisher, Ronald C. 1996. *State and Local Public Finance.* Chicago: Richard D. Irwin.

Fox, William F. and LeAnn Luna. 2003. "Subnational Taxing Options: Which is Preferred, A Retail Sales Tax or a VAT?" *Journal of State Taxation,* vol. 21, no. 3, Winter, pp. 1–22.

Fujii, Edwin, Mohammed Khaled and James Mak. 1985. "The Exportability of Hotel Occupancy and Other Tourist Taxes." *National Tax Journal,* vol. 38, no. 2, June, pp. 169–178.

Gade, Mary N. and Lee C. Adkins. 1990. "Tax Exporting and State Revenue Structures." *National Tax Journal,* 43, March, pp. 39–52.

Gentry, William. 1999. "Optimal Taxation." In: Cordes, Ebel, and Gravelle (eds.), *op. cit.,* pp. 261–264.

Hawaii Office of Tourism. 1978. *State Tourism Study, Public Revenue–Cost Analysis.* Honolulu: Office of Tourism, Department of Planning and Economic Development.

Kenyon, Daphne. 1999. "Tax and Revenue Effort." In: Cordes, Ebel, and Gravelle (eds.), *op. cit.,* 363–365.

Loyacono, Laura L. and Scott Mackey. 1991. "The Taxidental Tourist." *State Legislatures,* October, pp. 21–24.

Mak, James. 1988. "Taxing Hotel Room Rentals in the U.S." *Journal of Travel Research,* vol. 27, no. 1, Summer, pp. 10–15.

Mak, James and Walter Miklius.1990. "State Government Financing of Tourism Promotion in the U.S." In: *Proceedings of the National Tax Association and Tax Institute of America Meeting,* pp. 58–63.

Mathematica, Inc. 1970. *The Visitor Industry and Hawaii's Economy: A Cost–Benefit Analysis.* Princeton, New Jersey: Mathematica, Inc.

Miklius, Walter, James E. T. Moncur, and Ping Sun Leung. 1989. "Distribution of State and Local Tax Burden by Income Class." In: Hawaii Tax Review Commission, *Working Papers and Consultant Studies,* vol. 2. Honolulu: State of Hawaii, Department of Taxation, pp. 7–19.

Mok, Henry. 1986. *The Effectiveness of Destinational Advertising: The Case of Hawaii's "City Magazine" Campaign.* Ph.D. dissertation in economics. Honolulu: University of Hawaii at Manoa, December.

National Public Radio. 2002. "Starting School Earlier." *All Things Considered,* August 20. Accessed at www.npr.org.

Olson, Mancur. 1971. *The Logic of Collective Action.* Cambridge: Harvard University Press.

_____. 1982. *The Rise and Decline of Nations.* New Haven: Yale University Press.

Phares, Donald. 1980. *Who Pays State and Local Taxes?* Cambridge, Mass.: Oelgeschlager, Gunn, and Hain.

_____. 1999. "Tax Exporting." In: Cordes, Ebel, and Gravelle (eds.), *op. cit.,* pp. 381–383.

Rees, Robert. 1996. "Punchout on Punchbowl." *Honolulu Weekly,* vol. 6, no. 1, January 3, p. 5.

Seiglie, Carlos. 1990. "A Theory of the Politically Optimal Commodity Tax." *Economic Inquiry,* vol. 28, no. 3, July, pp. 586–603.

Tait, Alan. 1999. "Value-Added Tax." In: Cordes, Ebel, and Gravelle (eds.), *op. cit.,* pp. 422–426.

Travel Business Analyst, Market Intelligence for Management. November 1992. Asia Pacific. Hong Kong: Travel Business Analyst.

Ulbrich, Holley H. 1999. "Infrastructure Financing." In: Cordes, Ebel, and Gravelle (eds.), *op. cit.,* pp. 188–190.

U.S. Advisory Commission on Intergovernmental Relations (ACIR). 1989. "Intergovernmental Fiscal Relations in Hawaii." In: *Tax Review Commission, Working Papers and Consultant Studies,* vol. 2, December. Honolulu: State of Hawaii, Department of Taxation, pp. 139–314.

————. 1994. *Revenue Diversification, State and Local Travel Taxes,* M-189, April. Washington, D.C.: ACIR.

U.S. Travel Data Center and Forthergill/Beckhuis Associates. 1979. *Delaware Tourism Policy Study.* Dover, Del.: Delaware State Travel Service.

Wanhill, Stephen. 1995. "VAT Rates and the UK Tourism and Leisure Industry." *Tourism Economics,* vol. 1, no. 3, September, pp. 211–224.

Whitney, Scott. 2002. "The Automatic Tourism Money Machine." *Honolulu,* April, pp. 26–32.

World Tourism Organization (WTO). 1994. *National and Regional Tourism Planning.* New York: Routledge.

World Travel and Tourism Council (WTTC). 1997. *Travel & Tourism and Hawaii's Economy, 1997.* London: World Travel and Tourism Council.

CHAPTER 13

Adams, Marilyn. 2002. "Spoiling the Seas." *The Honolulu Advertiser,* November 10, pp. F1 and F2.

Amaro, Belisa. 1999. "Ecotourism and Ethics." *Earth Island Journal,* vol. 14, no. 3, pp. 16–17.

Anderson, Terry L. and Peter J. Hill. 1996. "Appropriable Rents from Yellowstone Park: A Case of Incomplete Contracting." *Economic Inquiry,* vol. 34, July, pp. 506–518.

Brandon, Katrina. 1996. *Ecotourism and Conservation: A Review of Key Issues.* Environment Department Papers, Paper No. 033. Washington, D.C.: The World Bank.

Briassoulis, Helen. 2000. "Environmental Impacts of Tourism: A Framework for Analysis and Evaluation." In: Briassoulis, Helen (ed.), *Tourism and the Environment,* revised 2nd edition. Boston: Kluwer Academic Publishers, pp. 21–37 .

Brown, Katrina, R. Kerry Turner, Hala Hameed, and Ian Bateman. 2000. "Environmental Carrying Capacity and Tourism Development in the Maldives and Nepal." In: Clem Tisdell (ed.), *The Economics of Tourism,* vol. II. Northampton, Mass.: Edward Elgar Publishing Ltd., pp. 546–555.

Cesar, Herman, Pieter van Beukering, Sam Pintz, and Jan Dierking. 2002. *Economic Valuation of the Coral Reefs of Hawaii.* Arnhem, the Netherlands: Cesar Environmental Economics Consulting.

Coccossis, Harry and Apostolos Parpairis. 2000. "Tourism and the Environment: Some Observations on the Concept of Carrying Capacity." In: Briassoulis, Helen (ed.), *Tourism and the Environment,* revised 2nd edition. Boston: Kluwer Academic Publishers, pp. 91–105.

Davis, Joyzelle. 2002. "Cruise Lines Fouling Coastline, Suit Charges." *The Honolulu Advertiser,* April 27, p. C2.

Dawson, Teresa. 2002. "They're Heeere!" *Honolulu Weekly,* December 11–17, p. 5.

Dimara, Efthalia and Dimitris Skuras. 1998. "Rationing Preferences and Spending Behavior of Visitors to a Scarce Recreational Resource with Limited Carrying Capacity." *Land Economics,* vol. 74, no. 3, August, pp. 317–327.

Dixon, John, Kirk Hamilton, Stefano Pagiola, and Lisa Segnestam. 2001. *Tourism and the Environment in the Caribbean.* Environment Department Papers, Paper No. 80. Washington, D.C.: The World Bank.

Dixon, J. A., L. F. Scura, and T. van't Hof. 1993. "Meeting Ecological and Economic Goals: Marine Parks in the Caribbean," *Ambio,* vol. 22, pp. 117–125.

Domroes, Manfred. 2001. "Conceptualising State–Controlled Resort Islands for an Environment–Friendly Development of Tourism: The Maldivian Experience." *Singapore Journal of Tropical Geography,* vol. 22, no. 2, pp. 122–137.

Ecotourism Society. 1998. *Ecotourism Statistical Fact Sheet.* Burlington: International Ecotourism Society.

Field, Barry C. and Martha K. Field. 2002. *Environmental Economics, An Introduction,* 3rd edition. Boston: McGraw–Hill/Irwin.

Forsyth, Peter, Larry Dwyer, and H. Clarke. 1995. "Problems in Use of Economic Instruments to Reduce Adverse Environmental Impacts of Tourism." *Tourism Economics,* vol. 1, pp. 265–282.

Hansen, John. 2002. "Cruise Industry Stands By Its Word." *The Honolulu Advertiser,* November 8, p. A20.

International Monetary Fund, United Nations Environment Programme, and the World Bank. 2002. *Financing for Sustainable Development.* Washington, D.C.: The World Bank.

Knapman, Bruce and Natalie Stoeckl. 1995. "Recreation User Fees: An Australian Empirical Investigation." *Tourism Economics,* vol. 1, no.1, March, pp. 5–16.

Lindberg, Kreg, Stephen McCool, and George Stankey. 2000. "Rethinking Carrying Capacity." In: Clem Tisdell (ed.), *The Economics of Tourism,* vol. II. Northampton, Mass.: Edward Elgard Publishing Ltd., pp. 556–560.

Mak, James. 1991. *The Benefits and Costs of Tourism in Palau.* Foreign Investment and Tourism Conference, January 9–11, Koror, Republic of Palau. Honolulu: Department of Economics, University of Hawaii at Manoa.

Mak, James and James E. T. Moncur. 1995. "Sustainable Tourism Development: Managing Hawaii's 'Unique' Touristic Resource: Hanauma Bay." *Journal of Travel Research,* Spring, pp. 51–57.

———. 1998. "Political Economy of Protecting Unique Recreational Resources, Hanauma Bay, Hawaii." *Ambio,* vol. 27, no. 3, May, pp. 217–223.

Mastny, Lisa. 2002. "Redirecting International Tourism." In: *State of the World 2002,* A Worldwatch Institute Report on Progress Toward a Sustainable Society. New York: W. W. Norton & Company, pp. 101–126 and 225–234.

Parkin, Michael. 2000. *Microeconomics,* 5th edition. Reading, Mass.: Addison–Wesley.

Pianin, Eric. 2002. "Giant Pandas in the Desert?" *The Washington Post National Weekly Edition,* July 31, p. 31.

Pigram, John J. 1980. "Environmental Implications of Tourism Development." *Annals of Tourism Research,* vol. VII, no. 4, pp. 554–583.

Seltzer, Michael. September 2002. "Travel the Talk." *The Conference Board, Business Enterprise for Sustainable Travel,* at www.sustainabletravel.org/traveler/news01.cfm.

Shirkey, Wade Kilohana. 2002. "Fat Fuels Laundry's 100th Anniversary Celebration." *The Honolulu Advertiser,* November 8, p. B3.

"Snowmobile Rules Rankle in Yellowstone." 2002. CNN.COM, November 12.

Suen, W. 1989. "Rationing and Rent Dissipation in the Presence of Heterogeneous Individuals." *Journal of Political Economy,* vol. 97, pp. 1384–1398.

Tabatchnaia-Tamirisa, Natalia, Matthew K. Loke, Ping Sun Leung, and Ken A. Tucker. 1997. "Energy and Tourism in Hawaii." *Annals of Tourism Research,* vol. 24, no. 2, pp. 390–401.

Todd, Graham. 2001. "World Travel and Tourism Today." In: A. Lockwood and S. Medlik (eds.), *Tourism and Hospitality in the 21st Century.* Boston: Butterworth–Heinemann, pp. 3–17.

The Travel Industry World 2002 Yearbook—The Big Picture. 2003. Spencertown, N.Y.: Travel Industry Publishing Company, Inc. Also 2001 Yearbook.

U.S. Environmental Protection Agency (EPA). 2000. *A Method to Quantify Environmental Indicators of Selected Leisure Activities in the United States.* Prepared by Abt Associates. Washington, D.C.: EPA.

Vieitas, Claudia F., Gustave G. Lopez, and Maria A. Marcovaldi. 1999. "Local Community Involvement in Conservation: The Use of Miniguides in a Programme for Sea Turtles in Brazil." *Oryx,* vol. 33, no. 2, pp. 127–131.

Waite, David. 2002. "Hanauma Fee Policy Ruled Valid by Judge." *The Honolulu Advertiser,* October 18, pp. A1–A2.

Wanhill, S. R. C. 2000. "Charging for Congestion at Tourist Attractions." In: Clem Tisdell (ed.), *The Economics of Tourism,* vol. II. Northampton, Mass.: Edward Elgard Publishing Ltd., pp. 561–567.

World Bank. 2002. *Sustainable Nature Tourism and Conservation: Towards a Nature Tourism Economy in Kwazulu Natal.* Washington, D.C.: The World Bank.

———. 2003. *Sustainable Development in a Dynamic World.* World Development Report 2003. Washington, D.C.: The World Bank.

World Tourism Organization (WTO). 2002. *Voluntary Initiatives for Sustainable Tourism.* Madrid: WTO.

World Travel and Tourism Council, International Hotel & Restaurant Association, International Federation of Tour Operators, International Council of Cruise Lines and United Nations Environment Programme. 2002. *Industry as a Partner for Sustainable Development: Tourism.* London: The Beacon Press.

Yamanouchi, Kelly. 2002. "Cruise Industry OKs Rules." *The Honolulu Advertiser,* October, 25, pp. A1 and A6.

CHAPTER 14

Briassoulis, Helen and Jan van der Straaten. 2000. "Tourism and the Environment: An Overview." In: Briassoulis, Helen and Jan van der Straaten, *Tourism and the Environment, Regional Economic, Cultural and Policy Issues,* revised 2nd edition. Boston: Kluwer Academic Publishers.

Butcher, J. 1997. "Sustainable Development or Development." In: M. J. Stabler (ed.), *Tourism and Sustainability, Principles to Practice.* New York: CAB International, pp. 27–38.

Cesar, Herman, Pierter van Bukering, Sam Pintz, and Jan Dierking. 2002. *Economic Valuation of the Coral Reefs of Hawaii.* Arnhem, the Netherlands: Cesar Environmental Economics Consulting.

Dollar, David and Aart Kraay. 2001. *Growth is Good for the Poor.* Washington, D.C.: The World Bank.

Field, Barry C. and Martha K. Field. 2002. *Environmental Economics,* 3rd edition. New York: McGraw–Hill/Irwin.

Fyall, A. and B. Garrod. 1997. "Sustainable Tourism: Toward a Methodology for Implementing the Concept." In: M. J. Stabler (ed.), *Tourism and Sustainability, Principles to Practice.* New York: CAB International, pp. 51–68.

Goodall, Brian and Mike J. Stabler. 1997. "Principles Influencing the Determination of Environmental Standards for Sustainable Tourism." In: M. J. Stabler (ed.), *Tourism and Sustainability, Principles to Practice.* New York: CAB International, pp. 279–304.

Hunter, Colin. 1997. "Sustainable Tourism as an Adaptive Paradigm." *Annals of Tourism Research,* vol. 24, no. 4, pp. 850–867.

Hunter, Colin and Howard Green. 1995. *Tourism and the Environment, A Sustainable Relationship?* New York: Routledge.

Imber, David, Gay Stevenson, and Leanne Wilks. 1991. *A Contingent Valuation Survey of the Kakadu Conservation Zone.* RAC Research Paper No. 3, vol. 1. Canberra, ACT, Australia: Resource Assessment Commission.

Industrial Economics, Inc. 2002. *Draft Economic Analysis of Proposed Critical Habitat Designation for the Kauai Cave Wolf Spider and the Kauai Cave Amphipod, Island of Kauai, Hawaii.* Prepared for the Division of Economics, U.S. Fish and Wildlife Service. Cambridge, Mass.: Industrial Economics, Inc.

McCool, Stephen F. and R. Neil Moisey (eds.). 2001. *Tourism, Recreation, and Sustainability.* New York: CABI Publishing.

Mitchell, Paul Cameron and Richard T. Carson. 1989. *Using Surveys to Value Public Goods: The Contingent Valuation Method.* Washington, D.C.: Resources for the Future.

Krautkraemer, Jeffrey A. 2002. *Economics of Scarcity: State of the Debate.* Unpublished paper. Pullman, Wash.: Department of Economics, Washington State University.

Naya, Seiji F. 2002. *The Asian Development Experience.* Manila: Asian Development Bank.

Perez-Salom, Jose-Roberto. 2001. "Sustainable Tourism: Emerging Global and Regional Regulation." *Georgetown International Environmental Law Review,* vol. 13, no. 4, pp. 801–836.

The Pew Research Center for the People and the Press. 2002. *What the World Thinks in 2002.* Washington, D.C.: At www.people-press.org.

Poon, Auliana. 1993. *Tourism, Technology and Competitive Strategies.* Oxon, U.K.: CAB International.

Sinclair, M. Thea and Mike Stabler. 1997. *The Economics of Tourism.* New York: Routledge.

Stabler, M. J. (ed.). 1997. *Tourism and Sustainability, Principles to Practice.* New York: CAB International.

TenBruggencate, Jan. 2002. "Saving Open Space Has Value." *The Honolulu Advertiser,* December 2, p. B1.

Tietenberg, Tom. 1994. *Environmental Economics and Policy.* New York: HarperCollins College Publishers.

United Nations Economic and Social Commission for Asia and the Pacific (ESCAP). 1999. *Guidelines on Integrated Planning for Sustainable Tourism Development.* New York: United Nations.

World Bank. 2003. *Sustainable Development in a Dynamic World.* World Development Report, 2003. New York: Oxford University Press.

World Commission on Environment and Development (WCED). 1987. *Our Common Future.* (Brundtland Report.) New York: Oxford University Press.

World Tourism Organization (WTO). 1994. *National and Regional Tourism Planning, Methodologies and Case Studies.* New York: Routledge.

_____. 1998. *Guide for Local Authorities on Developing Sustainable Tourism.* Madrid: WTO.

_____. 2000. *Sustainable Development of Tourism: A Compilation of Good Practices.* Madrid: WTO, 2000.

_____. 2002. *Tourism and Poverty Alleviation.* Madrid: WTO.

World Travel & Tourism Council, International Federation of Tour Operators, International Hotel & Restaurant Association, International Council of Cruise Lines, and United Nations Environment Programme. 2002. *Industry As a Partner for Sustainable Development: Tourism.* London: World Travel & Tourism Council.

CHAPTER 15

Bergsma, Maggie. 2001. "Travel Distribution Systems: One-To-One Marketing." In: A. Lockwood and S. Medlik (eds.), *Tourism and Hospitality in the 21st Century.* Boston: Butterworth-Heinemann, pp. 246–254.

Cetron, Marvin. 2001. "The World of Today and Tomorrow: The Global View." In: A. Lockwood and S. Medlik (eds.), *Tourism and Hospitality in the 21st Century.* Boston: Butterworth-Heinemann, pp. 18–28.

Chicago Fed Letter. 2002. Special Issue, no. 174a, February.

Clark, Colin. 2001. "The Future of Leisure Time." In: A. Lockwood and S. Medlik (eds.), *Tourism and Hospitality in the 21st Century.* Boston: Butterworth-Heinemann, pp. 71–81.

DRI-WEFA. 2002. *The Role of Travel and Tourism in America's Top 100 Metropolitan Areas.* Lexington, Mass.: DRI-WEFA.

Eberstadt, Nicholas. 2000. "World Depopulation. Last One Out Turn Off the Lights." *Milken Institute Review,* First Quarter, pp. 37–48.

Goodall, Brian and Mike J. Stabler (ed.). 1997. *Tourism and Sustainability, Principles to Practice.* New York: CAB International, pp. 279–304.

"Journey into the Future." 2002. *Conde Nast Traveler,* November, pp. 95–114.

Kleiman, Carol. 2003. "U.S. Urged to Enact Paid-Vacation Law," *The Honolulu Advertiser,* April 23, pp. C1 and C3.

Krautkraemer, Jeffrey A. 2002. *Economics of Scarcity: State of the Debate.* Unpublished paper. Pullman, Washington: Department of Economics, Washington State University.

Lenain, Patrick, Marcos Bonturi, and Vincent Koen. 2002. *The Economic Consequences of Terrorism.* OECD Economics Department Working Papers No. 334. Paris: Organization for Economic Co-operation and Development.

Leu, Walter. 2001. "National Tourist Offices." In: A. Lockwood and S. Medlik (eds.), *Tourism and Hospitality in the 21st Century.* Boston: Butterworth-Heinemann, pp. 265–272.

Lohman, Martin. 2001. "Coastal Resorts and Climate Change." In: A. Lockwood and S. Medlik (eds.), *Tourism and Hospitality in the 21st Century.* Boston: Butterworth-Heinemann, pp. 284–295.

Lomborg, Bjorn and Olivier Rubin. 2002. "Limits to Growth." FP *Foreign Policy,* November/December, pp. 42–44.

Mak, James. 1996. *The Future of Hawaii as a Tourist Shopping Destination.* Unpublished paper. Honolulu: Department of Economics, University of Hawaii at Manoa.

Mastny, Lisa. 2002. "Redirecting International Tourism." *State of the World 2002.* A Worldwatch Institute Report on Progress Toward a Sustainable Society. New York: W. W. Norton & Company, pp. 101–125 and 225–234.

Miller, Leslie. 2002. "Airport Hassles, Not Just Fear, Have Many Travelers Preferring Road." *The Honolulu Advertiser,* October 21, p. A3.

Moffett, Sebastian. 2003. "Anxious, Aging Population Stunting Japan's Growth." *The Honolulu Advertiser,* February 17, pp. C1–C2. Also in *Asian Wall Street Journal,* February 11.

Muller, Hansruedi. 2001. "Tourism and Hospitality into the 21st Century." In: A. Lockwood and S. Medlik (eds.), *Tourism and Hospitality in the 21st Century.* Boston: Butterworth-Heinemann, pp. 61–70.

Navarro, Peter and Aron Spencer. 2001. "September 11, 2001, Assessing the Costs of Terrorism." *The Milken Institute Review,* Fourth Quarter, pp. 17–31.

Newsweek International. 2002. "The Future of Travel," July 22/July 29, pp. 34–65.

Pizam, Abraham and Aliza Fleischer. 2002. "Severity versus Frequency of Acts of Terrorism: Which Has a Larger Impact on Tourism Demand?" *Journal of Travel Research,* vol. 40, no. 3, February, pp. 337–339.

Reed, Dan. 2002. "Passengers Return, But Revenues Haven't." *The Honolulu Advertiser,* April 14, p. G4.

Rhoads, Christopher. 2002. "Post-Sept. 11 Fears Carry Price." *The Honolulu Advertiser,* June 10, p. D1.

Sakai, Marcia, Jeffrey Brown, and James Mak. 2000. "Population Aging and Japanese International Travel in the 21st Century." *Journal of Travel Research,* vol. 38, no. 3, February, pp. 212–220.

Tarlow, Peter E. 2002. "Tourism in the Twenty-First Century." *The Futurist,* September–October, pp. 48–51.

TenBruggencate, Jan. 2003. "Coral Disease May Be Tied to Climate Change." *The Honolulu Advertiser,* January 6, p. B1.

"The Globalization of Tourism." 1999. *UNESCO Courier,* July/August.

Todd, Graham. 2001. "The World Travel and Tourism Today." In: A. Lockwood and S. Medlik (eds.), *Tourism and Hospitality in the 21st Century.* Boston: Butterworth-Heinemann, pp. 3–17.

Travel Industry World 2002 Yearbook. 2003. Spencertown, N.Y.: Travel Industry Publishing Co., Inc.

U.S. Department of Commerce. 1996. *Service Industries and Economic Performance.* Washington D.C.: Government Printing Office.

Wall, G. and C. Badke. 1994. "Tourism and Climate Change: An International Perspective." *Journal of Sustainable Tourism,* vol. 2, no. 4, p. 193–203.

World Bank. 2003. *Sustainable Development in a Dynamic World.* World Development Report 2003. Washington, D.C.: The World Bank.

World Tourism Organization (WTO). 1994. *National and Regional Tourism Planning, Methodologies and Case Studies.* London: Routledge.

———. 2001. *Tourism after 11 September 2001: Analysis, Remedial Actions and Prospects.* Madrid: WTO.

INDEX

 Production Notes for Mak/TOURISM AND THE ECONOMY

Cover and Interior designed by Trina Stahl in Adobe Garamond, with display type
    in Twentieth Century MT.
Composition by Trina Stahl

Printing and binding by Versa Press, Inc.

Printed on 60# Starbrite Opaque, 435 ppi.